Additional praise for *The Tr*

"This rigorously researched book pi
wonder what happens between political grandstanding and
meaningful action. It exposes how the illusions of change and
impressions of leadership offered by Justin Trudeau have in fact
protected vested interests. Martin Lukacs is a journalist I depend
on to inform me about what is really going on."

– **David Suzuki**, scientist and broadcaster

"Martin Lukacs's incisive examination of the machinations
behind the Trudeau Brand is an invaluable tool—both for those
looking for the real story about this country missing from the
corporate media, and for the social movements that are our best
hope for the future. Read this book and take action for the land,
the people and the planet."

– **Judy Rebick**, author of *Heroes in My Head* and activist

"To move forward in Canada, I've long said we need a
'Colonialism For Dummies' book on the shelves of major
bookstores. Turns out buying into that franchise is nearly
impossible, but Martin Lukacs has written this timely and
accessible book instead."

– **Ryan McMahon**, Anishinaabe comedian, writer,
and media maker

The Trudeau Formula

For Kate,

To incurring the
wrath of the
elite!

In appreciation of
~~your~~ our work,

The Trudeau Formula

Seduction and Betrayal in an Age of Discontent

Martin Lukacs

Montréal / Chicago / London

Black Rose Books No. TT405

Library and Archives Canada Cataloguing in Publication

Title: The Trudeau formula / Martin Lukacs.
Names: Lukacs, Martin, 1984- author.
Description: Includes index.
Identifiers: Canadiana (print) 20190137681 | Canadiana (ebook) 2019013772X | ISBN
9781551647500 (hardcover) | ISBN 9781551647487 (softcover)
| ISBN 9781551647524 (PDF)
Subjects: LCSH: Trudeau, Justin. | LCSH: Liberalism—Canada. | LCSH: Neoliberalism—
Canada. | CSH:
    Canada—Politics and government—2015-
Classification: LCC JC574.2.C2 L85 2019 | DDC 320.51/30971—dc23

C.P. 35788 Succ. Léo-Pariseau
Montréal, QC, H2X 0A4

Explore our books and subscribe to our newsletter:
www.blackrosebooks.com

Ordering Information

USA/INTERNATIONAL	CANADA	UK/IRELAND
University of Chicago Press	University of Toronto Press	Central Books
Chicago Distribution Center	5201 Dufferin Street	50 Freshwater Road
11030 South Langley Avenue	Toronto, ON	Chadwell Heath, London
Chicago, IL 60628	M3H 5T8	RM8 1RX
(800) 621-2736 (USA)	1-800-565-9523	+44 (0) 20 8525 8800
(773) 702-7000 (International)		
orders@press.uchicago.edu	utpbooks@utpress.utoronto.ca	contactus@centralbooks.com

Black Rose Books is a not-for-profit publishing project of Cercle Noir et Rouge

Contents

Introduction   1

PART I   The Elements of the Formula

1. More Radical Options   15
2. Real Change™   29
3. The Clickbait Prime Minister   43
4. In the House of Justin   57
5. Out of the Limelight, into Legislation   75

PART II   The Outcome of the Formula

6. How Justin Learned to Stop Worrying and Love the (Alberta Carbon) Bomb   95
7. The Reconciliation Industry   131
8. Stakeholders, Transparency, Democracy, and Other Obstacles   175
9. Sunni Ways   191
10. #WelcomeToCanada   213

PART III   The Undoing of the Formula

11. The Green New Deal of the North   226

Acknowledgements   253
Endnotes   255
Index   291

To my parents

Introduction

Not long after the media announced the Liberals' election victory the night of October 19, 2015, Justin Trudeau strode through the Queen Elizabeth Hotel in downtown Montreal. Entering the main hall, he wove his way slowly through a packed crowd. Prime Minister Stephen Harper had been vanquished. The room was boisterous. Reaching the podium, Trudeau skipped up the stairs, buttoned his blazer, flashed a thumbs-up, and began his speech.

"Sunny ways, my friends, sunny ways," he said. "This is what positive politics can do."

This wasn't Trudeau's first time invoking the famous metaphor for former Prime Minister Wilfrid Laurier's governing style—it was his favourite story, which he felt characterized his own political approach. When Laurier had spoken of "sunny ways," he was alluding to Aesop's Fable, *The North Wind and the Sun*. In the fable, the wind and the sun break into argument over which of them is stronger. A traveller soon appears on the road, and to settle their dispute the wind and sun decide to see who can get him to take off his jacket first. The wind blusters and blows, but its cold blasts only make the traveller grip his garment more tightly around himself. Then the sun takes a turn. Shining warmly, radiating heat, it is not long before the traveller willingly discards the jacket.

As fables go, it seemed apt. In Trudeau's telling, the wind evidently represented Stephen Harper. There was Harper's icy, plaster-stiff smile, his disdain for Indigenous peoples, parliamentary institutions, and life outside the suburbs—or the fear he tried to stoke of Muslim terrorists lurking around every corner. He had never quite shaken that notorious incident in 2006, when, dropping off his young son at school, he had offered him a handshake instead of an embrace. "We beat fear with hope, we beat cynicism with hard work," Harper's bright and glowing challenger told the cheering audience that October night. Trudeau, a politician who didn't look like he slipped his human skin on every morning, who actually liked coddling babies, had captured the excitement of millions. "Canadians from all across this great country sent a clear message tonight: it's time for a change in this country, a real change," he said. "You want a government with a vision that is positive and ambitious and hopeful. I promise that I will lead that government. I will make that vision a reality, I will be that prime minister."

The morning after the election, as if to underscore the fable, Trudeau turned up in a Montreal subway station. At the top of an escalator, he greeted surprised and delighted commuters with hugs and selfies. I consider myself an unsentimental political observer, but watching the episode on the news that evening, I was overcome with emotion. My experience was no doubt shared by many people in Canada, who breathed a collective sigh, yielding to a wave of relief at the end of nearly ten years of Harper's rule.

Sunny ways, hope and hard work, real change, a youthful prime minister faithful to the progressive wave that lifted him to power: all of them persuasive stories that today, nearly four years later, feel more like fairytales.

To valiantly make their case, Liberals insist that the economy is strong. And it's true, the stock markets are up, and so too is productivity. There are new jobs—a million since 2015—and unemployment is the lowest in decades. The Liberals have locked horns with the Conservatives over climate policies. They're passionate about their relationship with Indigenous peoples, which Trudeau never fails to remind us is his government's most important. But people are finding it hard to spot the link between hard work and hope. In surveys, only one in six people in 2019 say their lives have improved from the previous year, and only one in eight believe that the next generation will enjoy better prospects.[1] Hope may be difficult to quantify, but by these approximate yardsticks it is in vanishingly short supply.

Hoarding the Future

Most people in Canada used to feel assured life was getting better. Between the end of the Great Depression and the late 1970s, the standard of living increased, inequality and unemployment declined, and healthcare, pensions, and income-security were established. Wages, while not being split fairly across society, increased in lock-step with a growing economy. Not today. The dizzying growth that has made Canada extraordinarily wealthy has been captured almost exclusively by the richest among us. Between 1980 and 2015, the real market income of the richest 10 percent of Canadians went up by half, that of the richest 1 percent has more than doubled, and that of the richest 0.1 percent has almost quadrupled—while the real market income of those Canadians in the bottom 90 percent barely budged.[2] In other words, in the era between Pierre Elliott Trudeau and Justin Trudeau, the income of the overwhelming majority of Canadians basically flat-lined. The benefits of growth didn't trickle down; the wealthiest showered in all of them. In that same period, there has been an accompanying explosion in racial inequality. In Toronto, wage-earners regardless of their race made relatively similar salaries in the 1960s and 1970s. Today, in the poster-child city for diversity, a person of colour earns only 50 cents for every dollar earned by a white person.[3] And on reserves, poverty has barely budged: half of Canada's Indigenous children live below the poverty line.[4]

Since the 2008 recession, living standards have taken an especially dramatic tumble. Half of those who identify as working class today say they were middle class ten years ago—the bottom has dropped out from under them.[5] Personal debt, working hours, and mortgage payments have risen. Good job opportunities and leisure time have fallen. No wonder nearly one-third of Canadians don't have enough at the end of the month to cover their bills. There are as many food banks and agencies as there are Tim Hortons.[6] In rural towns and low-income inner cities and formerly thriving manufacturing regions, this intensified economic insecurity and distress has led to coping through doping, an epidemic of drug-use. Over the last three years, more than 11,500 people have died from opioid overdoses, stunting growth in Canadian life expectancy for the first time in several decades.[7] And if you're Indigenous, transgender, a refugee, or a person of colour, you face not just greater economic precarity but the threat of everyday discrimination, racism, and hatred—whether from police, employers and landlords, or emboldened white supremacist groups whose numbers in Canada have more than doubled since 2015.[8]

The hoarding of a secure, liveable future is felt intuitively by the young. They leave university, collapsing under the weight of student loans, to pick between poorly paid gig jobs. Forget about a reliable pension. Never mind owning a home. The chances even of renting a one or two-bedroom apartment in a major city on a minimum wage are mere decimals from zero.[9] They are the first generation in Canada to expect to be worse off than their parents. And the horizon doesn't merely look bleak, but is increasingly shrouded by smoke from forest fires, flooded by rising waters, or scorched by heat waves—climate change-fuelled extreme weather that has hit every part of the country. Every year since the Trudeau government signed onto the Paris climate agreement in 2015, the gap between our official carbon reduction targets and our actual emissions has grown wider.[10] I know people in their early twenties who attend "ecological grief" circles, where they discuss with dread the state of the planet they're inheriting. Others, even younger, are walking out of their high schools and marching in the streets. Squeezed by the end of the month, haunted by the end of the world: these are the signature marks of the anxiety and anger of a new Canadian generation.

Because so many are doing very badly, some are doing very well. Corporate profits are the highest they've been in the history of money. Two years ago, the top five Canadian oil-producing companies made $46.6 billion. Last year, the big six banks bagged $45 billion—nearly twice what they made in 2010, and the eighth galloping year in a row that they've set a new high. At Christmas in 2018, while you may have been fretting about credit card interest rates, bank executives awarded themselves $15 billion in bonuses (yes, that's billions, not millions). By January 2 of the New Year, before lunch-time, each of the 100 highest paid CEOs had already pocketed the average wage a Canadian worker will earn in all of 2019.[11] Since Trudeau came to office, the amount of money the richest Canadians have stashed away in offshore tax havens has leapt to an astonishing $353 billion—three times the government revenue of Argentina or Finland.[12] Meanwhile, 4,000 new foreign millionaires moved into the country last year, turning Canada into one of the most popular destinations for the uber-rich escaping higher taxes and regulations elsewhere.[13]

The divide in our society, assessed not in terms of income but overall wealth, is even more lopsided. According to a 2017 report by Oxfam, two Canadian men own as much as the bottom 30 percent of the Canadian population—eleven million people. The very richest, David Thomson the third Baron Thomson of Fleet, is worth a mind-bending $46 billion.[14] He got something of a head start by being born the son of Kenneth Thomson, the second Baron Thomson of Fleet, inheriting his father's properties, his media empire, and his hereditary peerage (his sister lost out, because their grandfather, Roy Thomson, stipulated that only male heirs could run the family business).[15] Having enlarged his bequeathal, he is currently a boss of 45,000 employees, owns *The Globe and Mail* and Winnipeg Jets, and paid a record $76.7 million for the Baroque painter Peter Rubens' *The Massacre of the Innocents*. Which come to think of it, is not the worst metaphor for what has happened to most people in our economy.

So this is where we stand, after four years of sunny ways. Justin Trudeau's Liberals remind us that you can't achieve everything you'd like in government. "Transitions to a cleaner future are hard," protests Environment Minister Catherine McKenna. "It is not easy to decolonize," adds Crown-Indigenous Affairs Minister Carolyn Bennett. And look at those Conservatives, say Liberals whenever they have a chance, throwing up obstacles at every turn to reason and progress and wise policy.

But eventually, you begin to reflect on Trudeau's favourite fable and realize that, regardless of the different approaches taken by sun and wind, the aim pursued is the same: relieving the traveller of his possession.

The Free World's Best Hope?

It all started so promisingly. It's hard to forget that bright, warm day in early November 2015, when Justin Trudeau, in a perfectly fitted suit and with perfectly tousled hair, strolled with his new cabinet to the steps of Rideau Hall, opened to the public to witness their swearing-in ceremony. Onlookers took in the equal number of male and female ministers, the first gender balanced federal cabinet in Canadian history. "Because it's 2015," Trudeau explained, a line soon celebrated in the columns of newspapers across the globe. His cabinet of outdoor enthusiasts promised to "give to our children and grandchildren a country even more beautiful, sustainable, and prosperous than the one we have now." His every speech was peppered with empathic nods to the struggle of Canadians with inequality, precarity, and poverty. He personally welcomed Syrian refugees at Toronto's airport, telling them "you are home, welcome home." Hope invested in Trudeau soared when Donald Trump, his own hair looking like a toxic gas flare, took over the White House. "At any moment I could leap into Justin Trudeau's arms," American comedian Samantha Bee said, summing up the feelings of many men, women, and more than a few liberal governments the world-over. *Rolling Stone* magazine splashed a large photo of him on their cover, asking "Why Can't He Be Our President?"

Trudeau's new government, we were frequently reminded, was filled with the best and brightest. He had won a convincing majority and everyone seemed to agree he was assured a second term in office. If he were to act on the clear mandate he had won for bold policies, the people of Canada would undoubtedly side with him. Everything was ripe for transformation.

That's not exactly what happened. Trudeau had promised to replace an antiquated 19th century voting system, but reconsidered when it became apparent the wishes of Canadians did not match his preferred model, favouring the incumbent government. He bought the old, crumbling Trans Mountain oil pipeline from American tycoons, spending far more on a single piece of fossil fuel infrastructure than on any renewable energy project. The Liberals announced that the United Nations Declaration on the

Rights of Indigenous Peoples was "unworkable," and instead dispatched heavily armed police to batter down a peaceful blockade erected by the Wet'suwet'en First Nation, who were trying to put into practice those rights in northwest British Columbia. This friend of labour legislated away the right to strike of a postal union that wanted safer working conditions; this champion of equality gave profitable multinational corporations billions in hand-outs and tax cuts; and this feminist set new records selling weapons to the misogynistic dictatorship of Saudi Arabia. Private affluence continued to soar, without any discernible benefit to the public good. New, desperately-needed universal social programs—like child care or pharmacare—never materialized. Within a year, we stopped hearing much at all about Trudeau's vaunted assault on income inequality.[16]

Now, we know it was a right-wing movement and the Progressive Conservative Party under Brian Mulroney that inaugurated the era of cutting taxes, deregulating business, privatizing the public sphere, and shrinking government. A half-century ago, the big business architects of this revolution began concertedly spreading a renewed fervour for the market, until it was finally adopted as the common sense of government, laying the seeds for the plutocratic society we now see around us. These days, the current incarnation of the federal Conservatives and their provincial party allies are consorting with hateful and racist far-right figures, stoking xenophobia toward refugees fleeing war and hardship, lurking at anti-abortion rallies, and burying their heads in the sand-bags that pile up around cities menaced by climate floods. They sully our political discourse with lies and fabrications. The enthusiasm of their proclaimed concern for workers and ordinary folk is matched only by the zeal with which they screw them over when in power.

But assigning the Liberal Party responsibility for the mess we're in is long overdue. After all, it's not like they've lacked for opportunities to change course. They've been in power 17 of the last 26 years. Is it possible that it isn't dastardly Conservatives who have thwarted their plans for change? That Liberal good intentions didn't simply go awry? Could the disappointment, disillusionment, and deception increasingly associated with this government not be an accident, but a feature, indeed a cyclical one, of the Liberal Party's politics?

This book is an attempt to explain how the Liberal Party under Justin Trudeau has lived large on its fables. The current state of our market society—the spiralling economic and racial inequality, the precarious jobs and stagnant wages, the towering power of finance, the deterioration in public services, the funnelling of wealth upward—was launched by Canada's right-wing. But the politics that justified this would never have triumphed in their hands alone. Every aspect of this corporate agenda—which we know today as neoliberalism—has been at odds with the values of most people in Canada. This progressive majority has always aspired to a society that pools and shares resources and looks after the collective good. The corporate agenda thus had to be repackaged as progressive, which is what the Liberals accomplished.

In the 1990s, the Liberals sawed off any of their party's previous inclinations to redistribute wealth and create universal social programs, and merely sanded the roughest edges of their right-wing embrace of unregulated markets. To this was fused an embrace of inclusive policies around multiculturalism, environmentalism, anti-racism, gay and women's rights, and diversity, whose limited realization was made compatible with the needs of corporate interests. In this manner, the Liberals signed the Kyoto climate protocol, but let oil giants get away with ballooning emissions; supported Sikh men wearing turbans in the RCMP, but escalated a "war on drugs" that criminalized and incarcerated black and brown people, and joined a "war on terror" that increased racism and police harassment toward Muslims; and inaugurated the discourse of reconciliation with Indigenous peoples, while continuing to dispossess them of their remaining land-base. It is not an accident that its emergence coincided with the fullest merger yet of marketing and politics. The tools of polling, focus groups, and advertising were applied to turning the leading politicians of these parties into brands whose progressive, seductive gloss could disguise how they were now accountable, above all, to the priorities and needs of corporate power.

The Liberal Party of the 1990s and early 2000s, more trusted than the Conservatives—and therefore a more effective partner to corporations—were thus able to advance the neoliberal agenda beyond the wildest dreams of the right-wing. Many of the economic and ecological problems we confront today—the perverse scale of inequality, a dire lack of affordable housing, the planet-wrecking boom in the Alberta tar sands, a welfare state that is now among the stingiest in the industrialized world—can be directly traced back to Liberal policies of that era.

A Shock-Absorber for the Establishment

Over the last ten years, something cracked. Faith in this political consensus, in the inevitability of progress, began to splinter. Discontent became more widespread, extending well beyond Stephen Harper or even the Conservatives, to the established order. Increasingly people questioned the stories that upheld this order, the politics that sustained it, the elites who most benefited from it. In 2014, the EKOS polling agency presented Canadians with the following statement: "If the current patterns of stagnation among all except those at the very top continue, I would not be surprised to see the emergence of violent class conflicts." Nearly two out of three people agreed.[17]

In every Canadian generation in which discontent has peaked, the Liberal Party has cushioned and subdued it, like a great establishment shock-absorber. Shedding tears about the injustices of our country's past, inveighing against the inequalities of the present, pledging a dynamic politics of the future: Justin Trudeau was a dazzling simulation of defiance against the social and economic order. It was an approach famously encapsulated by the aristocratic protagonist in Italian author Giuseppe di Lampedusa's novel *The Leopard*. Surveying Italian society at a moment of looming upheaval in the 19th century, he offered a piece of advice to members of his besieged class: "If we want things to remain the same, things will have to change."[18] The Liberal Party would update this for the 21st century, co-opting the language of social movements, offering focus-grouped challenges to the establishment, and entrancing the global press with skillful use of social media, as they practiced a new politics of hype.

As we will see, on every front they governed through a spectacle of activity that seemed to utterly disrupt politics as usual, but in fact mostly shored up prevailing disparities of wealth and power. With crisp rolled-up Oxford shirts, celebrity good looks, bright, empty words, and a reservoir of nostalgia for his father's name to draw on, Justin Trudeau was a marketing guru's dream messenger of this formula of changeless change. If he didn't exist, the most savvy of the elite might have tried to invent him.

Trudeau thus succeeded in masking how no impulse of his government would threaten the authority of corporate interests. Whereas Harper had made his loyalties to certain sections of the corporate class brazenly obvious, provoking widespread resistance, Trudeau struck a much more discrete compact with the oil and media barons, arms manufacturers, big banks and pharmaceutical companies, and Silicon Valley billionaires and Bay Street financiers.

Trudeau was keenly aware of his formula's early achievements, describing them in an interview to *The Guardian* on the first anniversary of his election: "We were able to sign a free trade agreement with Europe at a time when people tend to be closing off," he said. "We're actually able to approve pipelines at a time when everyone wants protection of the environment. We're able to show that we get people's fears and there are constructive ways of allaying them—and not just ways to lash out and give a big kick to the system."[19] Deftly winning support for pro-corporate trade deals or for climate-torching pipelines, and muting popular anger at a hoarding elite—rarely has Trudeau been so clear that his goal was not to transform the status quo but to smoothly defend it.

No wonder he became the darling of Davos, idolized by a global liberal establishment who had presided over an inequality-exploding era and were now under siege from a surging democratic socialist left and an ugly racist right. Trudeau was their great hope, a politician who might put a coiffed gloss on a system of fossil fuel-addicted capitalism whose legitimating stories were fraying. This jet-setting elite class of financiers, from whom Trudeau drew some of his closest advisors, were intent on crafting a new political consensus that would guarantee profit-making in an age of lagging growth, while making some rhetorical and material concessions to assuage an increasingly angry population.

But behind the allure of Canada's Camelot was an ordinary establishment politician of an extraordinarily successful establishment party. In 2019, revelations about how Trudeau's office sought to help corporate engineering giant SNC-Lavalin evade criminal prosecution for major corruption afforded a glimpse behind the cult of progressive celebrity. But the Liberals have not merely bullied one of their own ministers to aid a corporate titan close to the establishment. They have bullied critics that stood in the way of bank profits, First Nations in the way of resource projects, and entire European governments in the way of pro-corporate trade deals. And when necessary, they have played the role of junior partner to the biggest bully in the world, the United States government.

The Liberal Party's political philosophy, priding itself on its peerless, privileged access to realism, has proven to be blind to the damage it is causing to the welfare of millions and the health of the planet. Sharply constrained by corporate power, their policies—a carbon tax, the Child Care Benefit, better representation of women and people of colour at the top—provided marginal benefits but did nothing to address the root causes of inequality, racism, deteriorating public services, or climate breakdown. Canadian liberalism—with its unshakeable faith in the magic of markets, its abandonment of redistribution, its commitment to extractivism—offers ultimately no answers to the crises of our age.

Besides that, the formula may no longer even be an effective way to win office. Forty years of austerity and neoliberalism have left basic needs—decent wages, affordable housing, accessible education—out of reach for growing numbers. The resulting anger and insecurity, unaddressed by Liberal policies, have been seized on and misdirected toward scapegoats by a surging right, with even more extreme white supremacists in tow. This exemplifies a great peril in Canadian politics: while polls frequently document that our society has grown more open, compassionate, and social democratic in their values, in the absence of a visionary and bold response to establishment Liberal centrism, it is the ugly right who will triumph.

This is not only about the Liberal Party; it is also about us. In every generation, the Liberals' sway over Canada's progressive majority has stunted our imagination, persuading us that they are the best defence against the Conservatives, that they are our best hope for social change, and that there is no alternative to them, anyway. They have confused compassionate rank-and-file Liberal voters from understanding just how starkly and consistently the party's elite, and the establishment it serves, contradicts and flouts their values.

To win the country we deserve, we'll need to stop believing in their fables, speak to our deepest collective aspirations, and expand our sense of what is politically achievable.

But before any of this becomes possible, we have to understand how the Liberal Party speaks to the elite, when nobody else is in the room.

1

More Radical Options

In early May 2015, Justin Trudeau stood at a lectern in the dimly lit, chandeliered ballroom of the Canadian Club of Toronto, a guest of Bay Street's favourite luncheon speaker series. The 43-year-old was on the verge of his first federal election campaign as leader of the Liberal Party, but after a rapid climb to the top of the polls, he had tumbled back down to third place. Just days earlier, hoping to reverse Trudeau's prospects, the Liberals had unveiled their most dramatic-sounding policy proposal: a tax hike on the top one percent of wealthy Canadians, the very members of that afternoon's audience.

The major newspapers had quickly voiced their disapproval. *The Globe and Mail* warned against "redistributionist dogma," suggesting that "taxing the rich will not pay off for Trudeau." The *National Post* advised him to "ditch the 'soak the rich' rhetoric," because "pinning his hopes on a class war is a losing strategy."[1] But if the newly-announced policy had given anyone in the audience the impression that they were dealing with a socialist firebrand, Trudeau was here to clear things up. "I know people in your position get asked for a lot, and as evidenced by the thriving and generous philanthropic culture in Canada, you step up," he said in a deferential tone from the stage. "Your contributions to Canadian society have been appreciated—and I'm asking for one more."

Not to worry, he reassured them, corporate tax hikes were out of the question. That could have the "undesired effect of stifling innovation, investment, and growth," he said, repeating a business lobby talking point that disguised how it was in fact decades of cuts to corporate taxes that had led to tepid innovation, historic lows in investment and growth, and the unprecedented hoarding of profits. And, he added, the accusation from detractors that the Liberals were "trying to create a sense of envy" toward the wealthy was nothing more than "rank political nonsense." Trudeau was hoping, however, that they would indulge his proposal to raise the top income tax bracket, so that "those with the most do a little bit more to help those in Canada with less."

It was a declaration of intent to the country's corporate elite: he was not out for strident confrontation, but savvy collaboration. They had on their hands, when you got down to it, a "very real problem." The secret to the country's success, the "essence of the Canadian bargain," was that "we've always had a sense of fairness," he said. "Canada has thrived for generations on this fundamental idea. Yet recently, something has changed." While dominant wisdom held that Canada had been uniquely insulated from the impact of the financial recession, Trudeau ran through gloomy statistics that indicated otherwise: the economy had more than doubled in size over the last generation, but median incomes had "all but flat-lined." Household income had not kept up with household debt, more Canadians were living paycheck to paycheck, and a third of those nearing retirement had no savings at all. It was time, he believed, for policies "aimed squarely at restoring that sense of fairness."

Then, as if his speech cues read, *This is the message you want them to go home with*, his voice shifted dramatically. "And, I might say, if we don't deliver fairness, Canadians will eventually entertain more radical options," he said, slowly drawing out the sentence. The room had quieted, and a utensil clattered against a piece of china. "All of the time I've spent with Canadians tells me that the status quo is not sustainable. Change is coming, my friends. What we need is leadership and a plan to shape that change responsibly, for the benefit of all. Either we choose to act now, or we will be forced to react, later."

In such polite society, it was about as frankly-worded a warning as one could make: beware of the backlash against the elites. The signs were there for those paying attention, in the polls and in the rise of new social movements. In 2011, a local branch of the global Occupy movement had set up camp just a few blocks from here, in the park grounds of St. James Church; a year later, the Idle No More Indigenous uprising had shaken the country; another two years on, a small but politically forceful Black Lives Matter movement would spring up in Toronto. All raised uncomfortable questions about a country riven by deep inequalities. While Stephen Harper seemed oblivious to this rejection of politics as usual, Justin Trudeau wanted his audience to know that he, like certain capable Liberal leaders before him, had a finely calibrated radar for discontent.

Trudeau's pitch boiled down to this: he was the man who could stand between them and the backlash. He was the man who could responsibly shape change that appeared inevitable. A bit of change—a sprinkling of fairness, or even just the "sense of fairness"—could pay off handsomely. Coughing up a little more in personal income taxes, after all, would hardly shift the fundamental economic arrangement of Canadian society. But as part of a compelling package, it might take the edge off the hunger for more "radical options." Options that could entail paying much higher wages to workers. Or returning Crown lands to Indigenous peoples. Or redistributing excessive wealth to pay for universal child care, free public transit, or a rollout of renewable energy. On the other hand, if elites delayed for too long, those options might burst into the political mainstream—with or without their blessing.

Capitalism's Depleted Public Trust

Justin Trudeau had been honing this message with a group of advisors and Liberals for the previous two or three years, then testing it in elite venues—everywhere from the Calgary Petroleum Club, to the annual conference of the The Canadian Council for Public-Private Partnerships, to the Empire Club of Toronto. Prime among those advisors was eventual Foreign Affairs Minister Chrystia Freeland, whose 2012 book *Plutocrats: The Rise of the New Global Super-Rich and the Fall of Everyone Else* Trudeau often quoted from. A business reporter with *Reuters* and former managing editor of *The Financial Times* who moved in the rarefied circuit of five-star hotels, New York high-rises, and Silicon Valley boardrooms, Freeland was an unapologetic defender of capitalism. But she was also a clear-eyed chronicler of the rise of resentment and anger over its unequally divided spoils. "For more and more people, the plutocrats' technocratic paternalism seems at best weak broth and at worst an effort to preserve the rules of a game that is rigged in their favour," she wrote in *The New York Times* in 2013. "More radical ideas, particularly ones explicitly hostile to elites and technocratic intellectuals, gain traction." Freeland would later reflect that 2013, during which she accepted Trudeau's invitation to run for the Liberals, "was the year the revolt against the plutocrats began."[2]

One of her acknowledged gurus was Dominic Barton, who would eventually chair the Trudeau government's council on economic growth. He would be, until 2018, the head of the globe's largest management consultancy, McKinsey & Co., an organization so synonymous with the affairs of the corporate elite that it is known simply as The Firm. The boyish-faced, Canadian-born Barton was "one of the most connected people in the world," according to *The Financial Post*, fielding calls from "the Vatican to the Iranian government."[3] In 2016, he would chaperone Trudeau around the favourite stomping grounds of the plutocrats, the World Economic Forum in Davos, where journalists, in Freeland's words, play "Geishas" to crowds studded with statesmen, tech billionaires and pop stars.

For the past decade, this gathering at a ski resort high up in the Swiss Alps had been invaded by unease about the growing political turmoil far below. In the wake of the financial crash, Barton had conducted a globetrotting audit of capitalism, soliciting the opinions of 400 business and government leaders. An economic system hard-wired to pursue short-term profits as its highest priority was, in his unvarnished conclusion, "sick." Leaders could not ignore the "surge in public antagonism" that was jolting countries across the world. "Capitalism depends on public trust for its legitimacy and its very survival," he wrote, and that trust was increasingly in short supply. The annual Trust Barometer published by the Edelman polling agency showed this trend was being equally felt in Canada: since 2008, confidence in big business, CEOs, and the corporate media had plummeted.[4] "If the crisis remains unaddressed and the system fails again, the social contract between the capitalist system and citizenry may truly rupture with unpredictable and severely damaging results," Barton warned.[5]

But Barton's diagnosis was far more bracing than his prescription: a shift from what he called short-term to long-term capitalism, with the elite reducing CEO pay, accommodating themselves to slightly lower profits, and promoting environmental and social initiatives to restore a measure of faith in capitalism. For her part, Freeland believed a "bitter political fight between economic winners and losers" could be "inevitable," just as it had been in the 1930s and 1940s, when well-organized workers' movements and left-wing parties had forced major social reforms from governments in Canada, the United States and elsewhere. So what were "smart centrists" to do, she asked, to "fine-tune 21st century capi-

talism"? It might help somewhat to "shore up the welfare state."
But her main advice was to engage in "retail, bottom-up politics,"
building a "constituency among those who are losing out and
those who sympathize with them." Such politics didn't have to
"be extremist and nasty, but they have to grow out of, and speak
for, the 99 percent."[6] Capitalism, in other words, needed much
more effective salespeople.

Echoing this perspective, Trudeau directly addressed Canada's
elite in an op-ed published in *The Globe and Mail* shortly after he
won the Liberal Party's leadership race in 2013:

> "If you are among those few who have thrived, here is why you
> should care about the diminished fortunes of the middle class.
> The past 30 years' growth has been the product of a broadly
> supported economic agenda. Governments of all political stripes
> have been elected and re-elected, here in Canada and abroad, on
> a similar economic platform: openness to trade, fiscal discipline,
> tax competitiveness and investment in skills, research and
> infrastructure… Middle-class Canadians supported this agenda
> because, they were promised, it would create shared prosperity.
> The basic bargain was that growth was good for them, and they
> would share fairly in its fruits. That simply hasn't happened."

The agenda he was describing in the coded jargon of the business elite—privatization, deregulation, corporate tax cuts, pro-
corporate trade, shrinkage in the state's social spending, all part
of a bipartisan consensus defended by Liberals and Conservatives—had indeed hollowed out the living standards of the middle
and working classes, brought wages to a shuddering flatline, and
created an obscene concentration of wealth at the top. But this
agenda involved apparently "benign economic forces," in Freeland's words, "leading to a malign political result." Like her and
Barton, Trudeau was clever enough to gesture at the symptoms,

but not courageous enough to scrutinize their root causes, the sickness itself. In *The Globe and Mail*, he continued:

> National business leaders and other wealthy Canadians should draw the following conclusion, and do so urgently: If we do not solve this problem, Canadians will eventually withdraw their support for a growth agenda. We will all be worse off as a consequence. Deepening anxiety yields deepening divisions in every society, and we are not immune to that vicious cycle here in Canada. We will begin to vote for leaders who offer comforting stories about who to blame for our problems, rather than how to solve them."[7]

The consequences of that agenda, Trudeau was saying, were not principally injustices that needed to be confronted, but threats to the agenda's legitimacy that needed to be contained. The symptoms should be soothed, in other words, so as to prolong the sickness. "This is plainly the language of technocratic management, not moral urgency," journalist Luke Savage wrote in *The Guardian*, "first and foremost an appeal to the self-interest of elites rather than a coherent political demand directed at the powerful."[8]

In darkly alluding to leaders who offer "comforting stories," Trudeau was no doubt referring to right-wing politicians who sought to pin blame for people's economic plight on the most vulnerable—immigrants, people of colour, Muslims, Indigenous peoples, the poor. But there was also little question he was evoking figures on the left—like U.S. presidential nominee Bernie Sanders or U.K. Labour leader Jeremy Corbyn, to name two politicians who would soon enjoy a meteoric rise in popularity. If their equivalent emerged in Canada, he or she might instead point their finger directly at the millionaire and billionaire class listening to Trudeau in the Canadian Club on Bay Street in spring

2015. But Trudeau's speech ably identified the conditions for a potential surge in such anti-establishment politics in Canada, and proposed what should be done to avert that possibility. Which brought us to his pitch: if his elite audience would endorse his plan to slightly adjust the scales of an extreme societal imbalance, he could serve as an able defender of the system by which they had been so regally rewarded. It was a comforting, welcome message. At the speech's end, Trudeau received a long and loud standing ovation.[9]

The Party of One

There was a reason Trudeau's message went down so well with Canada's corporate elite: many of them had grown frustrated with Conservative Prime Minister Stephen Harper and were ready to give the Liberal Party another chance.

The last Liberal prime minister, Paul Martin, a successful corporate tycoon in his own right, had initially raised such high hopes. The corporate elite looked forward to the sort of tax cuts he had implemented as Jean Chrétien's Finance Minister—$100 billion alone in the budget for the year 2000, a corporate giveaway unlike anything in Canadian history. But as prime minister, Martin proved to be a disappointment. On the heels of a corruption scandal over a Quebec ad sponsorship program run by the Chrétien government, Martin was reduced to a minority. From 2004 to 2006, he was forced to rely on the support of opposition parties—and to eventually accept that he could only change the channel from sponsorship sleaze with social spending. With Jack Layton's New Democratic Party (NDP) applying pressure, Martin reached a $41-billion, ten-year deal with the provinces to maintain funding levels for healthcare—a move that Jack Mintz, the head of the right-wing C.D. Howe Institute, lambasted as a "spending orgy." In the 2005 budget, the New Democrats successfully pushed Martin to cancel planned corporate tax cuts and instead increase funding for social programs by billions of dollars. Martin also parted ways with the corporate elite on aspects of military policy, buckling to the anti-war movement's demand that Canada refuse to join the U.S. cruise missile defense program.[10] The British magazine *The Economist* wondered aloud about where the "old Paul Martin" had gone. The "tough and decisive deficit-cutter who transformed the public finances" had been replaced by a man "parading a generous social conscience."[11] Tapping into the disgruntled id of Canada's corporate elite, they branded him with a nickname that has stuck to this day: Mr. Dithers.

But better the politician you knew than the politician you didn't. Well before Stephen Harper defeated Martin in 2006 and formed a minority government, corporate lobbyists had been shuffling to Stornaway, the opposition leader's residence, to try to cultivate a relationship.[12] To many of them, however, Harper would remain an icy and inscrutable figure. He felt he owed no deference to corporate executives, least of all on Bay Street, and he certainly didn't expect to canvass them about his policies. His was a *Party of One*, as the title of journalist Michael Harris's book about the Harper years put it. When he took office, word quickly spread that Conservative MPs were giving the cold shoulder to business lobby-sponsored events in Ottawa, the cocktail circuit through which access and influence flows. *The Globe and Mail* reported that the corporate boxes at Scotiabank Place, the hockey arena where the Ottawa Senators play, had never been so empty of politicians and government officials.[13] Under Harper, CEOs could forget about their old missions abroad with Prime Minister Jean Chrétien, hobnobbing with provincial premiers while wooing foreign investment.

Not that Harper didn't often advance corporate interests. Several elements of his agenda—slashing corporate taxes, scrapping environmental regulations, signing trade deals, and seeking deeper economic, military, and security integration with the United States—overlapped with theirs. He even eventually plucked a chief of staff, Nigel Wright, from the elite investor class. But he was out of tune in other ways. His social conservatism clashed with a liberal ethos of diversity and tolerance that prevailed among the financial and corporate elite. His bare-knuckled, ideological hatred for the welfare state and universal social programs like healthcare was at odds with large parts of the corporate elite (who had long accommodated themselves to Canada's public system of healthcare, for instance, as an important competitive business advantage). Ultimately, Harper's allegiances were not to the corporate class broadly but to certain factions within it.

This composition could be discerned by the makeup of Finance Minister Jim Flaherty's exclusive policy retreats held every summer in Wakefield, Quebec. The guest list usually included a few lawyers, bankers, or financiers, but was heavily dominated by oil, resource, and construction companies, right-wing academics and economists from think tanks like the Fraser Institute and C.D. Howe, and retailers like Sears and Walmart. Also present was the Canadian Federation of Independent Business, a lobby group that represented medium-sized businesses and low-wage retail employers who were much more hostile than other large corporations to union organizing, taxation, and fair salaries for workers.[14] During an in-camera conversation held in 2009, described to me by one attendee, a dinner speech by a former Alberta finance minister was followed by an animated debate about privatizing healthcare. There was strong sentiment in the room in favour, tempered only by the recognition that it would be difficult to sell to Canadians. A leaked agenda in 2011 showed that Flaherty was urged yet again by that year's attendees to consider this highly inflammatory political move.[15]

Narrow alliances, a hermitic policy-making process, and a rigid neo-con world-view, wrapped up in a controlling and vindictive man: it was a prime ministerial blend bound to unsettle a corporate elite used to being treated like enlightened arbiters of the government's political direction. The frustration eventually slipped into the open. In 2010, Toronto Dominion Bank CEO Ed Clark complained in a speech that Harper wasn't listening to the emerging belief of executives that he should increase their personal taxes. Clark explained that at the last gathering of the Business Council of Canada, the organization representing the country's top CEOs, the room had been surveyed about how to reduce the deficit. "Raise my taxes," almost every person had said. But when Clark had done a consultation with Harper before that year's budget, he had gotten nowhere. "He doesn't listen, but you get to chat with him," Clark lamented.[16]

Harper was furious about being publicly challenged. The Conservatives fired off an email message to party members, later reported by the media, that tried to link the bank CEO to the Liberals. The email also pointed out that Clark had earned $11 million in 2009. "He can afford higher taxes. Can you?" Such a harsh rebuke by a prime minister of a sterling voice on Bay Street was unheard of. A senior banker at another big bank admitted anonymously that the Conservatives were "creating an environment in which corporate leaders are scared to speak up about policy."[17]

"Better for Business than Stephen Harper"

What had prompted Ed Clark and his fellow corporate executives to call for a hike to their taxes? Was it worry about the state of the deficit, another financial crash, or the bursting of the housing bubble? Or were they, like some of the strategists around Justin Trudeau, tuned into the rising anger about the spiralling inequality they had so benefited from? Whatever it was, they knew something had to give.

That was not Stephen Harper's way. When the financial recession had hit early during his time in office, he had briefly shown glimmers of practical adaptability, stimulating the economy through government intervention in violation of his professed right-wing libertarian principles. But he otherwise settled into a high-handed governing style that brooked few compromises with his many perceived foes. He provoked the biggest upswell of Indigenous mobilization in a generation, after brazenly gutting Canada's environmental laws. Then he prolonged the mobilization by refusing for weeks to accept the modest demand of hunger-striking Attawapiskat Chief Theresa Spence for a meeting with the Governor General. He turned Canada into an international climate pariah, and as protests grew he dispatched ministers to denounce critics as "radicals" and to bully foreign governments into accepting Alberta tar sands imports. Under his watch, no pipelines were built. No major trade pacts were inked. A giant weapons deal with Saudi Arabia received terrible press. To add insult to injury, Harper was a boorish embarrassment on the global stage. He let the G20 meetings in Toronto descend into police mayhem. He lost Canada's bid for a seat on the United Nations Security Council. He thumbed his nose at U.S. President Barack Obama. He had proved as much a liability to the self-image of Canada's elite as he was to their economic agenda.

An age of discontent needed a different kind of politician. A politician with a softer touch, more responsive to pain and grievances, more able to navigate protest and upheaval. A politician who could act proactively in concert with the elite, lest they "be forced to react, later." A politician, even, who could tell the wealthiest to their faces that he would raise their taxes, while still fundamentally serving their interests. Harper was unable or unwilling to make a pivot that a growing segment of the corporate elite now seemed to feel was necessary: to begin placating people's desire for climate action, for recognition of Indigenous rights, for getting a handle on inequality, and to make concessions, certainly symbolic but perhaps even material, to restore confidence in the economic system itself. The magazine of the corporate elite, *Canadian Business*, counselled their readers to take Harper's Liberal alternative seriously. "For those inclined to simply dismiss Justin Trudeau," the editor-in-chief wrote, "don't." Not only did the magazine believe he had "an agenda just as capitalist-friendly as the Conservatives," but it was willing to endorse an even stronger conclusion: "Justin Trudeau might be better for business than Stephen Harper."[18]

It was left to none other than Conrad Black—recently returned from domicile in a Florida prison—to more fully articulate the emerging consensus among the corporate elite. The former business titan, convicted of corporate fraud, had once bankrolled Brian Mulroney's run for the Progressive Conservative leadership, and used his media empire to promote the reunification of the Conservatives in order to challenge the reign of the Liberals. But Harper's government, he wrote in *The National Post*, had become "authoritarian and peevish" and was "frightening in its disregard for democratic institutions." On the other hand, he had been closely watching Justin Trudeau, and he liked what he saw. Trudeau had an "alluring personality" and was "flexible on public finance." Overall, the Liberals had shown that they were "adequately to the right of the NDP not to frighten the cautious Canadian bourgeoisie." Trudeau had deftly positioned himself, Black admiringly noted. "Trudeau seems to be regaining enough of the old Liberal dexterity of being just far enough to the left of the Conservatives as not to seem like tweedle-dee and tweedle-dum to voters of the centre-left," he wrote.[19] Harper "was a good prime minister, but it was time to see him off." Trudeau "has earned his chance."

This version of Trudeau certainly wasn't the man most Canadians had learned about in media portrayals during his rise to the Liberal Party leadership. This was, however, the politician who would eventually govern them. But if "responsible change" was what Trudeau had promised the audiences of the wealthiest one percent, the rest of Canada would need a different kind of slogan and story.

2

Real Change™

In April 2015, a few weeks before his speech to the Canadian Club of Toronto, as the Liberals stumbled in the polls, Trudeau travelled to Washington, D.C., for a meeting with a top official from the Obama White House. With him was his main advisor, Gerald Butts. No mere advisor, Butts was Trudeau's best friend since their undergraduate days at McGill University. They had immediately connected, and Butts had invited Trudeau along to join the debating club, where Butts's dogged style won him two national championships (Trudeau reportedly swayed judges by his reputation alone). They later traveled internationally together, and joined each other's wedding parties. Known to some as the "bearded guru," Butts was a keen political strategist who would serve a more important role than anyone in Trudeau's rise to power and in his method of governing.

Above all, Butts was the shepherd of Trudeau's political trajectory, and a keeper of the story that Trudeau would tell Canadians. In his late 20s, while Trudeau moved to British Columbia to become a high school teacher and snowboard in Whistler, Butts went to work for Ontario Liberal leader and eventual Premier Dalton McGuinty, acting for several years as his principal secretary. In his memoir, McGuinty fondly recalls that they did a "Vulcan mind meld" when they first met, and that Butts could finish his sentences.[1] In the same role he would later fill for PM

Trudeau, Butts showed a knack for intuiting and articulating the story his boss could excel in telling.

When Pierre Elliott Trudeau passed away, Butts helped his friend write the eulogy for his father's funeral, a speech that catapulted the young Trudeau into the national consciousness. As McGuinty's aide, Butts regularly fielded and deflected requests for Trudeau's services at fundraisers or events, admitting to a reporter as early as 2002 that he was careful about "misusing that potential." When pressed about what exactly Trudeau was saving himself for, Butts was coy about his best friend's political aspirations. "But if Justin Trudeau wants to run for office, I don't think he'll have any shortage of people who want to help him out," he told the reporter with a smile.[2]

In the meantime, Butts seemed to do everything to prepare himself for that eventuality. "Almost everyone who knows Mr. Butts describes him as one of the best networkers they have ever met, capable of making a lasting impression on members of the elite even before he joined their number," observed *Globe and Mail* journalist Adam Radwanski, who has written the most in-depth profile of Butts.[3] His rolodex—gathered during his time with McGuinty, followed by a four-year stint as the president of the World Wildlife Fund Canada—spanned Bay Street titans and corporate lawyers, economists and elite environmentalists, and high level figures in the U.S. Democratic and U.K. Labour parties. It was a world apart from Butts's working-class Cape Breton upbringing, though his friends and colleagues would "roll their eyes a bit at the small-town, humble-roots way he still presents himself," according to Radwanski. "He seems to enjoy being in the spotlight, and moving in elite circles, a little more than he'd care to admit," Radwanski wrote. "When he worked for Mr. McGuinty, there were running jokes among co-workers about his tendency to interrupt meetings by taking phone calls from very important people."

When Trudeau gathered his closest friends and advisors in 2012 in Mont Tremblant, Quebec, to decide whether he would run for Liberal leadership, observers agreed that the person in the room who already had Trudeau's pitch clearly mapped out was Gerald Butts. The following year, Scott Reid, an advisor to former Prime Minister Paul Martin, sat in on a speech that Butts gave to a Liberal riding association event in Belleville, Ontario, and noted that the contours of this story were clear. "He repeatedly told the crowd that Trudeau will only win if he stands for change," Reid wrote. "The subtext was unmistakable: a few daring policies are necessary."[4] This was the delicate political maneuver the Liberal Party would seek to pull off: building up buzz about how a Trudeau victory would represent an anti-establishment breakthrough, while simultaneously signaling to the elite that their interests were to be safeguarded.

Rebel Without a Cause

A key part of Butts's early strategy to present Trudeau as an agent of change was to play up a slightly maverick persona. As a striking contrast to the staid appearances and manner of Stephen Harper or NDP leader Tom Mulcair, Radwanski writes that Trudeau's team "would 'let Justin be Justin'—cheery, cocky, prone to dramatic flourishes and occasionally intemperate—rather than trying to make him more traditionally prime ministerial." Always in view of cameras, Trudeau struck an acrobatic yoga pose over a table in a decorous parliamentary committee room; en route to an evening event, he vaulted over a fence to give fans a chance for a selfie. Sometimes the flourishes could be too dramatic. In Ottawa in 2014, giving an on-stage interview at a conference put on by the Liberal-affiliated think tank Canada 2020, Trudeau was asked whether he would support a combat mission in Iraq against the Islamic State. "Why aren't we talking more about the

kind of humanitarian aid Canada must be engaged in, rather
than trying to whip out our CF-18s and show them how big
they are?" Trudeau ad-libbed.[5] To some, it was an edgy and apt
critique of macho generals who play at war. To Butts, it undermined Trudeau's credibility in the eyes of the corporate and media
establishment. Standing at the back of the room, he shook his
head at Liberal staffers who, titillated by the comment, wanted
to spread it on social media.

All this was accompanied by a few ambiguous policy moves
designed to give the impression that Trudeau was bucking political orthodoxy. The Liberal leader reversed his position on mari-
juana and called for its legalization. While giving off a whiff of
cultural non-conformism, it was by that time being eyed by top
cops, Bay Street legal firms, and the corporate sector as a lucrative new market. Then Trudeau kicked Liberal senators out of
the party's caucus, obliging them to sit as independent members
of the chamber. News headlines raved that this "plants seeds
of 'revolution,'" and that it was a "bombshell," even though
senators acknowledged that "nothing has changed" in their voting patterns, and "business as usual continues."[6] In repeated
speeches, he also made it appear that "he sees a return to a bigger, more interventionist federal government," *The Globe and
Mail* noted, though Trudeau left details to the imagination.
On the whole, Butts consciously steered away from elaborating
any clear, core political and economic policies—which *Toronto
Star* reporter Susan Delacourt dubbed "the no-policy policy."[7]
Instead, the Liberals would let the focus on Trudeau's identity
stand in for a concrete program, allowing his personal story to
evoke vaguely transformational politics. He was a rebel, but
without an identifiable cause.

The strategy paid off initially. Before Trudeau launched his
campaign for leadership, most mainstream commentators proph-
esied that the Liberal Party—tainted by the corruption scandals

of the Chrétien years, hobbled by the atrophying of the organization—was heading toward its demise. Peter C. Newman, the best-selling bard of the country's political history, wrote a book-length eulogy entitled *When the Gods Changed: The Death of Liberal Canada*. But Trudeau would oversee an incredible reversal. That reversal didn't rely only on his personality, celebrity and fundraising prowess, or Butts's political savvy: it also came down to sheer hard work. When Trudeau won his seat in the riding of Papineau in Montreal in 2008, he wore out his shoes knocking on thousands of doors. After taking over the party leadership, he insisted this basic axiom of effective, grassroots organizing be scaled up nationally. To do so, the Liberals mimicked the decentralized organizing structure used by Obama's 2008 presidential campaign. Known as the "snowflake" model, it empowered neighbourhood teams of volunteers to take initiative rather than waiting on directives from staffers. Over one weekend alone in May 2015, volunteers knocked on 200,000 doors across the country.[8] All the information gathered was fed back into a sophisticated database, also borrowed from the Obama Democrats. The organizing was supported by a digital team numbering 50 people at its height, and by some estimates reached 18 million Canadians.[9] Both Trudeau and the party soon jumped massively in the polls. It was a complete rebuke to their critics. The brand was rebooted. Infighting seemed a thing of the past. The Liberal Party's prospects had been resuscitated.

Where the Liberals eventually stumbled was on matters of core policy. In early 2015, the Liberals supported Stephen Harper's Anti-Terrorism Act, Bill C-51, which expanded policing and spying powers in the wake of a shooting attack on Parliament Hill. Amnesty International warned that it "could be used to target environmental activists and aboriginal protesters."[10] The legislation was backed by the media and seemed popular, but as scrutiny mounted, public opinion turned resoundingly against it. Even three former Liberal Party leaders—Paul Martin, Jean Chrétien, and John Turner—soon decried its "serious problems for public safety and human rights."[11] While party pollsters insisted it wouldn't hurt them with voters, party organizers saw a significant drop in enthusiasm and recruitment among volunteers—not long after record highs in door knocking. And on the fundraising circuit, Liberal MPs got grief from anxious high-level donors. Meanwhile, the New Democrats were rewarded for their early, principled opposition to Bill C-51 by leaping over the Liberals in the polls (and when the provincial NDP upset the Conservatives in Alberta, they jumped to the top spot—the first time the federal party had occupied that position since a brief moment in the late 1980s). It was a sign that Canadians would vote for a party willing to subscribe to initially unpopular but undeniably progressive stances.

The Theatre of Class Warfare

As Butts and Trudeau travelled to Washington, D.C., in April 2015, they had this lesson on their minds. There they met with John Podesta, former chief of staff to Bill Clinton and, until a month before, the top advisor to President Obama, a position he had left to chair Hilary Clinton's upcoming presidential campaign. The meeting, an advisor to the Liberal Party told me, "straightened out the Canadians' plans." On their return, Trudeau introduced the tax hike on the one percent, a policy straight out of the Obama playbook. Indeed, Trudeau's pitch to the Canadian Club of Toronto was cut-and-pasted from Obama's line, in a television ad in 2012, to "ask the wealthy to pay a little more so the middle class pays less."[12] Obama's own tax hike, as well as his denunciations of "fat cats" on Wall Street, elicited howls from the Republicans and made it seem like he was a champion of working people. But it was couched in a wider set of policies—including a reduction to corporate tax rates that deepened Republican President George Bush's cuts, and a trillion dollar public bailout of the banks—that ushered in the highest corporate profit rates in a century, and which ensured that the overall wealth of the top one percent didn't diminish but actually grew.

Butts had Trudeau employ a similar kind of light Liberal populism, repeating "taxing the one percent" as often as possible, rhetorically channeling the demands of the Occupy movement that had so impacted the public discourse. In one television ad during the 2015 election, Trudeau rode an escalator the wrong way, evoking the tough economic battle for Canadians. And in their most-played ad, he responded to attacks from the Conservatives that he was "not ready" with the message that he had a plan that "works not just for the few, but for everyone." Walking with Parliament Hill in the background, Trudeau pronounced himself "not ready to watch hard-working Canadians lose jobs and fall further behind," but ready instead, echoing Obama again, to "ask our wealthiest to pay more tax so our middle class can pay less."[13] Butts, who closely monitored the New Democrats' announcements to ensure they would not seize the change mantle, knew this would starkly differentiate Trudeau from Mulcair, who had sworn never to raise taxes on the wealthy.[14] The fulminations of the corporate media about Liberal "class war" only reinforced the anti-establishment brand Butts coveted.

Even though the Liberals were finally unveiling seemingly clear policies, there was less to them than met the eye. One needed only to inspect Trudeau's tax policy, for instance, to realize that its brand of class war was more than anything an affected simulation. Economists pointed out that the small increase to the top income bracket for the wealthiest might not even be collected by the government, because the Liberals were not closing other loopholes that the wealthy used to evade paying what they owed. And most of the gains of the accompanying tax cut for the "middle class" in fact went to individuals with incomes between $89,200 and $200,000, who constituted not the middle class but the top ten percent.[15] When Trudeau had told the Bay Street audience that the rich would "help those in Canada with less," he had apparently meant those with almost as much.

Yet, as a rhetorical strategy, it was the appearance of progressivism that counted. This hearkened back to the strategy that Butts had used to help Ontario Liberal leader Dalton McGuinty win his 2003 and 2007 campaigns. In 2007, a splashy promise to create a vaguely defined poverty-reduction strategy—which included a small hike in the minimum wage—helped McGunity acquire an "activist profile," court the progressive vote, and differentiate the Liberals from the provincial New Democrats, which under leader Howard Hampton was nipping at their heels. "We put Hampton in a hell of a box in 2007. We outflanked him on the left," said a former McGuinty advisor.[16] But in government, as the Liberals oversaw fresh corporate tax cuts, persistent wage stagnation, and a growing number of precarious jobs, inequality boomed to rates in Ontario not seen since the Great Depression.

Running Left, Governing Right—A Part of Our Heritage

Feigning to the left during elections wasn't a tactic Butts had invented. It was a Liberal move so much a part of their tradition that it was worthy of a Canadian Heritage Minute. Amidst the anger of depression-wracked Canada in the 1930s, Prime Minister William Lyon Mackenzie King had bemoaned to Winston Churchill that the Cooperative Commonwealth Federation (CCF)—the precursor to the New Democrats—was the "common enemy" of Liberals and Conservatives alike, and campaigning to his left would "see to it that I did not lose any members through the CCF."[17] In the early 1960s, Lester Pearson sensed the shifting mood of the country, and facing pressure from assertive workers' unions, brought in universal public healthcare, pensions, and the 40-hour work week. "I don't intend to let the NDP steal the popular ground of the left," he said. Pierre Elliott Trudeau echoed the New Left in 1968 and won over young voters with promises of "participatory democracy" and a "just society." After losing to the Tories in 1979, he swung left again, this time adopting economic nationalism as the progressive battle cry of the day. The Heritage Minute could be rounded out by an appearance from Jean Chrétien in the early 1990s, introducing a Red Book full of promises on child care and Indigenous rights, and pledging that the Liberals were "not the party of the big corporation... but the party of the little people in Canada." This left-ward posture was as reliably successful during campaigns as it was reliably abandoned in office.

In the spring of 2015, the New Democrats almost made this tactic too easy for the Liberals. As Mulcair visited the Empire Club of Toronto to stress that his government would be the furthest thing from a threat to elite corporate interests, Trudeau made big promises to usher in sweeping democratic reform, starting by replacing the first-past-the-post election system. The advisor to the Liberal Party—the same one in the loop on Trudeau's meeting in Washington, D.C.—urged Butts to add another key plank to Trudeau's pitch to be Canada's progressive option: deficit spending. For decades, politicians across the spectrum had been gripped by a right-wing economic orthodoxy that held that budget deficits were an assured disaster. This dogma was so powerful that parties scrupulously presented detailed costings of their plans, bowing before the altar of the balanced budget, living in fear of being branded as fiscally irresponsible. Yet, deficit-spending in an economic downturn was common sense: it increased demand, stimulated business activity, and helped the government build projects or provide much-needed services. With increased economic activity came greater government revenue, and the ability to pay down deficits. Its political use, however, was an ideological ruse to constrain governments from acting ambitiously in the interests of ordinary Canadians (when it came to doling out corporate tax cuts or bailing out banks, concerns about deficits mysteriously disappeared).

Trudeau, however, continued to passionately defend fiscal conservatism. "Our platform will be fully costed, fiscally responsible, and a balanced budget," he said in April. In July, he repeated his message: "I've committed to continuing to run balanced budgets… Liberals balance budgets. That's what history has shown." And in the first televised leaders' debate in early August, he criticized Stephen Harper for turning the budget surpluses of the Jean Chrétien and Paul Martin governments into Conservative deficits.[18] Meanwhile, economic advisors like Chrystia Freeland were putting the finishing touches on an infrastructure plan to court progressive voters. Journalists Tristan Markle and Sarah Beuhler point out that when the Canadian economy began to enter an official recession at the end of the summer, it gave the Liberals a chance to super-charge the plan's progressive symbolism. "A technical recession provided the perfect rationale to jettison a balanced budget policy proving more unpopular every day," they wrote.[19]

Besides the shift in the economy, a play to the centre by the New Democrats created an opening for the Liberals to orchestrate a dramatic reversal of their position. At the end of August, Mulcair, campaigning in Tory-friendly ridings in southwestern Ontario, promised New Democrats would finance their promises without running a deficit. Besides the promise not to raise taxes on the richest, any tax increases on corporations would be "slight," "graduated," and "reasonable." The New Democrats' star economics candidate Andrew Thomson, a former Saskatchewan finance minister, followed up with an admission that some cuts would be "inevitable."[20] On the Liberal tour bus, passing through southwest Ontario at the same time, it was hard to suppress the joy. It was obvious to them immediately that this was a major strategic error, making the New Democrats seem too much like the Conservatives. "I don't get it," one Liberal insider said at the time. "They had a foot on our throat and they took it off."[21] A few months later, Justin Trudeau admitted his team realized this was the decisive turning point of the election campaign. "When they said we're going to balance Stephen Harper's budget, we realized 'OK, you know what? That's probably the election right there,'" he recalled in an interview at the end of 2015. "My one worry was actually that the NDP was going to have heard the same things that we did and pitch an even more ambitious program. We were worried that the NDP was going to go really big."[22]

The Liberals pounced. "The choice in this election is between jobs and growth or austerity and cuts," Trudeau shot back while speaking at an evening rally near Brampton, Ontario. "Tom Mulcair chose the wrong side." The next day, former Prime Minister Paul Martin was trotted out to attack Mulcair for endorsing an austerity agenda. "If the NDP has decided to move to the far right, so be it—that's their decision," Martin said.[23] In the 1990s, Martin had been the primary architect of the most inequality-exploding right-wing austerity program in Canadian history—which made his criticism of the New Democrats akin to an arsonist reprimanding boy scouts for starting campfires outside town. "Stephen Harper won't help you, and Tom Mulcair can't help you, because he's signed on to Harper's budget," soon became one of Trudeau's main campaign refrains. "Ours is the most progressive platform in this election."

Two days later, Trudeau gamely operated a giant crane at a construction site in Oakville, and then announced what the Liberals called the biggest infrastructure investment in Canadian history—including transit, affordable housing, child care, and clean energy—on double Harper's annual infrastructure spending. To do so, the Liberals would go into deficits, reversing a stance that Trudeau had passionately defended up until just three weeks before. They would run $10-billion deficits for each of the next three years, before balancing the budget in 2019.[24] Suddenly, the Liberals looked like a people's party.

There was some dudgeon from the usual right-wing media quarters: the cover of the next day's *Winnipeg Sun* screamed, "Political Suicide." But polling numbers soon confirmed strengthening support for deficits, and by October, four out of five Canadians supported stimulating the economy this way.[25] Nor were there cries of apoplexy from corporate quarters. This was in large part because Bay Street, in recent years, had itself started calling for deficit spending to jumpstart economic growth. Nova Scotia MP and former Martin cabinet minister Scott Brison and others fanned across the country, reassuring Chambers of Commerce that Liberals would be responsible economic managers.

The beginning of the Liberal ascent in the polls began at that moment, over a gesture that seemed to clarify who was ready to act on behalf of the interests of a majority of Canadians. Over the following days, the New Democrats' lead in the polls evaporated. They had risen in popularity by embracing a critical stance toward Harper's draconian security legislation. They crashed by deserting that kind of boldness. An honest election postmortem overseen by the outgoing New Democrat president Rebecca Blaikie later faulted the party for essentially offering

Canadians "cautious change," no match for Trudeau's pledge of "real change."[26]

In September, a few weeks before an election that the Liberals were now coasting toward, the advisor who had been on Butts's case in the spring about deficit spending wrote him a satisfied email. "How do the polls look now, Gerry?" he asked cheekily. He says he received a short response: "well, if we had done it when you told us to do it, it wouldn't have worked as well," Butts wrote.

It was a fascinating, revealing peek into the mind of a master strategist who, drawing on a long-standing Liberal practice of out-maneuvering the New Democrats, was yet again about to catapult the Liberal Party into power. The marketing of Justin Trudeau's Liberal Party, which had seemed in jeopardy only a few months before, had been pulled off with resounding success. The party had renewed its allegiances to Canada's corporate elite, while selling itself, yet again, as the vehicle for a dramatic break with the status quo. And it had a leader who was about to become a globally viral image of fresh, progressive leadership.

3

The Clickbait Prime Minister

In one corner stood Patrick "Brazz Knuckles" Brazeau—an Indigenous Senator appointed by Stephen Harper, muscular and heavily tattooed, with a black belt in martial arts. In the other corner, with the bookie odds 3-1 against him, stood a lighter Justin "the Canadian Kid" Trudeau, at the time still a Liberal backbencher. It was a charity boxing match in March 2012, but it also had much bigger stakes. In Ottawa's political bubble, it had transformed into a weighty drama, a decisive test of an MP dismissed as a "reed-thin," "pedigreed," "young Dauphin," the unproven son of a famous father.[1] The right-wing media were relishing the prospect of the cocky Brazeau clobbering both Trudeau and his political aspirations.

In the first round, Brazeau charged, swinging wildly and connecting on a few big punches. Trudeau seemed momentarily shaken, but soon found his feet. When Trudeau walked to his corner after the bell, there was a big smile on his face. He had let Brazeau slug himself into exhaustion. By the third round, with Trudeau landing heavy blows on a stunned and out-skilled Brazeau, it was all over, as the referee called it a technical knockout.

In his Liberal red boxing shorts, Trudeau had shown that he could match Stephen Harper's controlling, steely hardness with his own version of pugilistic masculinity—and that his party, despite a devastating electoral collapse in 2011, could perhaps even make a comeback. Pundits in all the major newspapers agreed, describing the fight as a turning point. In their eyes, Trudeau's rise to Canada's top political office was now practically ordained.

Charity boxing matches are usually bar room larks. Not this one. Unwittingly, Brazeau had become a pawn in a piece of very effective political theatre. Trudeau, who had amateur-boxed all his life, had not merely trained methodically, practically guaranteeing a victory over an out-of-shape opponent. He and his advisors had crafted the optics of the stunt from the start, including selecting his Conservative opponent. "It wasn't random," Trudeau mischievously told a journalist from *Rolling Stone* magazine in 2017, five years later. "I wanted someone who would be a good foil, and we stumbled upon the scrappy tough-guy senator from an Indigenous community. He fit the bill, and it was a very nice counterpoint... I saw it as the right kind of narrative, the right story to tell." According to the magazine feature, which otherwise heaped praise on Trudeau, he had said this with all the "calculation of a CFO in a company-budget markup session."[2]

In 2012, during a training session in the gym before the fight, Trudeau had given another interview to a documentary film crew that revealed some of this acute self-awareness. "Never underestimate the power of symbols in today's world," he told them.[3] Trudeau would rely on this knowledge not merely to spin a story around a boxing match, but to forge a powerful super-brand to revive and varnish the progressive image and allure of the Liberal Party.

Candid Moments with a Celebrity Statesman

They were all real headlines, some from the world's most prestigious newspapers, reading like a parody of the most over-the-top internet stories. "The New Young Face of Canadian Politics," swooned *Vogue*. "Justin Trudeau does 'jazz hands' at G20," exclaimed *The Huffington Post*. "Justin Trudeau's 7 Secrets to Being Extraordinarily Charming," read another. "Meet the prime minister of Canada, our new man crush," read yet another. "Can Justin Trudeau's Socks Save the World?" asked *The Guardian*, seemingly only half tongue-in-cheek. And there was even the prototypical *BuzzFeed* listicle: "Literally Just 27 Really Hot Photos of Justin Trudeau."[4]

A bit of fawning over a young, good-looking, newly-elected statesmen is unavoidable, but Trudeau's team had sought out this sort of coverage, running the most image-focused campaign in Canadian history. Through the summer and fall of 2015, the media had trouble keeping up with Trudeau, as he hiked up mountains, paddled down rivers, and balanced his son Hadrian over his head, always inviting the gaze of the camera. But when Trudeau took office and the global media clued in, the stream of viral-ready images and videos went through the internet's stratosphere. Sightings of a vigorous, shirtless prime minister became a national social media past-time. There he was, getting caught with a surfboard interloping at a beach wedding (bare chested), photobombing teenagers preparing for their prom during his morning jog in Vancouver, or posing for selfies with a family hiking in the Gatineau woods (bare chested again). When no new material could be generated, old images—such as of Trudeau doing a peacock yoga pose in a parliamentary committee room back in 2013—resurfaced and took global media headlines by storm.[5]

It's standard for modern politicians to carefully market themselves, but the Liberal government's efforts were unprecedented both in their intensity and skill. As with the most effective marketing, the symbolism of Trudeau's brand catered to widespread desires: for social and political change, for a new kind of emotive and unscripted anti-politician, and for an open and progressive government in touch with ordinary people's perspectives. Harnessing his celebrity, nostalgia for the prior wave of Trudeaumania, and fatigue over a decade of vindictive rule by Stephen Harper, Trudeau's team had turned him into the world's first clickbait prime minister.

Trudeau's team drew on his authentic strengths, but highlighted them shrewdly. Besides his physical attributes, they directed media attention to activities that displayed his likeability, compassion, and delight for people and fauna: welcoming refugees at the airport, hugging pandas at the zoo, or taking patients from a children's hospital to view the latest *Star Wars* (which also alluded to famous coverage of an outing he had taken with his father to see *Return of the Jedi* as an 11-year-old in 1983).[6] It helped that a lifetime under the media microscope had given him a consummate sense of how to play to the media's impulses. "I see images as a way to communicate," he told journalist Susan Delacourt in an interview a few months after the election.[7]

The day throngs awaited his cabinet's swearing-in at Rideau Hall, Trudeau was captured on a CBC camera telling communications director Kate Purchase that they were "tricking" the media by having the bus drop off ministers at a distance. "Getting off the bus is such an ugly shot that we're making sure they get the walk over from 24 [Sussex Drive]," he said.[8] And when CBC's Peter Mansbridge mused about how the bus that was ferrying ministers to their first meetings made him think of campers "singing kumbaya," Trudeau got a perfect chance to playfully chastise him for being out of touch. "Well, maybe that's your experience on a bus Peter," he said, "but a lot of people take the bus every day to go to work."[9] (The Chrétien government had used a similar tactic in 1993 to signal that the lavish Mulroney era was supposedly over: ministers were driven to parliament in mini-buses on their first day; then, out of the view of the cameras, the passengers jumped out of the vehicles and into chauffeured limousine sedans.)[10] In CBC footage of Trudeau's first morning in his office, you can catch another remark: Gerald Butts saying that the best way to respond to questions about the cabinet's gender balance would be to reference the current year, which Trudeau promptly turned into the "quip" about it being 2015.[11]

Few of Trudeau's seemingly candid moments were ever out of the reach of his full-time personal photographer. A *Maclean's* journalist observed that, in order to capture Trudeau jogging past the prom-bound teenagers, photographer Adam Scotti would have had to rush ahead of an agreed-upon route, set up the frame of his shot, and make sure he was ready just as Trudeau ran by. "What once appeared like a pleasant coincidence of timing for whomever gets to pose with the prime minister, is starting to feel even more like a staged exercise than it was before," wrote Aaron Hutchins.[12] The staging of Trudeau's candid moments reached its peak when a video went viral of him giving an audience an "off-the-cuff" explanation of quantum computing; the riff had in fact been prepared, and the question planted.[13]

And it wasn't just Justin Trudeau's image that the Liberals focused on. Staffers from the entire Liberal cabinet blasted out endless flattering photos and memes on social media, underlining everything apparently progressive, green, and innovative about the government. They seemed to spare no expense. According to access-to-information documents obtained by *Blacklock's Reporter*, the Liberals spent $212,000 on the cover of the 2017 Budget alone (including $89,500 for talent fees and photos of "models posing as middle class Canadians").[14]

These calculated facets of the brand made one rethink even the most seemingly spontaneous gestures, like that visit Justin Trudeau had paid to the Montreal metro station in his riding the morning after his election victory. The trip was no doubt motivated in part by the instincts of a sincere, sociable guy keen to connect with his constituents as they headed to work on the subway. But all the same, it was a gesture sure to communicate spontaneity and accessibility, the antithesis of the rigid stage management associated with Stephen Harper. And more subtly, it made a visual connection to the Liberal television ad that had been in heavy circulation during the election campaign, in which Trudeau, evoking how hard life had gotten for many Canadians, tried to ride a down-moving escalator. Here he was, the day after the election, greeting people at the top.

Trudeau's government represented a new pinnacle in the merger of corporate branding and political campaigning. For decades, celebrities had been conscripted to create a familiar and alluring personification of faceless corporate giants. "The blander and more homogenized the product, the more distinctive the mask it needs to wear," *Guardian* columnist George Monbiot writes.[15] Cars, cigarettes, alcohol, watches, deodorant, razors: the allure of each is enhanced by the sense of connection and trust imparted by an associated celebrity. Barack Obama was the first great celebrity statesman of the 21st century, the charismatic face of a Democratic party that implemented the blandly lethal dictates of Wall Street.

Trudeau would play a similar celebrity role, using his dazzling image to fulfill a pledge he had made to the corporate elite at the Canadian Club of Toronto: restoring faith not only in the Liberal Party, but in the tattered legitimacy of capitalism. And in the wake of Trudeau's 2015 election, it seemed to be working: the Edelman Trust Barometer showed that trust in government and big business, which had plummeted in the years after the financial recession, had jumped back up.[16] As millions clicked and consumed his beaming smile, as loving crowds swarmed him again and again, Trudeau offered an easy and cheap simulation of the openness, dynamism, and change that his government claimed to stand for.

A Weapon of Mass Distraction

"Canada is back, my friends," Trudeau announced to a roar of applause at the United Nations climate summit in Paris, in December 2015. It was not long after he had come to power, and he had arrived in France with a delegation of 300 people in tow (he had even invited opposition leaders to hitch a ride on his plane). His speech to the summit, in which he declared that Canada would "act based on the best scientific evidence and advice," received a standing ovation. *The New York Times* heralded the "swift about-face" from the Canadian government, congratulating Trudeau for "reversing course" on climate change.

Trudeau's lead negotiator at the talks, Environment Minister Catherine McKenna, certainly made it seem that way: in a surprise move of the summit, she was instrumental in pushing for the Paris accord to establish as its goal a limit of 1.5 degrees of global warming. At the last major negotiations in Copenhagen in 2009, governments had agreed to limit warming to 2 degrees—which African leaders had called a "death sentence," and low-lying Pacific Island nations a guarantee of their disappearance. Even though the new 1.5-degree target wasn't binding, it was a powerful and important pledge. Yet when Trudeau returned to Canada, his practical steps would walk back the symbolic ones: a frenzy of fossil fuel developments that was utterly incompatible with what he had just signed onto. Over the next year alone, he would approve the Kinder Morgan and Line 3 tar sands pipelines and a massive liquefied natural gas plant in British Columbia; allow seismic testing to continue in the Arctic; and permit deepwater oil and gas exploration in the Gulf of Saint Lawrence.[17]

On one of the last days of the negotiations in Paris, a group of Canadian youth delegates had staged a protest in the conference halls to inject a note of skepticism about Trudeau's brand of selfie diplomacy. "We want to be heard, not just seen," they chanted. Trudeau had refused their request for a meeting, but he had offered them a photo opportunity. "If he only wants photo-ops," 27-year-old delegate Katie Perfitt said, "we have serious concerns about his ability to develop sound policies that are justice-based and in line with climate science." Media coverage noted patronizingly that the youth seemed out of tune with the ecstatic reception Trudeau had received.

His brand was serving its core political function: distraction and deflection. A key strategy of Trudeau's government was to make dizzyingly bold proclamations to audiences abroad—a pledge to tackle corporate globalization, take on climate change, compassionately open Canada's doors to desperate refugees, or reverse the denial of the rights of Indigenous peoples. These unfailingly elicited fawning international coverage, bolstering their domestic credibility. What would follow next were not policies to ambitiously fulfill these pledges, but ploys to quietly evacuate them of any meaning. In France, this tactic even has a name: *effet d'annonce*. If a politician delivered a significant announcement in a splashy enough way, its effect in netting widespread praise could distract from the fact that they never get around to making that announcement meaningful.

Trudeau put a different spin on his global media seduction. The magazine spreads and international coverage was a way to reach citizens at home and abroad. "I need people to stay involved and stay engaged and stay positive about what we're doing," he told *The Canadian Press* in late 2015. "The idea of checking in every four years to say whether you like the person in government or whether you want to change them is not what engaged citizenship is in the 21st century. So the more I can stay attentive to people and close to them, the better I will be at serving them."[18] But what the Trudeau government was cultivating looked more like brand loyalty than engaged citizenship—like a fanbase instead of a critical electorate.

For the first years of Trudeau's time in office, the media seemed to be his most steadfast fans. "This is *our* Camelot," a Canadian reporter remarked, only half-jokingly, to journalist John Powers, as they watched the swearing-in ceremony at Rideau Hall in the fall of 2015. A few months later, in the final days of the Obama presidency, a giddy troupe of Canadian reporters traveled with Trudeau for a state visit to the White House. The reporting neglected to mention how Obama had fallen far short of his own brand: the uptick in drone warfare, the deportation of nearly 2.5 million immigrants, and his entrenchment of mass surveillance. The Twitter account of CBC News Alerts focused its attention on more weighty matters: the designer outfits Sophie Gregoire Trudeau would be wearing ("Lucian Matis dress, Ela handbag, Zvelle shoes, John de Jong earrings, Dean Davidson ring").[19]

Canada's corporate and state media were not merely suckered by Liberal PR tricks. More fundamentally, many in the elite media had a shared stake in Trudeau's political project. After a decade of crudely social conservative politics under Stephen Harper—not to mention the global coverage of crack-smoking Toronto mayor Rob Ford—their self-image on the global stage had been battered. In Trudeau, they had found a source for its rehabilitation. The praise from liberal writers reached absurd heights. *GQ* writer Stephen Marche declared that the "political vision through which Trudeau has attained and maintained power is unique in the world as it stands… It's not the same as a Clinton or a Bush running for President. It would be closer to a Washington or a Jefferson."[20] The conservative wing of Canada's media class, meanwhile, raged about Trudeau's supposedly tax-and-spend and anti-oil agenda—thereby feeding the myth about the Liberals' left-wing impulses, enabling their very communications strategy.

All the while, Trudeau returned time and again to the international stage to burnish his brand. In the spring of 2018, Trudeau signed a partnership with French President Emmanuel Macron in a ceremony at the presidential palace in Paris, vowing to intensify his climate efforts. "Trudeau and Macron promise to double down on climate-change fight," a CBC headline uncritically read, quoting Trudeau's announcement that the pact would "encourage and accelerate the achievement of the Paris Agreement targets through concrete measures to make this agreement in principle a reality."[21] But the only thing he had doubled down on was his support for the Kinder Morgan tar sands pipeline—which, the very day before meeting with Macron, he had offered to publicly bail out. Like with a web-surfer scrolling disappointed through a piece of clickbait, image had triumphed over content.

The Politician Without Qualities

It wasn't a main-stage TED talk, but it might as well have been. Justin Trudeau gazed meaningfully at the crowd, turned to each side, and then began his address. He reminded them that "diversity doesn't have to be a weakness." He exhorted them to "develop common understanding across divides." He stressed that it was within their grasp to "eliminate extreme poverty" or "end terrible diseases." Changing the world will require courage, he said with a clench of his fist, but being "anchored in their sense of rightness, willing to pit their ideals against all comers," wouldn't cut it. "To let yourself be vulnerable to another point of view—that's what takes true courage."[22]

There was little to disagree with in Trudeau's commencement speech to the 2018 graduating class of NYU. Like a hallmark

TED talk, everyone could nod along to its Big Idea. It scorned polarization, positioned itself beyond ideologies, and imagined irreconcilable material interests resolved by a can-do, win-win attitude. It left you with warm, fuzzy feelings, rather than concrete proposals for systemic change. And it was geared to go viral—which it promptly did, carried in media outlets in the U.S. and around the world, reinforcing the impression that Canada's prime minister could not be a more vivid contrast to Donald Trump.

Much of Trudeau's success relied on this ideological versatility, which strongly echoed Barack Obama. The U.S. President, Matt Taibbi wrote, had cultivated a persona that was like "an ingeniously crafted human cipher, a man without race, ideology, geographic allegiances, or, indeed, sharp edges of any kind. You can't run against him on the issues because you can't even find him on the ideological spectrum."[23] One of Trudeau's most lampooned statements, made during a 2015 stump speech, was in fact a poorly paraphrased version of a comment made by Obama: "We're proposing a strong and real plan. We can grow the economy not from the top down... but from the heart outwards."[24] (Obama had said that the "economy grows not from the top down but from the middle out and the bottom up").

You can search the entirety of Trudeau's memoir *Common Ground* for a clear articulation of a political philosophy or a social program or even just a few bedrock principles: you won't find them. There are careful disavowals of "resentments" and "extremes." His favourite line of attack against parties to his left and right is to accuse them of "divisiveness." "Serious inequality isn't a myth, as some conservative commentators claim, nor is it a slogan for promoting class warfare," he writes, to point out he cares deeply about inequality but would never dare suggest it entails winners or losers.[25] Instead, we "need to be open to shared prosperity just as we are open to diversity." Denying fundamental social conflicts in society serves a particular function: it disguises the profound disparities of power and wealth that are the truest source underlying the country's divisions, and veils the power of the corporate elite that have helped create them.

Trudeau's glossy political versatility wasn't natural, but had been developed in his thirties, on the inspirational corporate speaking circuit. Between 2006 and 2008, he was in demand as an "Education, Environment & Youth Advocate"—according to the billing on Speakers' Spotlight agency, his "electric charisma and inspirational message leaves audiences educated, entertained and ready to make a difference."[26] He made a tidy sum, pulling in $290,00 in 2006 and $462,000 in 2007.[27] In a speech in 2008, you see on display the rhetorical mode he would deploy as prime minister a decade later (as well as the stool that would become a staple of all his town halls). "So we have a whole new set of challenges and we have to start thinking differently," he says. "Everything is connected. Everything we do and do not do affects the entire system." He continues in the same vein. "Humanity is going to have to break out of this pattern that has been the story of our lives, of our entire history. How do we do it? We do it by opening our eyes and opening our hearts: to others, to difference, to diversity, to discovery."[28] All of it sounded like vintage Trudeau: oratory without political content, hazy idealism without clear substance, and moral ambition without distinct purpose.

For the elite media, the honeymoon ended with the so-called India disaster. On a few occasions on that trip, Trudeau's family wore traditional Indian clothing commissioned from top designers. But it didn't have the desired effect. "Fashion diplomacy is only ever somewhat notable when it goes right, but it's possible the Trudeaus are doing it too right," Vanity Fair suggested. As Omar Abdullah, the former chief minister of the north Indian state of Jammu and Kashmir, put it on Twitter, "Is it just me or is this choreographed cuteness all just a bit much now? Also FYI we Indians don't dress like this every day sir, not even in Bollywood." There is, however, little proof in polling data to back up the idea that that Trudeau took a hit for his overseas fashion choices. It's not as if Canadians cared when Stephen Harper donned an ungainly, ill-fitting powder blue sari. India wasn't the moment when Canadians turned on Trudeau; it's when the elite media did. What really rankled the Canadian pundits was the sense that Trudeau had embarrassed them. Trudeau's meme machine had finally backfired.

4

In the House of Justin

"This is revolutionary, it really is," gushes Omar Raza, the policy secretary of the Liberal Party. "We're in new territory. We are trailblazing like you won't believe." Raza is on stage on the first morning of the national convention in Halifax in April 2018, describing the new Liberal policy-making process to a few hundred delegates. Hair slicked to the side, hands gesturing vigorously, shirt adorned with buttons saluting his leader, he's like an eager young preacher getting warmed up at Sunday service.

"This is a policy process that is not about words on paper, but the people it represents," he says as he opens a policy workshop in a break-out room. "From the grassroots, from someone who is perhaps your neighbour, who had an idea and brought it forward as a resolution, it will now form party policy for eight years."

It sounds like everything Justin Trudeau promised the Liberal Party would become: a dynamic and democratic vehicle designed to usher in bold, progressive change. To help achieve this vision, in 2012 the Liberals had created a new class of "supporters" who could vote in the leadership race without paying membership fees. Hundreds of thousands of people had joined the party to vote for Trudeau. Then, at their convention in 2016, the party voted to get rid of paid membership fees entirely. Widely-reported in the media, it was a signal that the Liberals were the "most open political movement in Canada," Trudeau had said, "a modern, responsive, wide-open organization that anyone can join and shape and work to build." According to the president of the Treasury Board, Scott Brison, the New Democrats and Conservatives remained "traditional old-style political clubs." But "young people in particular don't want to be part of a club, they want to shape a political movement that reflects their progressive values."

The new policy process, Raza explains, unfolds as follows: individuals had submitted resolutions that were put to an online vote, in which nearly 6,000 members participated. The top 30 resolutions moved ahead. At the convention, voting would whittle the resolutions down to 20, and on the plenary floor, members would approve 15 becoming official party policy.

"In plenary tomorrow you'll see what you've usually seen at conventions: heated debate in front of the full national caucus, national membership, national party," Raza promises. "This will then inform platforms, discussions, and ideas moving forward with our members in parliament and our government." The voice of a party's base—channeled via internet technology, harnessed by genuine democracy—finding clear expression through the party's top representatives. Who wouldn't be ready to jump up and join in some hallelujahs?

After his speech, Raza gives the floor to party members who have sponsored resolutions—a chance for them to make their last pitch. The president of the Young Liberals, Mira Ahmad, makes an impassioned plea to decriminalize sex work. Other resolutions are just as unequivocally left-wing: they call for the government to create a Seniors' Ministry, sign the UN Treaty to ban nuclear weapons, develop comprehensive services in restorative justice, and take measures against tax avoidance, including by shutting down tax havens.

The resolution to shut down tax havens is presented by Judith Quinn, an elderly healthcare worker from Montreal, who accompanies her pitch with a cartoon slideshow. She speeds through the slides, landing on an image of a Kochtopus, visualizing the U.S. billionaire family's moneyed tentacles spreading through think tanks, government, lobby groups, and the media. "I'm picking on the Koch brothers, but it could be any number of extremely wealthy companies or individuals with undue political influence," she says. Her presentation wouldn't have been out of place at an activist gathering in a community hall, rather than in Halifax's gleaming new convention centre.

An Old Boys' (and Girls') Club

If Quinn wanted Canadian examples of "undue political influence," she wouldn't have had to look far. Down the hall, a group of Liberal staffers paced the entrance of the Laurier Club lounge, carefully checking badges. To enter, you had to be one of the party's high-level donors, having given the party $1,500—just short of the maximum allowable annual donation. Money in exchange for political access and influence was baked into the Laurier Club's creation. It had been founded in 1986, after John Turner's defeat by Brian Mulroney ended a nearly unbroken 20-year Liberal stretch in power. It was the twilight of the first Trudeau era, when the party's brief flirtation with economic nationalism in the early 1980s had disconcerted their allies on Bay Street and antagonized Alberta's oil barons. The Laurier Club served to patch up and rekindle relationships between corporate leaders, wealthy patrons, and senior party officials and parliamentarians. Its founder, Leo Kolber, was a businessman with deep pockets who was one of the party's chief fundraisers. In the late 1970s, Pierre Elliott Trudeau's Quebec lieutenant Marc Lalonde had asked Kolber if he could raise $50,000 for the party. "Tell you what," Kolber said, "you get Trudeau to come to my house for a fundraiser, and I'll get you a hundred." He hosted garden parties at 24 Sussex Drive and intimate dinners for Trudeau and other Liberal leaders at his posh Westmount home atop the Mont-Royal mountain. Rewarded later with a Senate appointment, he would take credit for convincing Prime Minister Chrétien and Finance Minister Paul Martin to cut the capital gains tax used by Canada's wealthiest from 75 to 50 percent (and in 2017, *The Toronto Star* reported that his name was associated with an offshore tax haven account worth tens of millions of dollars).[1]

Men fraternizing in smoke-filled rooms decked out with landscape art and Mission furniture may be a thing of the past, but lobbying firms in the country's capital still advise their clients to join the Laurier Club. What you gain are invitations to exclusive events year-round, attended by prominent MPs and sometimes the prime minister, and access to the special lounge at convention. I've often heard Liberals say this a way to "appreciate" their donors. But having attended Conservative and New Democrat conventions, I know that those political parties seem to have figured out appreciative gestures without offering a suite set apart from the rest of the delegates.

In Halifax, the Laurier Club lounge is packed and noisy through the entire day. Journalists are prohibited, but I found a way to sneak in. There were tables laden with a buffet of veal and mushroom burgers and finely arranged salads. As I piled some food on a plate, I made small talk with a woman whose business card, which she quickly handed me, detailed her Liberal credentials: former Senate staffer, president of a Provincial Women's Association, and recent candidate for a nomination in an Ottawa riding. I asked if she thought it was ironic that the "most open political movement" in the country still offered the perks of a private club. She looked at me, and then she looked at the mushroom burger on my plate.

Next to us, waiters skipped from one group to the next, collecting empty glasses served at the open bar. Former justice and Natural Resources Minister Anne McLellan was reclining on a leather couch, white wine in her hand. Past me walked former Foreign Affairs Minister Pierre Pettigrew, tan as a pumpkin. Over there were current ministers Ralph Goodale, Ahmed Hussen, François-Philippe Champagne and Jane Philpott. The room smelled of spilled beer and raw power.

For every parliamentarian, you could count nearly a dozen lobbyists in the room, sometimes awkwardly circling ministers like teenagers at a high school dance. But more often than not, they blended seamlessly into the socializing. I bumped into an executive assistant from a major union, who helped me identify others in the room. He pointed to lobbyists for Kinder Morgan and the Canadian Association of Petroleum Producers. There were others from fertilizer and potash companies, hovering around Agricultural Minister Lawrence McAuley. There was also Robert Sutherland, the spectacled director of government relations for Innovative Medicines Canada. His presence was perhaps to be expected, considering his pharmaceutical association's lobbying in 2018 had jumped by 500 percent from the previous year, as the Liberals struck an advisory council to consider a universal pharmacare program that could potentially eat into drug company profits.[2] And in the corner, there was a loud clique from the Liberal-friendly Summa agency, which represents clients like Google, Boeing, and Canadian National Railway. None of these lobbyists had officially announced their presence at the convention, weren't showcasing themselves at booths, and certainly hadn't proposed policy resolutions. Why should they? With a bit of money, direct access to the party's decision-makers was guaranteed here.

If Omar Raza is a public face of the Liberal Party, the lobbyist I struck up a conversation with is its private face. I found him standing alone at a bar table, nursing a beer, wearing a bespoke suit and alligator skin shoes. A card-carrying Liberal, he worked for a Conservative-linked lobbying firm, National

Public Relations. They boast a hefty corporate portfolio. They manage the Canadian media profile of U.S. fighter-jet manufacturer Lockheed Martin, help car manufacturer Ford sell luxury SUVs to millennials, and won approval from the Liberal government for a major liquified natural gas plant in British Columbia. They had some notorious contracts in their recent past: in the early 2000s, they ran the "Canadian Coalition for Responsible Environmental Solutions," an astroturf campaign funded by oil companies that tried to kill Canada's ratification of the Kyoto Protocol. Though identified most closely with the Conservatives, their website advertises that they've even done speech-writing for Prime Minister Trudeau.[3]

After complimenting his shoes, I asked him how being a Liberal helps with his lobbying. "It's useful for me to understand how Liberals think," he said. "I can help a firm speak the language of Liberals, to fit their objectives to the party's priorities."

He told me about a contract with a major construction and appliance company. While completing it, he had given a group of Liberal parliamentarians a tour of the company's plant, where they tested Virtual Reality goggles that simulate working on a construction site. "They loved that. Innovation has been big with this government, so we showed them how we're 'innovative,'" he said, making bunny ears with his fingers and chuckling.

"People have a sinister image of lobbyists whispering in politicians' ears," he said. "But that's mostly just stereotypes. It's all much more straightforward." He put down his beer and looked around. "This is a great place not for lobbying, but for building relationships. It's where the party gels."

Perhaps it was more straightforward. These lobbyists had a discreet presence here not merely because they didn't want to attract attention, but because they didn't consider themselves altogether distinct from the Liberals. Corporate power isn't extraneous to the Liberal Party. Corporate power is integral to it. That power didn't have to go to great lengths to bend the party to its shape, because the party was already willingly and comfortably bent that way. That power simply had to cheerfully co-exist with Liberal activists denouncing the undue influence of corporations a few rooms over.

Grassroots Democracy, Liberal-Style

After a night of revelry at a waterfront party, where free drinks and Halifax's iconic donairs were generously furnished, members trickled into the plenary hall the next morning for the policy debate. But of the more than 3,000 people attending the convention, in the end, barely a hundred showed up. Next to me a journalist, looking confused, reached for her phone. Surely the voting would be delayed, she tweeted.

Not so. The top 15 resolutions were quickly passed, almost all of them without any debate, most unanimously. Five were voted to the highest priority: implementing a universal pharmacare program, increasing mental health services, decriminalizing drug possession, decriminalizing sex work, and improving employee pensions. The Liberal leadership had endorsed none of these policies to date, which raised the obvious question: what would happen now to the democratic will of the party?

We got a sense that afternoon at a media Q&A with Justin Trudeau, to which he arrived buoyant after his convention speech was received with boisterous standing ovations. A journalist asked how he would move forward with the plan to decriminalize drugs. "We're proud about the opportunity to draw on the ideas from all across the country," he said, beginning a long roundabout politician's answer. "This is the exciting part of being a really open movement. We look forward to seeing what the grassroots have to say about where their priorities are. We will of course reflect on next steps for a broad range of issues they bring up. We're still going through the process of prioritizing resolutions."

"On that particular issue," he concluded, shrugging his shoulders, "it's not part of our plans."

The previous morning, Raza had neglected to mention the last stage of the policy-making process: after the membership's vote, resolutions are sent to a national platform committee for that final act of "prioritization." That committee, we would find out several months later, would be made up of a few select MPs, chaired by Ralph Goodale and Mona Fortier, and the prime minister—not exactly the grassroots base. With a shrug, Trudeau had just consigned the third-highest priority of Liberal members to policy oblivion.

Nor had Raza mentioned that the new Liberal constitution approved in 2016—after being developed by party president and Trudeau's close friend, Anna Gainey—granted more power than ever to the prime minister and party insiders. Previously, chairs of the committee responsible for overseeing the party's platform had been elected democratically at conventions. Now they would be appointed by the party's board of directors, who were given sole authority to run the policy process. The national campaign committee, which oversaw nominations, candidate vetting, and the promotion of the platform, had previously been appointed by the board of directors. But now they would be exclusively appointed by the party leader. The constitutional changes had briefly ignited controversy during the 2016 convention, before members were placated by minor amendments and Trudeau's reassurances. "If I believed for a second that the new constitution was about taking power away from the grassroots, I would be right there with you, shoulder to shoulder, speaking out against it," he had dramatically told party members from a microphone on the convention floor.[4] But there was simply not much power to take away from the grassroots, because they had so little to start with. It was one thing for the Liberal Party to empower their members when they were not in government, as they had in the run-up to the 2015 elections—that's when they needed volunteers to energetically knock doors and get out the vote. It was another thing entirely for members to get any input into the matter of governing.

In 1968, a certain other prime minister had made grand promises about introducing "participatory democracy" to the Liberal Party. Pierre Elliott Trudeau, after arousing incredible hope during his election that year, had given officials a mandate to design an ambitious new party process that "reaches out to absorb the ideas and to reflect the aspirations of all Canadians…to encourage the widest possible participation by those interested in questions of public policy." At the 1970 policy convention, resolutions passed by the grassroots membership included a call for a guaranteed annual income and a review board to monitor civil rights abuses unleashed by Trudeau's invocation of the War Measures Act in Quebec. But Trudeau quickly made clear that he had reconsidered his earlier commitment. "When the dust had settled by the early 1970s, the Liberal Party's internal organization remained democratic in its constitutional form but autocratic in its day-to-day practice," writes Liberal Party historian Stephen Clarkson.[5] Behind the participatory window-dressing, the policy process became increasingly centralized in the hands of the party centre.

As I watched Justin Trudeau stroll away from his media Q&A, some part of me wondered if pitchforks and torches would appear. But the betrayal of his democratic promises barely seemed to register. The journalists on hand didn't seem interested to press the point that Trudeau had just inverted the premise of a widely-advertised democratic policy process. And the membership weren't exactly marching on the convention centre. While such moves by the party leadership would dampen morale over the following year, for now Liberal members were carousing at a concert and in Halifax's outdoor bars.

It struck me that what I'd witnessed over the last two days was a dizzyingly successful exercise in political disorientation. Lobbyists misled politicians, party officials misled activists, government misled the public. A swell of grassroots members had engaged in a full-throated democratic enterprise, which turned out to be little more than a stage-managed technocratic spectacle. The tent was big enough to encompass certain Liberals passionately discussing the promotion of principles alongside other Liberals actively violating them, reminding me of an old line of Wilfrid Laurier's that Trudeau would be unlikely to ever quote: "principles without organization may lose, but organization without principles may often win."[6] It was a remarkable achievement, repeated with each generation. The demonstration of this pliable capacity of the modern Liberal Party was like a drawing by M.C. Escher of a building of impossible dimensions, where stairs that are supposed to ascend in fact descend, doorways in plain sight recede or vanish, and an upside-down world convinces you, with a few brilliant tricks of perspective, that it is right-side up.

But if what's experienced is not so much prosaic membership in a party but collective rapture in a church, it's easy to forget about the state of the structure, what pays for upkeep, and who shuffles in and out of the backdoor after service. I remembered standing in the main convention hall earlier that day, bathed in a warm sea of red lights, my eyes expectantly fixed to the stage. I gripped a noise-maker I'd been handed, which, when unfolded, doubled as a poster emblazoned with the year 2019, the '0' replaced by a contour of Trudeau's face and wavy hair. In the minutes before the prime minister arrived, the clatter of excitement gave me a rush of unanticipated pleasure. I waited for inflated platitudes about democracy to descend like balloons from the ceiling.

Harper's Zombie Bureaucrats

On a sunny spring day in 2016, over a hundred people, many of them former top-ranking civil servants, gathered to celebrate the life of environmental trail-blazer Jim MacNeill, at a chapel in Ottawa's Beechwood cemetery. By the city's standards, it would not be an ordinary funeral.

When Justin Trudeau had come to power six months before, media coverage made it seem like civil servants were of unanimous feeling: relieved, liberated, jubilant. The Liberals quickly re-introduced the mandatory long-form census and gave the green-light to ministers and federal scientists to speak more freely to media. In the first days of the new government, a video went viral of employees at the Ministry of Global Affairs mobbing Trudeau as he made his way through their lobby, crowding around him for handshakes and selfies.[7] Just as Justin Trudeau had promised he would open up and democratize the Liberal Party, he had made it clear that the civil service itself could expect a great, progressive airing out.

But the feeling among those gathered at MacNeill's funeral appeared to be different. MacNeill, for one thing, hadn't been a typical bureaucrat. "Jim was like a junkyard dog," close friend and long-time colleague David Runnalls said. "He was one of the last of a breed of great Canadian public servants who wasn't afraid to speak truth to power."[8] MacNeill had grown up poor in a depression-era prairie dust bowl and worked in government for Premier Tommy Douglas. He then moved to Ottawa alongside a group of progressive-minded civil servants who helped create Canada's welfare state. Appointed to special advisory roles by Pierre Elliott Trudeau, he wrote the federal government's first environmental policies and headed up preparations for the historic 1976 UN Habitat conference in Canada. Later, he was the chief architect of a major UN commission that popularized the concept of "sustainable development."

According to a friend of MacNeill's who attended the funeral, Runnalls's eulogy offered a few details to spoil the rosy story about the transition from Harper. Many former senior civil servants, far from being overjoyed with Trudeau, were disgruntled and dismayed. What Trudeau had done was keep on so many of Harper's senior bureaucrats that it would help derail his bold promises, Runnalls predicted.

There was a murmur from the crowd, first of surprise, then agreement. "Does this usually happen at Ottawa funerals?" MacNeill's friend whispered to Green Party Leader Elizabeth May, who was sitting next to her in the chapel row. "Definitely not!" May whispered back. Other eulogists soon joined in, transforming an occasion of mourning into a session critiquing a sitting prime minister—a turn of events that MacNeill's friend says the tough, truth-telling civil servant would have been perfectly happy about.

May, who was mentored by MacNeill, told me in the spring of 2018 that she had been a firsthand witness to the shadow cast by an unreformed Harper-era bureaucracy. "The people who became senior in the civil service under the Harper administration were ones that when Harper said 'jump,' they asked 'how high?'" she said. "People who were prepared to say 'no' to Harper didn't last long; people who were prepared to say 'yes' got promoted faster."

According to May, there hadn't been a "dramatic change" in the civil service since Trudeau formed government. "I sometimes call it an army of marching zombies," she said. "Harper is no longer giving them their instructions, but they were true believers in what they did under him. And a lot of the bureaucracy has now figured out how to give Harper advice in Trudeau-speak."

Many of MacNeill's colleagues had resigned in protest over the years, including under Harper, after being asked to implement policies they were opposed to. They believed that Trudeau should have fired those deputy ministers that had either been appointed, or stuck around, during the Harper years—and that anything less was a clear sign of a looming betrayal of many of the progressive causes that inspired Canadians to vote for the Liberal Party. While civil servants rarely become household names, there was one major exception under Trudeau: Michael Wernick, the Clerk of the Privy Council, would become a major character in the SNC-Lavalin affair, and be obliged to give high-profile testimony in front of the Justice Committee. Before Trudeau appointed him to that position, he had been deputy minister of Indigenous affairs for eight years under Harper, a role in which he was frequently criticized by Indigenous communities.

In many cases where the Trudeau government had left Harper-era policies unchanged, May saw the imprint of Harper's zombie bureaucrats. It was there, in her view, in how the Ministry of Environment and Climate Change maintained Harper's paltry climate targets. It was there in how the Canada Revenue Agency continued to investigate charities. It was there in how the Ministry of Immigration, Refugees and Citizenship dragged their heels in bringing in Syrian refugees and allowing family reunifications. It was there in how the Ministry of Justice had still not gotten rid of the cruel mandatory minimum sentencing brought in by the Conservatives. In 2017, a survey by the Professional Institute of the Public Service of Canada found that more than half of federal scientists still felt they could not speak freely (in Harper's time, it had been 90 percent). The report indicated that "some respondents attribute this slow rate of change to managers who are misinformed or even unwilling to change."[9]

May didn't think civil servants should have been fired, but they should have at least been shuffled. "Move them around, anything to make sure you don't get retread Harper advice," she said. "Retread Harper advice has dominated since 2015 for all ministers and all departments." After being out of power for ten years, many of the new ministers as well as their staffers lacked the experience to defy the bureaucracy when necessary, she felt. "It's tough if the mandate letter to a new minister tells you to listen to senior civil servants, because if they are giving you bad advice, and they control your access to good advice, it becomes a self-fulfilling prophecy," she said. "You still end up with Harper-style policies."

Electoral Reform: the Ecstasy and the Agony

When Justin Trudeau laid out his party's platform, *Maclean's* columnist Paul Wells was provoked to ask: "Do fans of democratic reform have a single itch that Justin Trudeau didn't promise to scratch?"[10] But one announcement carried particularly positive shock value. "We need to know that when we cast a ballot, it counts," Trudeau said in the summer of 2015. "We are committed to ensuring that the 2015 election will be the last federal election using first-past-the-post."[11] The platform was unequivocal: "Within 18 months, we will introduce legislation to enact electoral reform," it said. Coming from a party that had historically benefitted the most from an antiquated electoral system, the statement grabbed the attention of many progressive and potential voters, and even won Liberals support from youth-driven activist organizations like LeadNow. The "last election under first-past-the-post" slogan quickly became a mainstay of Trudeau's stump speeches. When the New Democrats claimed that the Liberals had repeated the promise 1,813 times, no one disputed the figure.[12]

Once in power, the Liberals were no less vociferous, continuing to attack the Conservatives' disregard for—and erosion of—election laws, while reiterating their promise. "We are focused, as we made the clear commitment to do during the election campaign, on making sure that this election will be the last one held under first-past-the-post," Trudeau told Parliament in May 2016.[13] But while most of the popular campaigning around electoral reform supported a proportional system—based on the simple, democratic principle that the number of seats a party wins in parliament should reflect the number of votes they receive—the Liberals had something else in mind. Their preference was for a ranked ballot system. In this complicated system, voters don't choose one candidate, but rank the candidates according to preference. The winner is the first to receive a majority of votes, thus giving the advantage to the party that is the second choice of the largest number of voters. A simulation based on polling data suggested that under a proportional system, the Liberals would have won 50 fewer seats; under a ranked ballot, they could have increased their seat count to a 224-seat super-majority in Parliament.[14]

Consultations began, with Minister of Democratic Institutions Maryam Monsef conducting 22 well-attended town halls over the summer of 2016. Members of Parliament hosted discussions in their ridings. Experts appeared before a parliamentary committee on electoral reform. But the first indication of a dampening of Liberal enthusiasm came in October 2016. "With the current system, they now have a government with which they're happier," Trudeau said about Canadians to *Le Devoir*. "The need to change the electoral system is less compelling."[15] With results pouring in from consultations that were not to the Liberals' liking, it was time to cool expectations.

Monsef and the Liberals were cagey about what they were hearing at the town halls. In December 2016, Monsef said the data from the town halls would be released, "as soon as we've compiled it."[16] But a month earlier, volunteers from Fair Vote Canada had already managed to gather and publish the results from the range of consultants. The consensus was striking. In the Parliamentary committee, 88 percent of the experts who testified supported a proportional system. Among speakers at the town halls, it was 87 percent. And even in MP-hosted discussions, which likely involved many Liberal voters, it was still 69 percent.[17]

With a deadline looming, the Liberals decided to host a second round of consultations. It was like they were channeling one of Bertolt Brecht's satirical poems about democracy: Canadians had forfeited the confidence of the government, and could win it back only with a more favourable consultation result. On the website MyDemocracy.ca, the Liberals posed a series of questions about people's values—which a critic likened to a "pop-psych survey"—rather than directly asking which voting system they preferred.[18] Soon after, Liberals on the parliamentary committee refused to sign on to a call for a referendum on a proportional voting system, suggesting this exercise in democracy would be "rushed" and "too radical." By now it was obvious what was coming. Trudeau dispatched his newly-installed Democratic Institutions Minister Karina Gould to deliver the news: "It has become evident that the broad support needed among Canadians for a change of this magnitude does not exist," she claimed.

When Trudeau eventually answered for his betrayal in the House of Commons, his voice quivered, showing more bluster than bravado. "There is no consensus," he said, though that had hardly been a condition of his promise of electoral reform. "There is no clear path forward. It would be irresponsible for us to do something that harms Canada's stability when, in fact, what we need is to move forward on growth for the middle class and support…" He sat down abruptly without finishing his last sentence, as neighbouring Bill Morneau looked around confused. "Would it not just have been easier," Brecht had written, "for the government to dissolve the people and elect another?"[19]

A week later, Trudeau had regained his wits and put on one of his theatrical performances at a town hall on electoral reform in Yellowknife. While a lesser politician would announce the bad news on a Friday, take their lumps, and move on to other themes, Trudeau literally leaned in. When an audience member asked him to explain his reversal, he listened attentively, head tilted forward, one foot on his signature stool. His answer—several minutes long—summed up his view of the whole saga, casting himself as a leader making a difficult sacrifice for a higher calling. "Great question, and it's one that I have been struggling with over the past months," he told the audience. "The commitment that I made on electoral reform, repeatedly and explicitly, I made because it really mattered to me."

A ranked ballot, Trudeau explained, would be a good idea because "it favours parties who are good at reaching out to find common ground." And that would be threatened by proportional representation, he explained, a right-wing talking point with no evidence to support it. He acknowledged that breaking a promise might promote cynicism. "I recognize a higher responsibility even than that," he said, pausing to swivel and make eye contact with each part of the crowd. "And that is the responsibility every Canadian prime minister has to keep this country together and united and focused on the things that unite us rather than the things that divide us."[20]

Trudeau had raised huge hopes of progressive reform, then cynically betrayed each in turn—within the Liberal Party, within the civil service, and within the electoral system itself. But somehow, the prime minister had turned a black mark on his democratic record into an opportunity to strengthen the core elements of his brand.

5

Out of the Limelight, into Legislation

In early 2016, Finance Minister Bill Morneau announced he was abandoning a key pledge in the Liberals' much-promoted war on inequality. In their election platform, the party had pledged to close a major tax loophole that was being exploited by corporate executives to pay less on their earnings. The stock option loophole, which had been passed by the Mulroney government in 1984, had been justified as a way to help young companies find their feet. Instead, it was being used by CEOs at well-established, large corporations—who increasingly paid themselves in stock options that were taxed, thanks to the loophole, at just half the rate of taxation on a regular salary. In this way, the federal government's coffers were being drained of almost $1 billion every year, while the country's highest paid executives made off with a bundle (in 2013, for instance, 75 CEOs alone had pocketed $495 million).[1] Capping what executives could claim through this loophole was described in the Liberals' *Real Change* platform as a good "starting point" for generating new revenue.

When Morneau was asked by reporters to explain his backtrack, he told them that he made the decision because of feedback from "small firms and innovators" who wanted to adequately compensate their employees.[2] But that wasn't the whole story.

Not long after the 2015 election, Morneau had received a private letter about the stock option plan. It was written "urgently" by John Manley, the former Liberal finance minister under Jean

Chrétien and the president of Canada's biggest corporate lobby—not exactly a small firm or innovator. In the letter, which was obtained through access to information by *PressProgress*, Manley warned Morneau that the changes raised "significant uncertainties" and could lead to "sharp market reactions."[3] Investment decisions had already been made that year with the existing loophole in mind, so he hoped that Morneau, at the very least, would ensure that the changes would not be applied retroactively.

Not more than a week later, Morneau did exactly as Manley advised, announcing publicly that "any decision we take on stock options will affect stock options issued from that day forward."[4] (By the new year, he would scrap the stock option plan entirely). Within days, he received a thank-you letter from Manley. Morneau responded in kind, thanking "John" for his "support" in a handwritten note. "I look forward to working with you on issues of mutual concern," he concluded.

Several years before, during an interview in his office in 2010, John Manley had lamented that ignorance about the Canadian political system was damaging the country's democracy. "A knowledgeable public is a fundamental requirement for a democracy," he told a documentary film crew, "and I worry greatly about the fact that people are, in many cases in our modern democracy, willfully uninformed." His face had scrunched up in the pained expression of someone delivering a hard truth. "It's not that the information isn't available, especially with the internet. You can get information if you want it. But people just aren't interested."[5]

Considering his role, it was like the Wizard of Oz bemoaning how Dorothy had kept herself in the dark about the workings of Emerald City. From 2009 until the moment he was giving policy directions to Morneau, Manley was the man behind the curtain: the head of the Business Council of Canada.

What Big Business Wants

If you haven't heard of the Business Council, it's probably not for lack of interest. The lobby group, a common front of executives of the 150 largest corporations in the country, has never been a household name. It prefers it that way. Like the arrangements of its sparse office in Ottawa, it doesn't draw attention to itself, evoking none of the imposing presence of the Parliament building two blocks away. Instead, it relies on keeping Canadians unaware—willfully uninformed, one might even say—of its purpose. All the better to ensure it can continue quietly operating, as it has since its formation in the late 1970s, as a kind of parallel government in Ottawa.

When Manley became its president, he took over from Tom d'Aquino, an energetic and self-confident businessman who had spent the previous thirty years elevating the organization to an exalted sphere of access and influence. D'Aquino once told journalist Peter C. Newman that he didn't mind being called a lobbyist, since "the Pope is a lobbyist too." In a rare interview in the late 1990s, d'Aquino boasted about his success. "If you ask yourself, in which period since 1900 has Canada's business community had the most influence on public policy, I would say it was in the last twenty years," he said. "Look at what we [at the Business Council] stand for and look at what all the governments, all the major parties…have done, and what they want to do. They have adopted the agendas we've been fighting for in the past two decades."[6]

The Business Council arguably has even more power today, concentrating within its ranks a stunning and swelling amount of wealth. In 2005, its members—among them the big banks, automakers, oil, mining and insurance companies, and high-tech firms, whose heads are required to meet regularly in person—represented $2.3 trillion in assets. By 2009, that had grown to

$4.5 trillion, and by 2015, $7.5 trillion.[7] But that was the last time they publicly advertised it. When I called their office to find out the most up-to-date figures—information that wasn't, as per Mr. Manley's advice, available on the internet—Ross Laver, their senior vice-president of communications, told me that they were no longer updating them. Nowadays, Laver said in a genteel voice, they prefer underlining that they contribute the largest share of federal corporate taxes, employ more Canadians than anyone, and are responsible for most of Canada's philanthropy. It was perhaps no surprise. When you have for 40 years so success- fully been winning the war of the rich against everyone else, it is wise to be more circumspect.

Though the organization has gone through a few rebrands— going by the "Business Council on National Issues" until 2001, as the "Canadian Council of Chief Executives" until 2016, then changing to its current name—its *modus operandi* has remained unswervingly consistent. It has tried not merely to react to pro- posed policies of any government, but instead to proactively define their entire agenda. By establishing CEO-chaired policy task forces that mirror the key issues confronted by governments, it has often preemptively upstaged them with its own compre- hensive proposals.

With rare exceptions, most governments have become willing stage-hands. As Liberal finance minister in the late 1970s, Jean Chrétien admitted, "I don't do my budgets without consult- ing with the Business Council on National Issues." In the early 1980s, Trudeau's Finance Minister Allan MacEachern was look- ing to end certain corporate tax breaks and loopholes. The Busi- ness Council warned the government they would stop investing in Canada. Trudeau soon replaced MacEachern with Marc Lalonde, and the new finance minister paid a visit to d'Aquino at his home, an architecturally dramatic house elevated by thin steel columns that appears to float over McKay Lake, in Ottawa's posh Rockcliffe village.[8] Lalonde pledged the government's support to the Business Council.

Under Conservative Prime Minister Brian Mulroney, policy was directly outsourced to the task forces of the Business Council. This included adopting their proposals on tax cuts and defence policy. The greatest coup of d'Aquino's, however, was over Ottawa's Competition Act, intended to regulate corporations. The Business Council spent years developing a 236-page report and then handed it over to Mulroney. It became Canada's new law, the "only time in the history of capitalism," Newman writes with only a little exaggeration, "that any country allowed its anti-monopoly legislation to be written by the very people it was meant to police."

When the Liberals opposed the corporate-led trade agenda, they were briefly offside with the Business Council. At a dinner one night in the home of a European ambassador in the late 1980s, a shouting match broke out between d'Aquino and Chrétien, who had returned to Ottawa as the Liberal opposition leader. "You know the business community of Canada, it's done me in," Chrétien was overheard grumbling. "I've been trying to raise money for the party and I can't get no pennies out of those guys, after all I did for them… See that big shot d'Aquino over there? He's my problem 'cause he's leading those big business guys!"[9]

Not long after the Liberals returned to power in 1993, and abandoned their opposition to free trade, the two men patched things over. On a pleasant summer night, Chrétien and his wife were hosted for an evening at d'Aquino's house.* Soon after,

---

* In 2018, Environment Minister Catherine McKenna designated the house a "site of national significance," a status more fitting than she may have known: Liberal pilgrimages to the chambers of this corporate authority are truly a Part of Our Heritage.

d'Aquino produced a ten-point economic plan for Finance Minister Paul Martin. Journalist Murray Dobbin, author of a book documenting Martin's record, says their "list of demands is a virtual summary of what Paul Martin accomplished, or tried to, in his nine years as finance minister."[10]After the September 11, 2001 attacks on the World Trade Center in New York, d'Aquino and a group of North American CEOs called for a deepening of economic and security integration with the U.S. John Manley, in his first corporate assignment after leaving office, joined d'Aquino in co-chairing the Canadian task force, styled after the Business Council's task forces. Though it was eventually defeated by a cross-content social movement of opposition, the Council's proposals for the "Security and Prosperity Initiative" had negative implications: it would have stripped farmers in Canada of protections, raised the level of pesticides allowed in imported food, allowed Canadian police and security agencies to share private info with the U.S., entrenched greater U.S. control over Canadian energy, and obliged Canada to spend even more on its military. Like in so many cases before, the Liberal government of Paul Martin cut-and-pasted the Business Council's recommendations, slightly changed its name—to Security and Prosperity Partnership—and embraced it as its own public policy.[11]

When Harper came to power, the Business Council suddenly lost its exalted status. In 2010, as TD Bank CEO Ed Clark criticized Harper for not listening to corporates voices, he could point to an entire Business Council gathering of disgruntled executives to back up his point. Their frustrations would only grow. When Harper went after the profitability of telecommunications giants Bell, Rogers, and Telus by inviting the American Verizon into Canada to offer more competitive rates, the Business Council sought an emergency audience. They were shunned. In part to mend this hobbled relationship, Manley was picked as a successor to d'Aquino. He identified as "post-partisan," had sat on corporate boards after his political office, and had found favour with Stephen Harper by leading a panel, set up by the Conservative government, to make the case for extending Canada's involvement in the military occupation of Afghanistan. And even if the Business Council's status remained diminished under Harper, Manley would no doubt prove effective when the Liberals returned to power.

Although Manley had no problems lamenting Canadians' supposed ignorance about the political process, he aimed to make the activity of the Business Council even more secretive. "When you're a minister, you don't like an open letter telling you something that you'd be perfectly happy to hear in a private setting, and in fact might apply," he explained to *The Globe and Mail*, on first becoming Business Council President. "I think if you want your advice to be taken, you'd better give it in a private fashion."

"If the president of the [Business Council] says the government should do X, and they do X, then you're going to have a whole bunch of people jumping on them saying 'Oh, they're just doing what big business wants them to do. When you're actually trying to achieve something with government, sometimes it's better to stay out of the limelight and work behind the scenes."[12]

It was a prescription he would follow to the T in his lobbying of the Trudeau government, starting with his efforts to minimize the repercussions of the Liberal plan to close the stock option loophole. The Business Council would soon also push for a new infrastructure bank that would turn over public infrastructure to private profiteers. They would encourage the Liberals to cement trade deals that were as favourable to their members. They would apply pressure to win massive corporate tax cuts. And they would watch as Trudeau implemented a climate plan that they themselves had essentially designed a decade before, in order to let big polluters off the hook. Dislodged by Stephen Harper as the primary influence over the approach of government, the Business Council had been restored to what they viewed as their rightful position: helping enshrine broad corporate interests as public policy in Canada.

The Big Red Money Machine

Last year in Ottawa, a long-time Liberal fundraiser recalled when his job was much easier. He can't be named, because his remarks were made under Chatham House rules. "Corporate donations built the Liberal Party," he told a room of young, aspiring political operatives. It wasn't a boast or a shameful admission, more a matter-of-fact observation. "We used to head down to Bay Street in an election year, go into every single bank and get them to cut us cheques. By the end of the block, we'd have a few million dollars." And it wasn't only banks. It was equally normal for corporate executives to fork over $50,000 or $100,000 to the party or a Liberal politician. Fundraising, he added wistfully, hadn't been the same since those halcyon, glory days—a mere two decades ago.

All that was spoiled by the Liberal sponsorship scandal. From 1996 to 2004, a Liberal program to promote Canadian federalism within Quebec turned into a scheme to funnel money to Liberal Party-linked communications firms and Crown corporations. An investigation by Auditor General Sheila Fraser revealed that $100 million of public money had gone to firms who did little or no work. Meanwhile, the firms kept Liberal organizers and fundraisers on their payrolls and donated back portions of the money to the party. A year before the full, damning scale of the corruption was revealed in Judge Gomery's inquiry, Jean Chrétien attempted to head off the damage to the Liberals. He brought in sweeping changes to how parties could raise money, capping corporations, union, and individual donations at just a few thousand dollars.

To partially compensate for the money lost, parties would receive a public subsidy, earning money for every vote they received in the prior election.

Before then, political scientist Jamie Brownlee points out, donations to the Liberal Party came from the biggest banks and industrial firms, whose management was drawn from a broad network of the corporate class. Their birds-eye view took in the interest and welfare of not merely a particular part of the corporate class, but its entirety. Generally, however, most corporations gave consistently to the Conservatives and Liberals, in equal measure. This served as a corporate insurance policy: it guaranteed that their agenda would be looked upon with favour, regardless of which party formed government.

Chrétien's reforms not only failed to preserve the party's hold on power, the Liberal fundraiser says, but they ended up being an act of financial self-denial. (Though they did have a personal side-benefit: they threw a wrench into the corporate fundraising machine of Paul Martin, his arch-rival and soon-to-be successor.) Apart from those fundraising trips to Bay Street, Jean Chrétien had raised much of his money for the Liberal Party through corporate dinners. He had pulled in more than $30 million from $500-a-plate shindigs, doing the circuit like clockwork, ten each year, one in every province. 95% of the tickets were purchased by the corporate sector.[13] His reforms, however, "decreased the ardour of certain corporations for the Liberal Party of Canada," party president Stephen LeDrew bemoaned at the time.[14] Several banks boycotted Chrétien's last Ottawa dinner, a popular corporate mainstay since the mid-1990s, to show their displeasure. At his last leader's dinner at a downtown hotel in Montreal in May, 2003, with Martin in the audience, Chrétien proudly hailed his new rules. It was fitting that his announcement was made to a room full of businessmen who were, one last time, paying the going rate of $5,000 a table. It was a taste of how unlikely it was that his Liberal successors would, in the long-run, kick the habit of corporate money.

For the time being, however, the changes ruined the party's finances, the Liberal fundraiser says. The party turned to the Laurier Clubs, relying on cultivating wealthy donors who received generous tax write-offs and a cocktail with Prime Minister Paul Martin. Over the next few years, the Liberal Party set itself to rebuilding its fundraising power. It was a hard slog, the fundraiser says. In 2007, the Liberals launched a fundraising campaign called The Victory Fund, which, inspired by Barack Obama's success in connecting with millions of donors, tried to broaden fundraising to small-scale donations from grassroots members. But before the arrival of their Canadian Obama, money only slowly trickled in.

The Liberal leadership race in 2006 was the first under the new rules. Michael Ignatieff stumped for $100 cheques at barbecues, Stephane Dion sipped tea in living rooms, and Scott Brison became the first Canadian politician to host a web-a-thon, which involved an electronic ticker on his campaign website tallying up the online donations made over a single day.[15] But with new rules came new loopholes: money has a way of finding its way to a point of influence. During the leadership race, it was revealed that candidate Joe Volpe had received donations of $5,400 each from 11-year-old twin boys. It turned out that the boys, as well as several other donors, were in some way connected to executives at Apotex Pharmaceuticals, Canada's most powerful generic drug company owned by billionaire CEO Barry Sherman. Apotex had funnelled a total of $108,000 through several people, children included. This "strawman" donation strategy of Apotex would also eventually be used by SNC-Lavalin. Between 2004 and 2011, the Quebec company's senior executives would illegally donate $110,000 to the Liberal Party, its ridings, or its leadership candidates by soliciting employees to make political contributions. These contributions were in many cases then reimbursed through false refunds for personal expenses or the payment of fictitious bonuses.[16]

After Judge Gomery published his inquiry, Harper further tightened the fundraising rules. He shrewdly reduced the amount individuals could contribute, and banned corporate and union donations entirely. Once he had secured a majority, he eliminated public pay-per-vote subsidies. Since the merger of the Progressive Conservatives and Canadian Alliance—really, a take-over by the latter, with its roots in the Reform party—the corporate elite had become much more wary of the Conservative Party. So by necessity, Harper's Conservatives had already spent years building up a fundraising machine that relied on a steady flow of small individual donations, in place of corporate money. They could count on a base of 30,000 party donors; in contrast, the Liberals had to make do with between 1,000 and 2,000 members of the Laurier Club.[17]

In Ontario, skirting the ban on corporate donations continued with such regularity that fundraisers for the Liberal Party talked breezily about the details—until recently, when exposés forced ex Liberal Premier Kathleen Wynne to bring in reforms. Speaking to a trade publication in 2014, Karen Miller explained that when a law firm wanted to donate a high amount, she would receive not just the cash, but the names of several partners at the firm. She would then divide the total donation amongst them. "If a law firm—say Heenan Blaikie—gives you $10,000, it's not in Heenan Blaikie's name," she said. "They would give me 10 names, 20 names, 30 names that would make up the $10,000."[18] The final public disclosure of the amount would list not the firm but the partners' names. A year after this admission, many of the strategists and officials in Ontario's Liberal government would decamp to the new federal government, bringing with them their habits and considerably lower ethical standards on party finance.

The Pay-to-Play Government

In early 2016, news broke that a high-end law firm in Toronto had quietly hosted a private $500-a-head fundraiser with then Justice Minister Jody Wilson-Raybould.

When Trudeau had unveiled his plan to modernize government a few months earlier, he promised it would bring about a "sweeping agenda for change." A new rulebook, titled *Open and Accountable,* stated that "there should be no preferential access or appearance of preferential access." But it soon emerged that the event with Wilson-Raybould was not a one-off, but part of a massive, secret cash-for-access machine that rivalled anything Chrétien or Martin had ever created. Through 2016, the Liberals had scheduled more than 100 fundraisers and "appreciation events" at private homes or clubs, where donors could pay for exclusive facetime with Liberal ministers for anywhere from $400 to $1,500 a head. It was the Laurier Club model, expanded nationally.

The most popular special guest through the fall of 2016, in the lead-up to the next budget, was Finance Minister Bill Morneau. He was hosted at the waterfront mansion of Halifax mining tycoon Fred George, where he was joined by several land developers, bankers, and mortgage brokers who chipped in $1,500 each.[19] Apotex got in on the action again, with CEO Barry Sherman organizing a $500-per-ticket fundraiser—though after it hit the news, he claimed the fundraiser was unrelated to his firm, then clarified he was not in fact hosting it, and finally, entirely withdrew.[20] There was another $1,500-a-head fundraiser in Calgary (also later cancelled) at the home of Shaw president Jay Mehr, whose telecoms giant had directly lobbied the Finance

Ministry several times. Morneau insisted that the events "are in fact open" to the public. Only a yacht-owning millionaire would imagine that an ordinary Canadian couple could consider dropping $3,000 on a weekday to enjoy a cocktail with the finance minister. And even if they wanted to, they would have had difficulty finding the venue: for many of the events, the Liberals had used a special internet code to block details from turning up in online searches.[21]

The only greater prize than Morneau was hobnobbing with the prime minister himself. A photo emerged of Trudeau raising a glass of beer at a dinner at the mansion of a wealthy Chinese-Canadian business executive in Toronto, with several Chinese billionaires in attendance. One of the guests was a donor who was seeking Ottawa's final approval to begin operating a new bank aimed at Canada's Chinese community. Just a few weeks later, another of the guests donated $1 million to the Pierre Elliott Trudeau Foundation and the University of Montreal Faculty of Law. Trudeau was also to be hosted by the CEOs of a large construction firm and an automotive parts company, both of whom were looking to benefit from the Liberals' infrastructure and manufacturing policies—though the event was quickly cancelled when it was reported on by the media. A Bay Street insider said he had gotten a private email from the organizers alerting him to the event and providing a link for how he could buy a $1,500 ticket.[22] Trudeau's explanations were even more creative than Morneau's. He said he was being criticized for "engaging too much" with Canadians, suggested that his mingling with millionaires and billionaires was an opportunity to champion the middle class, and insisted that, while he might get lobbied, he couldn't be influenced.[23]

Having admitted that lobbying did in fact happen at these events, Trudeau stressed that donation limits were so low that the

Liberals "don't have money influencing political decisions." This discounted the fact that there was a special class of Liberal fundraisers, the Leaders' Circle, to which one gained entry by signing up ten new Laurier Club members at $1,500 a head—a practice known as "bundling." The Leaders' Circle website acknowledged their importance to skirting the rules: "with limits on political fundraising, donor networking and bundling are of the utmost importance to growing the Party." Whereas in the U.S. bundling had to be reported, there was no such oversight in Canada over amounts that could be as high as $15,000—hardly a tiny sum. And in insisting that money bore no influence, Trudeau must have been aware of something that Canada's wealthiest people were not, because their individual donations continued to pour in. Of the richest 100 Canadians, 56 have donated to the Liberals and 61 to the Conservatives. And many of the very wealthiest tycoons—the Thomsons, the Desmarais, the Irvings—donated to both parties. It was a sign of an enduring corporate insurance policy in action.[24]

Direct donations aren't the only way to use money as a means of influence. Ministers and civil servants know that if they are accommodating to corporations while in office, they may themselves be accommodated after retirement. Few options are as attractive as a lucrative directorship on a corporate board, pulling in a five or six-figure salary and stock options for a few meetings a year, a fraction of the work parliamentarians do while in government. Several ministers from Paul Martin's last Liberal cabinet had soft landings. Natural Resources and Justice Minister Anne McLellan got a directorship at an oil company. International Trade Minister Jim Peterson got a directorship at a mining company. Industry Minister David Emerson got directorships at a forestry and a gas company. But no one did as well as Pierre Pettigrew. Within a few years of office, the former minister of foreign affairs had joined no less than a dozen boards of investment banks and oil, gold, iron, and potash companies. He described how the connections he built up as a cabinet minister—"a rolodex like few Canadians have," he boasted—had proved useful to an oil company operating in occupied, war-torn Iraq.[25] And within a few weeks of resigning from Trudeau's cabinet in early 2019, Scott Brison, the President of the Treasury Board, had received a high-paying post as a vice-chairman of the Bank of Montreal.[26] None other than Foreign Affairs Minister Chrystia Freeland, in her previous days as a journalist, explained the allure of such gigs: "One thing that isn't in dispute is the material value of a political career after leaving elected office," she wrote in *Plutocrats*. "Politicians can't fully monetize their plutocratic networks until they retire. When they do, they can become multimillionaires."[27]

Bullying for Bay Street

In April 2018, an insurance company association based in Ottawa got the first of two phone calls—both unlike anything they'd received in 25 years of working on Parliament Hill.

On the line was Ian Foucher, a senior policy advisor in Finance Minister Bill Morneau's office. The tone was "angry," recalled Normand Lafrenière, president of the Canadian Association of Mutual Insurance Companies. Lafrenière had started publicly raising concerns about potential amendments to the Bank Act slipped into the 2018 budget, but Foucher was clear: do not meet with MPs and senators.

Deciding not to heed the aggressive message, Lafrenière prepared to testify to a Senate banking committee the following month. He was worried that if the amendments went through, Canada's big banks could begin selling customers' private data to unregulated companies, who would use the data to target those same customers. The night before testifying, his colleague Steve Masnyk received another phone call from Foucher.

"He was repeating the same thing…over and over and over," Masnyk said. "He said: 'Are you going to play ball with us or not? You better not appear in front of committees, and stop talking to senators and stop talking to MPs.'"[28] Masnyk and Lafrenière still testified, but the amendments soon passed. The "amendments satisfy calls from bankers for modernization to legislation," Canada's Lobby Monitor later reported.

This bullying on behalf of the banking sector might have surprised Lafrenière, but likely not another group: the bank lobbyists who had made Foucher one of the most heavily-visited officials in the Trudeau government. Since Trudeau had come to power, lobbying by Canada's big banks had risen sharply, nearly doubling.[29] Foucher himself had been visited close to 150 times by banks and corporate lobbyists—including dozens of times by the Canadian Banking Association that was pushing for those amendments that had concerned the insurance companies. The banks had big profits to protect: in 2018 alone, Canada's big six banks had made $45 billion, a sum that had grown higher every year since 2010. So it was perhaps no surprise that, according to the calculations of the transparency group Democracy Watch, they retained 100 full-time lobbyists across the country, and spent about $500 million annually on lobbying, advertising, and promotions.[30]

In order to squeeze out increasing profits every year, the tactics of Canada's big six banks have become more and more cutthroat. A public call from CBC for testimonials from bank workers netted an incredible result: private messages from hundreds of current and former bank employees confessing to an astonishing range of unscrupulous behaviour. The employees admitted that in order to meet the push by their banks for ever higher profits, they were pressured in dealings with customers to not disclose interest rates, to push credit cards with hidden fees, to sell insurance to people who didn't need them, and to lie about products.[31] A TD agent told CBC, "We are straight up told to tell false stories to sell products." A RBC financial adviser added, "We are all doing it." These tactics, alongside the hiking of fees, rising credit card interest rates, cuts to services, and the lay-off of thousands of people, is a major reason why, under the Liberal government, bank profits had climbed to record highs.

But the cosiness of the banking industry with the Liberal government would protect them from any repercussions. On the heels of the CBC reports, Canada's independent financial regulator launched an investigation. But the report from the Financial Consumer Agency of Canada (FCAC), issued in 2018, concluded that the big banks had not in fact caused widespread harm to consumers. Bank employees contacted by CBC were astonished— until access-to-information research showed that several drafts of the report had been sent to Minister Morneau's office and to the very banks who were being investigated, and edits had been made after. The edits watered down or removed recommendations for action, including a proposal that the banks work in the best interest of consumers.[32] While the report was being prepared, the bank lobbyists had been meeting with officials in the Trudeau government as many as eight times a week, including several times with the director of the supposedly independent regulator, up to a day before the report's release.

The lobbying frenzy hasn't been limited to the banking sector. In the first year of Trudeau's office, the activity of lobbyists in Ottawa underwent an astonishing spike, doubling in frequency of contacts with federal officials. Liberals and Liberal-friendly lobbyists stressed this was because of the new government's "openness" to Canadians. And consultations had indeed gone up. But in every year, lobbying activity has remained at least twice as high as it was under Stephen Harper, and in some areas, it has jumped by an even greater margin.[33] The year Trudeau was elected, the top 60 corporations on the Toronto Stock Exchange alone had nearly 1,000 lobbyists registered across the country. Among the top ten of those who most lobbied the Prime Minister's Office was a parade of corporations and major corporate lobby groups: Bombardier, Innovative Medicines Canada, the Mining Association of Canada, Irving Shipbuilding, Rio Tinto, and Shell. SNC-Lavalin was 14th.

Some have had a more frank take on the shift under the Liberals. Perrin Beatty, CEO of the major business lobby group Canadian Chamber of Commerce, described being "astonished and very pleased at the amount of outreach they have done." It was "very refreshing," says the long-time Tory MP and former cabinet minister under Brian Mulroney's government. "Ministers…have taken the initiative to call me with nothing more on their minds other than to say, 'Look, I'm new to the portfolio. I just wanted to introduce myself and to say that we welcome input.'"[34]

Officials in ministers' offices, rather than ministers themselves, have become the main conduit for the corporate lobby. The most lobbied government official is David MacFarlane, the policy director for Innovation Minister Navdeep Bains, with whom hundreds of contacts have been made each year. His job, according to one lobbyist interviewed by *The Hill Times*, was "basically to be lobbied."[35] His most frequent contacts have been with Telus, Shaw, and Rogers, the big three corporations that dominate media, internet, and cell phone service. According to one survey of Canadian attitudes, their profit-gouging has earned them the worst reputation among industries, lagging behind even banking and oil companies.[36]

This increased demand for lobbyists has been a boon for firms like Earnscliffe, one of Ottawa's oldest, who in the past enjoyed such proximity to power that one of its partners was hired to head Paul Martin's transition team in 2004. Earnscliffe's business had taken a hit after the sponsorship scandal, when allegations spread that they had taken in $10 million worth of government research contracts, sometimes for nothing more than "oral" reports. Business proved challenging under Harper. But by the end of 2018, they announced they were expanding onto a fourth floor of their Elgin Street building, which overlooks the East Block of Parliament Hill.[37]

Much has changed since the early 1980s, when there were only a few dozen firms in Ottawa and no oversight of the wining, dining, and gift-giving that took place in the city's restaurants and homes. After changes brought in under Harper in 2008, a federal registry notes all formal contacts. Gifts have been banned. Another Harper-era rule mandates a five-year cooling-off period before politicians or senior insiders can join a firm (recent departures from office often evade this by getting hired as "strategic consultants," rather than as lobbyists). As a consequence, the trade has become much more professionalized. While still mostly populated by ex-senior civil servants and politicians, lawyers, and political staffers—poaching a current government official remains the masterstroke—young people can now attend university programs with an eye toward a lobbying career. They have options in a growing industry: by the mid 1990s, there were 450 firms in the country's capital; by 2006, over 700; and today, by some estimates, there are close to 1,000. Canadians have underwritten this expansion: corporations deduct lobbying expenses from their taxable income.

Yet, we know little about how much corporations spend on such activities, since they are not obliged to reveal it. Under Trudeau, that is unlikely to change. In 2017, the prime minister hand-picked a new Lobbying Commissioner, who pledged not to "shake things up" and to work to "show Canadians the importance of lobbying."[38]

6

How Justin Learned to Stop Worrying and Love the (Alberta Carbon) Bomb

From across the table, Stuart McCarthy glares at me. He speaks in the slow, deliberate manner one uses to try to reason with someone who has just asked something utterly daft. "You have to impose the rule of law," he tells me, "otherwise the country will simply descend into anarchy."

It's June 2018, and we're eating lunch in Ottawa at a day-long confab hosted by Canada 2020, a think tank tied to the Liberal Party. Around me sit a group of lobbyists, including McCarthy, the Senior Vice-President at BlueSky Strategy Group, which has lobbied the Liberal government on behalf of the Canadian Association of Petroleum Producers, among other corporate clients. It'd be hard to find a more Liberal in-crowd. McCarthy's firm was founded by some of the same people who founded Canada 2020, and they both occupy the same building on O'Connor Street near Parliament Hill. According to a *Maclean's* report, the connections between BlueSky, Canada 2020, and the Liberal Party look like a "Venn diagram on steroids."[1]

A week before, the Trudeau government had announced it would buy the Kinder Morgan tar sands pipeline for $4.5 billion. As conversation drifts to the news, I wonder aloud: even if the government owns the pipeline, how will the Liberals possibly overcome the fierce opposition in British Columbia? McCarthy, disturbed by the question, insists that not pushing it through would jeopardize basic law and order. And what he says next is all the more striking because his gleaming shaved head and high-arched eyebrows give him an uncanny resemblance to Dr. Evil from the film *Austin Powers*.[2] "You don't need the military, just use the police. And send in some fire trucks."

You mean, to hose down protestors?

"Yeah, exactly. It's not going to be pretty. But we have to draw the line." He slices aggressively through a piece of chicken on his plate.

"The protestors are a noisy minority," he says confidently. "There's maybe 300 hardcore activists. Most of the Indigenous ones are imports. Once you deal with the leadership, the rest will collapse. And declaring the project part of the 'national interest' means you could deal with them as a terrorist threat." No one at the table bats an eye. Soon after, they congratulate each other on the conversation and wander off to look for dessert.

Was it all just Liberal locker-room talk? In a word, yes: it's how some Liberal partisans speak their mind when they think non-Liberals aren't around. Listening to McCarthy, I thought to myself that a Liberal-tied organization named BlueSky was a perfectly apt misnomer: far from imaginative, visionary thinking, he had just given us a demonstration in cynical realpolitik. Yet at the heart of Liberal circles, such a perspective seemed all too reasonable. In December 2016, just days after Trudeau had first approved Kinder Morgan's expansion, Natural Resources Minister Jim Carr mused about summoning the Canadian military to deal with protests. "If people choose for their own reasons not to be peaceful, then the government of Canada, through its defence forces, through its police forces, will ensure that people will be kept safe," he said to applause at an event with a construction lobby group in Edmonton. "We have a history of peaceful dialogue and dissent in Canada. I'm certainly hopeful that that tradition will continue. If people determine for their own reasons that that's not the path they want to follow, then we live under the rule of law."[3]

A week after the meal with McCarthy, it didn't surprise me when David Dodge, former Governor of the Bank of Canada, made similar remarks. "We're going to have some very unpleasant circumstances," he told an Edmonton audience of lawyers in June 2018. "There are some people that are going to die in protesting construction of this pipeline… We have seen it [in] other places, that equivalent of religious zeal leading to flouting of the law in a way that could lead to death… Inevitably, when you get that fanaticism, if you will, you're going to have trouble. Are we collectively as a society willing to allow the fanatics to obstruct the general will of the population?"[4]

The Sinister Seniors Call the Question

Two months later, in August 2018, Dodge would have something of an answer. A group of five women, their arms and legs tightly cuffed and shackled, were squeezed into a police van lined with steel mesh. Hunched in four-by-four-foot cages, they were driven for two hours, until they reached the Alouette Correctional Centre in Maple Ridge, British Columbia. On arrival, their clothes were swapped for green prison sweatsuits, and they were shuffled into a cellblock. The women were known as the "Sinister Seniors," a name right out of McCarthy, Carr, and Dodge's worst fantasies.

They had been sentenced to seven days in jail for a crime that many others were committing that summer—a crime, in fact, that as many as one in ten British Columbians were willing to engage in. Their motive? Justin Trudeau's decision to approve, promote, and then buy the Kinder Morgan pipeline. Initially owned by a

Texas oil company, and funded massively by Canadians banks, the project would twin an existing 1,100-kilometre pipeline that runs from Edmonton to Burnaby, nearly tripling the flow of diluted bitumen from Alberta's tar sands to the coast. It would increase seven-fold the tanker traffic in Vancouver's Burrard Inlet, imperil Canada's largest salmon run, and infringe upon Indigenous rights and title along the pipeline's route. The increase in yearly carbon emissions would amount to the equivalent of three million new cars on the road.[5]

Opposition, led by First Nations along the coast and in the interior of BC, had been strong from the start. Legal challenges had been filed. Thousands had rallied in the streets. But when the oil company put up razor wire fences around its terminal in late 2017 and began initial digging, the resistance shifted to more dramatic action. Starting in the spring of 2018, waves of people marched on the company's facility on Burnaby Mountain. Kinder Morgan had won an injunction that prohibited anyone from standing within a few metres of its work site. In defiance, groups of people would remain at the gates, in a coordinated and civil manner. Even though they were not in fact obstructing workers, this constituted a criminal act. When the Trudeau government purchased the pipeline in June, the numbers engaging in civil disobedience mounted.

By the end of the summer, the arrestees would top 500, including Green Party Leader Elizabeth May, then-NDP MP (now Vancouver Mayor) Kennedy Stewart, and even a former employee of Kinder Morgan. A third of those arrested were above 60 years of age. Among them were the five women who were entering the prison in Maple Ridge: a retired teacher, a theatre producer, a basket-weaving artist, a former president of the BC Teachers' Federation, and an anti-poverty advocate who would soon be elected to Vancouver's city council.

The retired school teacher was a slim, 74-year-old named Sachiko Charlotte Gyoba. Gyoba had signed petitions, written letters, visited her MP's office, and joined marches, but decided she needed to do more. It was her first time being arrested. "I won't be here much longer, but I worry about what kind of planet the next generation will inherit from us," she said, after serving her jail sentence. "People have to stand up when they see an injustice. If they don't, then democracy doesn't work for anybody." This was something she knew about firsthand: in 1943, she had been born in a Japanese internment camp in BC, and spent her first years growing up in a tarpaper shack.[6]

Her group of elderly female arrestees had picked up their nickname in court during the sentencing, when the Crown prosecutor accused them of making a "particularly sinister challenge to the court's authority." Yet it could easily be argued that the Sinister Seniors were acting on a greater authority: the province's popular will. A majority of British Columbians had voted for political parties who were opposed to the pipeline. The NDP government, in an electoral coalition with the Green Party, had pledged to "employ every tool available" to stop it in its tracks. And a poll found that no less than ten percent of the population said they were willing, if necessary, to engage in civil disobedience.[7] That amounted to a potential army of nearly half a million people prepared to wage a non-violent war in the woods—not exactly a few die-hard activist imports.

On the women's first day in jail, they saw a disturbing sight through the narrow cell window that confirmed their decision to get arrested: the sky was covered in a haze of smoke, as if shrouded by a grey veil. British Columbia was on fire.

Across the province, nearly 600 wildfires raged. By the summer's end, 13,000 square kilometres of land would burn and thousands of people would be evacuated. In some cities, breathing outside felt like jamming a fistful of cigarettes in your mouth and lighting all of them at once. The wildfires broke records set the previous year, when the province had become so hot and dry that a forest in Kelowna had erupted suddenly like a volcano, belching out flames and billows of smoke.[8] Through the summer of 2018, the horizon became eerie and unfamiliar: angry blood suns during the day, fried orange moons at night. On the women's second day in prison, the sky turned pink. "It was bizarre, like living on another planet," Vancouver city councillor Jean Swanson recalled.

This was the "new normal," a BC government report laid out: a world of natural disasters exacerbated by climate breakdown. The number of wildfires in Canada had doubled since the 1970s and increased in intensity and size as a direct result of the warming of temperatures, according to University of Alberta wildfire expert Mike Flannigan. "My colleagues and I attribute this to human-caused climate change," he said. "I can't be more clear on that. Human-caused climate change." A study showed that wildfires in Canada could jump by a further 75 percent by the end of the century.[9]

When the women were released after serving their sentence, wearing bead bracelets younger prisoners had made for them, they held a press conference outside the correction centre. The sky behind them remained a sooty grey. Having lacked access to computers, they read out a statement hand-written on lined paper. "Yes, prison conditions are harsh, but we are political prisoners," Jean Swanson said. "We are not criminals. We violated the injunction because we are so terribly aware that emissions from fossil fuels are destroying our climate, our planet, and our children's future. The impacts of this pipeline are more criminal than anything we've done."

Two months later, the Intergovernmental Panel on Climate Change of the United Nations published a landmark report. The world's leading scientists concluded that the impacts of the climate crisis were hitting harder and faster in the present than they had ever expected. If current rates of carbon emissions kept up, the dire impacts scientists had expected toward the end of the century would in fact occur in our lifetime: agricultural breakdown, deadly heat impacting hundreds of millions of people, and economic damage in the tens of trillions of dollars. Global emissions would need to be slashed in half in less than 12 years to keep warming from catastrophic levels, an undertaking that would require "rapid, far-reaching and unprecedented changes in all aspects of society."[10]

Which meant that Swanson had implicitly posed a question: what made a fanatic? Was it blocking a pipeline, or promoting one? Promoting a pipeline involved, after all, remaining in denial about the indisputable scientific consensus telling us to stop building new fossil fuel projects. And it involved shutting one's eyes to a fearsome warning from a living, imperilled planet: keep destabilizing the climate, and things will get a whole lot worse.

Is Canada Back?

If there was a global leader who was supposed to have understood the urgent need to transition from fossil fuels, it was Justin Trudeau. But like many establishment politicians who had taken on the mantle of climate champion, he couldn't seem to say "no" to oil companies. U.S. President Barack Obama had made climate change his legacy issue, passing a new Clean Power Plan, but simultaneously presided over a historic expansion of fossil fuel production. ("That whole 'suddenly America's like the biggest oil producer'...that was me, people," Obama would boast in 2018.)[11] German President Angela Merkel had overseen an accelerated transition toward renewable energy, but authorized the continuing extraction of the world's dirtiest coal. This approach simply would not—and will not—reduce emissions quickly enough to avert further climate disaster. But with his ubiquitous catchphrase— "we can protect the environment and grow the economy at the same time"—Trudeau would give this "all of the above" energy strategy the most optimistic gloss yet.

In March 2016, Trudeau told a conference that the "choice between pipelines and wind turbines is a false one. We need both to reach our goal, and as we continue to ensure there is a market for our natural resources, our deepening commitment to a cleaner future will be a valuable advantage."[12] It had an evasively progressive ring, until you realized it was like a nicotine addict insisting that, to build the courage to quit their habit, they had to chain-smoke. The benefits of one were undermined by the other.

There were other options. Trudeau had been elected on a widely popular mandate, not just to fight climate change, but to embark on an infrastructure-driven stimulus plan. It seemed like the perfect foundation for an energy transition, creating hundreds of thousands of jobs in a roll-out of wind and solar energy, a national high-speed rail program, and an ambitious retro-fitting program for houses and buildings. Contrary to relentless oil industry propaganda, a study by the Canadian Centre for Policy Alternatives showed that we could create far more jobs through investment in a clean energy transition than in oil and gas—as many as 34 times more.[13]

But Trudeau had no intention of pursuing such a transition. The Trudeau government would maintain the emission reductions targets of the Harper government, which was far less serious than comparable European countries. When Trump reversed Obama's decision and revived the Keystone XL pipeline, Canadian government officials secretly cheered, touting Donald Trump's election as "positive news" for Canada's energy industry.[14] In 2017,

Trudeau received an award from oil and gas industry executives at a summit in Houston, Texas. "No country would find 173 billion barrels of oil in the ground and just leave them there," he said to a standing ovation.[15] And toward the end of his first term in office, Trudeau would spend billions of public dollars buying the Kinder Morgan pipeline—buying a pipeline outright was something even the Climate Denier-in-Chief in the White House didn't have the gall to do.

What climate policies he would pass were rooted in the incremental, market-based approaches that centrist Liberal politicians—and, it would turn out, the corporate oil lobby—had embraced. But as the UN report had made clear, small nudges were utterly inadequate to the scale of the climate crisis. Deserving the title of a real climate champion would require government taking an ambitious role, imagining and implementing solutions at the necessary scale and speed. It would require something that Justin Trudeau and his most trusted advisors had long shown they were unwilling to do: take on the power of the oil corporations.

Green and Keen, Until Bay Street Says Otherwise

When veteran climate analyst Keith Stewart arrived at his office at the Toronto headquarters of the World Wildlife Fund Canada in the spring of 2010, he was in for a shock. Turning on his computer, he realized that the campaign he had been directing and working on for years—raising the alarm about the unsustainable exploitation of Alberta's tar sands—had disappeared from the organization's website.

Stewart hadn't received any warning, and would not be offered an explanation. Later, he would learn that a decision to shut down the campaign and wipe the website had come from the top of

WWF-Canada. The organization's leadership was abandoning its advocacy on an issue that, thanks in part to their efforts, was finally capturing global attention. When the decision was made, the organization's president was none other than Gerald Butts, Justin Trudeau's close friend and primary advisor, who would soon become one of Canada's most powerful officials.

In his role at WWF-Canada, Butts initially embraced bold climate policies. But before long, he would appear to succumb to limits on action prescribed behind closed doors by corporate power-brokers. It was a striking omen of how he and Trudeau would eventually run the Liberal government—and an instructive parable for those seeking to understand Trudeau's rapid shift from ostensible climate champion to pipeline-nationalizing oil booster.

When Butts arrived at WWF-Canada in 2008 as its new President and CEO, the first campaigns to slow down the break-neck expansion of the tar sands had just been launched by nearby Indigenous communities, who were suffering from downstream pollution. International media had begun taking notice, publishing reports of hundreds of ducks mired in a Suncor tailings pond. WWF-Canada was ahead of the curve of most organizations. Stewart, who holds a PhD in environmental policy and teaches at the University of Toronto, oversaw their climate campaigning. They sponsored a tour by journalist and fierce tar sands critic Andrew Nikiforuk. Their website featured commentary from the world's top climate scientist, James Hansen, who had warned that fully exploiting the Alberta tar sands would spell "game over" for a liveable climate.[16] Butts and Trudeau flew to northern British Columbia with funders to visit the Great Bear Rainforest, which would soon be threatened by Enbridge's proposed Northern Gateway pipeline. In an op-ed in *The Toronto Star*, Butts didn't mince words: "From hewers of wood and drawers of water to makers of moonscapes and creators of toxic tailing ponds: what a face for

Canada to show the world."[17] And in 2009, he would sign a joint public statement from several environmental groups calling for the government to "declare a moratorium on expansion of tar sands development and halt further approval of infrastructure that would lock us into using dirty liquid fuels."[18]

Just before Butts joined the organization, WWF-Canada had also opened an office in Edmonton and launched another campaign to try to curb the staggering amount of water that tar sands companies were drawing from the Athabasca river.[19] That campaign was led by Rob Powell, a mild-mannered scientist who had previously worked at an industry-friendly regulatory agency of the Alberta government. "What we were looking for from tar sands companies was mild steps toward sustainability," he told me on the phone from Alberta. "We wanted to ensure that the water outtakes would not drive the Athabasca river below a level of flow that would be catastrophic. Below that, everything falls apart, killing the fish, leaving enormous ecological destruction." Though Butts inherited this campaign, Powell says he was enthusiastic about it and had a hunch that the issue would rise in profile. He delegated several people to work on it.

While some companies resisted the campaign, others eventually agreed to make changes. The province's water management improved, and WWF-Canada's scientific modelling of water flows was heralded as an example for elsewhere in the country. The Toronto head office was delighted, Powell says. He began preparing another campaign, this time to challenge an outlandish exercise in green-washing by tar sands companies. To fulfill their obligation to remediate destroyed land, the industry was proposing to pipe toxic sludge from tailings ponds into giant mining craters, pour fresh water over them, and claim they would become thriving "end-pit lakes." "It might look like a lake, but it wouldn't act like one," Powell says. "It was a horrendous excuse for reclamation."

As the notoriety of Alberta's tar sands grew thanks to public education and campaigns, the mood shifted in some parts of the WWF-Canada headquarters. "It seemed like powerful people were not thrilled that we were working on this," Powell says. Stewart remembers that staff began hearing from the fundraising department that their tar sands campaigns were hurting donations. "Corporate funders started freaking out," Stewart recalls. "They'd tell us, 'I don't understand what you're doing. Can we figure this out?' Big donors weren't saying straight-out that they were opposed to our work. It was more like, 'I thought we had a partnership here.'" After all, WWF-Canada had a long history of friendly collaborations with corporations. Those now pushing more aggressive advocacy were beginning to jeopardize a safe brand.

Stewart says he heard that some members of the board of directors grew increasingly anxious. The board was populated by CEOs, corporate lawyers, and bankers, as well as future Liberal MP Seamus O'Regan.[20] It also included Blake Goldring, a member of the Business Council of Canada who had previously donated $500,000 to WWF-Canada.[21] He was the CEO of investment firm AGF Management, which advised an Oil Sands Sector Fund worth hundreds of millions of dollars.[22] He would not rejoin the board in 2010, for reasons unknown.[23] All that remained was for Gerald Butts to exercise his widely-praised skills in reading the tea leaves.

Powell says support for his work from his directors suddenly vanished. Every new campaign idea was rejected. "It was rather strange, when you have put a lot of effort in, and you have something to show for it," he says. "Wiping it from the map seemed a very odd choice."[24] At the same time, in the spring of 2010, Stewart came into the office to discover that all signs of the tar sands campaign had vanished from the WWF-Canada website.

Some staff demanded answers. One never came from Butts, Stewart says, but a director quietly told him: "We're not doing that anymore. Priorities have shifted. The focus will now be on corporate engagement."

Stewart says this exemplified a pattern of leadership from Butts. "He would be gung-ho about something, but after talking to Bay Street types and realizing they wouldn't go for it, he would drop it." Stewart believes Butts's commitment to climate action was real and profound. "But he came from a world of politics in which you get the best deal possible given the prevailing balance of power," he says, "while I come from the world of social movements, where we try to change the balance of power so the necessary becomes possible." Stewart could understand this strategic difference, but Butts's latest move was the last straw. He resigned in protest.

About a year later, Powell received a phone call from Butts. The Edmonton office, Butts told him, would be closed. After the financial crash of 2008, WWF-Canada needed to save money. "I don't think that explanation held water," Powell says. "It was years after the crash. And it so happened that a number of people in Toronto were hired afterward. I think for some reason he didn't believe we should be engaged in what we were doing."

Not long after, in 2012, Butts gave a talk in Calgary to an oil industry group. He was still president of WWF-Canada, but by now he was juggling frequent work with Justin Trudeau. In line with that drift, it seemed like he was workshopping the new pitch of the Liberal Party. The speech was titled "Dog catches car"—an old saw about someone not knowing what to do with power once they've secured it. He told the audience that they shouldn't be too pleased with the government of Stephen Harper, whose belligerent promotion of the oil industry had alienated many Canadians who desired policies addressing the climate crisis. "You guys have gotten everything you've ever wanted, and you're going to find it's way more difficult to get things done," he told them.[25] It sounded like the tough love message of a new confidant: the oil barons would need to smarten up.

Butts soon left WWF-Canada to begin working full-time with the man he evidently believed could become a more effective interlocutor to the oil industry. He wrote a letter to WWF's members announcing his departure, touting the work they had done on the Arctic, on ocean and freshwater protection, and on climate change. He didn't mention the tar sands.[26]

Around the same time that the WWF-Canada's tar sands campaigning was shut down, Butts forged ahead with a very different sort of campaign: a collaboration with Loblaws, Canada's largest grocer, owned by the billionaire Weston family. Starting in 2009, Loblaws began charging customers five cents for plastic bags in order to reduce their usage in their stores, and gave some of the proceeds to WWF-Canada. (Alexandra Schmidt Weston, the wife of Loblaws CEO Galen Weston Jr., sat on WWF-Canada's board of directors.) The hype associated with such campaigns is out of proportion to their impact, which is puny compared to just about anything else we might do. Reducing plastic bag usage did little of substance to stop the trashing of the environment—indeed one could argue that it distracted from the root causes, substituting for the radical measures that are needed. The initiative, however, worked out well for some. It made money for both Loblaws and WWF-Canada (which pocketed $3 million) and bolstered the green credentials of a multi-billion dollar corporation. And unlike WWF-Canada's tar sands campaigns, it didn't threaten the interests of anyone powerful.[27]

The sequence of events that transpired at WWF-Canada was an uncanny harbinger of how Trudeau, with Butts ever-present at his side, would eventually act in power. When the Liberals dealt with corporate giants, they would aim to collaboratively boost both their interests. When reckoning with the impact of the Alberta tar sands, they would do nothing that might cause ripples on Bay Street. In the span of a few years, Butts would go from bemoaning how a destructive mega-project had tarnished Canada's reputation, to helping make Trudeau its beguiling new face.

Friends in Unexpected Patches

In early October 2012, Justin Trudeau gave a press conference in Montreal announcing he would run for the Liberal Party leadership. The first stop on the campaign trail was Alberta. At a packed event in Calgary the next day, Trudeau called the province's tar sands a "blessing" and disavowed the energy policies of his father. "I think any policies and any politics that divides this country against itself, within itself, has been unhelpful in the past, is unhelpful today, and will be unhelpful going forward," he told cheering Liberal supporters.[28] Though none of the satisfied media observers characterized it this way, Trudeau's act underlined how he himself would govern: loyal to the interests of the corporate oil giants.

Back in the 1979 election, pushed by strong labour unions, the rise of the Quebec sovereignty movement, and stirring economic nationalism among Canada's corporate elite, Pierre Elliott Trudeau had run promising big changes to an oil industry dominated by profit-hungry U.S. companies. The policies he then brought in have been caricatured and ridiculed ever since by oil companies, political parties, and the corporate media. But they were the last gasp of a governing mentality snuffed out by the neoliberal age: that we could embark on an epic national project, using the power of government to shape the economy and regulate the pace of resource development.

Trudeau's National Energy Program, which built on the purchase of crown corporation Petro-Canada earlier in the 1970s, had many benefits, says Gordon Laxer, an emeritus professor of political economy at the University of Alberta. It provided for Canada's own energy needs, increased public ownership of a major industry, lowered oil prices for most Canadians, secured a greater share of oil company profits for government revenue, and even helped with the conservation of energy. So it was no surprise that secret polling at the time by oil lobby groups showed the policies were enormously popular, supported by 84 percent of Canadians, including a majority of Albertans.[29] Many Canadians in fact wanted the government to go further in the Canadianization of the oil industry, purchasing more U.S. oil companies. But the plan was reviled by the corporate media, U.S. oil companies, and Ronald Reagan—who, driven by a belief in the total supremacy of the market, couldn't stand the thought of such targeted government intervention in the economy in aid of citizens. But with public support being what it was, the U.S. government and U.S. oil giants—whose profits became merely "handsome, not astronomical"—eventually accommodated themselves to the changes.[30]

Trudeau, however, had made a mistake that opened up the program to attack: the program's revenue-sharing measures to keep the oil price the same across the country over-reached its jurisdiction in Alberta (the other major fault of the program was that it completely ignored Indigenous rights). "Opponents were hysterical," explains Laxer. "They raged about the 'East's' plan to steal Alberta's resources, stoking a sense of victimhood. They dubbed the Calgary headquarters of Petro-Canada 'Red Square.' They were out to kill the National Energy Program. When a downturn struck Alberta, they falsely pinned it to these policies, even though all oil producing regions in the world were affected.

The spin has stuck to this day." With the help of Tom d'Aquino's Business Council of Canada, Brian Mulroney quickly dismantled the National Energy Program when he came to power in 1984. What most people remember today is the bumper sticker slogan that stoked western revulsion: "Let the eastern bastards freeze in the dark."

Yet the program remains one of the most ambitious and far-ranging interventions of the Canadian government in our economy, and a model of what we might do.[31] Trudeau was on the right track—he just didn't go far enough. "Despite the program's egregious faults on provincial resource control, it deserves credit as the only time Ottawa ever stood up to Big Oil and its allies in Washington," Laxer writes.[32] If we want to avert climate catastrophe, our governments will need to recover this ability and willingness to carefully manage our oil reserves, to massively tax corporate profits, to regulate oil operations, and yes, perhaps even to publicly own and control some of them—at a scale exceeding what Pierre Elliott Trudeau was ever willing to do. That would be the surest way to ensure we get maximum benefit as we wind down fossil fuel use and transition to a renewable energy economy.

But such an idea couldn't have been further from Justin Trudeau's mind when he returned to Alberta in 2013 to address the Calgary Petroleum Club, not long after winning the leadership of the party. His speech laid out a vision not for challenging the country's most powerful and destructive industry, but for intimately collaborating with it.[33] Trudeau's speech echoed the one Butts had given to a similar crowd in Calgary a year before, but the tone was warmer. Stephen Harper might have run the "so-called friendliest government that the Canadian energy industry has ever had," Trudeau told the oil executives, but it had been a total failure. "Alberta's interests have been compromised more than just about anyone else's by Mr. Harper's divisiveness," he said. Harper hadn't been able to move "the yardsticks on one of the most important infrastructure projects of our generation, the Keystone XL pipeline." He had turned the tar sands into an "international poster child for climate change." Stymied by a growing cross-continental movement, Harper had not been able to "open markets to our resources, and facilitate the creation of pathways to those markets in responsible, sustainable ways," Trudeau added.

In other words, Trudeau did not differ from Harper over his support for the tar sands—he simply questioned the methods by which he had promoted them. Harper's government had antagonized Obama, instead of appealing to him. It had demonized First Nations and environmentalists, instead of building partnerships with them. "It has made enemies of people who ought to be your friends, and turned what should have been a reasonable debate into an over-the-top rhetorical war," Trudeau said. "Most importantly, it has impeded progress." This was Trudeau's pitch to the oilmen: he would be a more sensible salesman, a prime minister who could soften the ranks of opposition with a cheerful disposition and diplomatic touch.

He laid out his vision. "Market access, more and more, will depend on how well we manage our domestic policy, especially when it comes to the environment," he said. "I believe we can solve these problems a lot faster, a lot better, and a lot more cheaply if we see each other as partners in that national effort." The trick would be a few policies that would give cover for tar sands expansion. "If we had stronger environmental policy in this country—stronger oversight, tougher penalties, and yes, some sort of means to price carbon pollution—then I believe the Keystone XL pipeline would have been approved already," Trudeau said. When elected prime minister, he would help build this "national energy strategy."

If the heads in the room weren't vigorously nodding, it was probably only because oilmen know better than anyone to not reveal when they've been dealt an unbeatable hand. During all the years that Stephen Harper had spent in government, they had been waiting for a prime minister to endorse a carbon tax, while uttering those magic words: national energy strategy. It was their phrase more than Trudeau's, evoking a plan to protect and preserve the business model that they had been honing and promoting for several years in alliance with Conservative and Liberal politicians, right-wing think tanks, business-friendly academic institutes, and the country's biggest corporate lobby groups.

The note on which Trudeau ended his speech at the Calgary Petroleum Club must have sealed their confidence. "Keep an open mind," he said. "You can find friends in the most unexpected places."

Corporate Canada Waters their Wine

In the late 1980s, the environment barely registered as a concern for Canadians, when surveyed by pollsters. But by the mid 2000s, it was among their highest priorities. As these concerns mounted, the more savvy thinkers among the corporate elite realized a shift in strategy was necessary: if they had lost the battle over whether climate change was in fact happening, they could yet win the war over what should be done about it.

Tom d'Aquino of the Business Council of Canada was a practiced hand in this realm. Former SFU professor of communications Donald Gutstein points out that, as early as 1989, d'Aquino had told a gathering of business leaders in New York that if they were not proactive in defining environmentalism, "others will, and business will have to live with the results."[34] Ever since they helped dismantle the National Energy Program, the Business

Council had fought vigorously against any other attempt to regulate the oil industry. When an early draft of Brian Mulroney's
Green Plan included a small carbon tax, they reacted quickly with
calls and visits to the Prime Minister's Office.[35] Mulroney dropped
the idea. Through the Chrétien years, they supported only voluntary measures and funded an astroturf group to prevent the
ratification of the Kyoto Protocol.

But the growth in public awareness and activism necessitated
a new strategy. In 2006, d'Aquino seized on an idea pitched by
Roger Gibbins, a right-wing political scientist at the University of
Calgary and president of the oil-funded Canada West Foundation
think tank.[36] A few years later, Gibbins explained his thinking at
the time. If the industry was "going to go sort of mano-a-mano
against opponents in the U.S. and so on, it's just going to have
a lot of trouble," he said. Which is why "it needs the protection,
or cover, of a Canadian energy strategy…even if it means, in the
final analysis, that we have to water our wine a bit."[37]

Led by d'Aquino, a taskforce of corporate CEOs took up Gibbins's idea. But the National Energy Strategy, to paraphrase a
joke from literary critic Harold Bloom, was like the Holy Roman
Empire: not holy, not Roman, and not an empire. It wouldn't
advance the national prospects of Canada, but those of foreign-
controlled or multi-national companies who aimed to keep
vacuuming profits out of Alberta; it wasn't about energy sources
broadly, but the tar sands specifically; and it wasn't so much a
strategy as it was a doubling-down on the frenzied and reckless
exploitation and export of raw, unrefined resources.

A year later, the Business Council of Canada published a report
that laid out their goals. Titled "Clean Growth: Building a Canadian Environmental Superpower," it proposed a national plan
that would include investment in new technologies, emissions
targets that wouldn't limit their planned growth in oil production,

and—the water in their wine—a carbon tax.[38] They were willing to accept a policy they had previously reviled, but only because they hoped to head off regulations that would be more intrusive, or take a bigger bite of their profits.

Judging by today's polarized debate, one might think there were mixed feelings among the corporate elite over a carbon tax. That wasn't the case. When business professor Kaija Belfry Munroe conducted interviews in 2008 with the executives of Canada's corporate lobby groups and the largest companies in the heaviest-emitting industries, she discovered a remarkable consensus. Shell, Suncor, Nexen, ConocoPhillips, gas and steel companies, forestry giants like AbitibiBowater and Weyerhaeuser, the major cement makers, the Canadian Association of Petroleum Producers, and the Mining Association of Canada all "strongly supported" either carbon taxes or cap-and-trade.[39]

Not long after launching their report, the Business Council helped create a new organization, the Energy Policy Institute of Canada (EPIC), to act as a gathering point for Liberal and Conservative politicians and as a lobbying arm to win broader political support. Its president for a period was Dan Gagnier, whose wide-ranging career embodied the ease with which members of the Canadian establishment passed between the political and corporate worlds. He had been vice-president at Alcan, chief of staff to Quebec Premier Jean Charest, chief of staff of the premier's office for Dalton McGuinty, and a federal corporate lobbyist. Gagnier had also known Justin Trudeau since he was a child, through friendship with his father. Along with Gerald Butts and Katie Telford, he was part of Trudeau's innermost circle.[40]

Another member of EPIC was Bruce Carson, one of Stephen Harper's most trusted operatives, who for years shuttled between the oil patch and Ottawa. Much of what we know about EPIC emerged when Carson was charged with illegal lobbying and influence peddling, after securing contracts for his 22-year-old girlfriend. During Carson's subsequent trial, d'Aquino laid out EPIC's plan during questioning by the RCMP: get corporate leaders on board, recruit sympathetic academics, cultivate "public sensitivity" in the media, and win support at all levels of government.[41] "In effect, EPIC was founded with the ambition of capturing the energy policy of a nation, with the oil industry *de facto* in a privileged position," writes former leader of the Alberta Liberal Party Kevin Taft, who closely followed the trial's revelations.[42]

A network of corporate forums, oil-funded think tanks, and academic institutes were soon promoting the plan, including at the University of Ottawa's Sustainable Prosperity Network (where Dan Gagnier was a steering committee member). At a meeting in Winnipeg in 2009, business and political leaders met and "reached a broad consensus on the need for a pan-Canadian energy strategy." In Banff the following year, another meeting was convened on a "truly Canadian clean energy strategy," where all the key players of EPIC met with executives from oil companies and a select group of representatives from mainstream environmental organizations, including Gerald Butts (then-resident of WWF-Canada) and Marlo Reynolds, a director at Pembina Institute and later the chief of staff for Environment Minister McKenna. John Manley was there, as the new head of the Business Council of Canada. And so were future Natural Resources Minister Jim Carr and the omnipresent Dan Gagnier.

But the plan soon hit a major roadblock: Prime Minister Stephen Harper. In 2011, Alberta Premier Alison Redford had become the first mainstream political leader to sign on to a pan-Canadian climate plan that included a modest carbon tax, alongside coordinated support for pipelines. She was soon joined by other premiers, but federal support was missing. Harper was ideologically dead set against any policy containing the detested three-letter word. When TD Bank funded a report by the Pembina

Institute and the David Suzuki Foundation promoting a limited carbon tax, alongside a doubling of tar sands production, as part of the coordinated corporate lobbying push, the Conservatives responded angrily. Environment Minister Jim Prentice blasted the report as "irresponsible" and questioned why TD Bank would associate itself with proposals that would "harm the economy."[43] It was around this time that Trudeau and Butts began making the rounds with their pitch: the vision hatched by the corporate and oil lobby would need a more-aligned prime minister.

Just days before Trudeau's victory in the 2015 election, it was revealed that Gagnier—then serving as the Liberal Election Campaign Co-Chair—had been working as a lobbyist for pipeline company TransCanada. A letter he had written to several company officials was leaked, showing he had advised them on how they should lobby the incoming government. Gagnier resigned soon after, but not before Trudeau tried to mount a defence of his close friend, suggesting to the media that he had done nothing wrong. Gagnier's work for TransCanada, Trudeau said, had been known publicly for months—as if this made it less inappropriate, rather than more so.

Too little attention was paid to the contents of Gagnier's letter to TransCanada. It made clear that his principal allegiance was to the wider corporate and oil lobby, and that the goal they had been working toward together for nearly a decade was now, finally, within reach. "An energy strategy for Canada is on the radar and we need a spear carrier for those in the industry who are part of the solution going forward rather than refusing to grasp the implications of a changing global reality," he wrote. "The last point is critical as Federal leadership and a discussion with Premiers will take place earlier. This is where we can play and help them get things right."[44]

In Trudeau, they had finally found their spear carrier.

The Neoliberal Oil Rush

It wasn't the first time the federal Liberals had provided the Alberta tar sands a lifeline. 25 years ago, the industry was a dwarf of what it is now, with oil companies operating a few projects that produced a modest 350,000 barrels a day. Prices then were too low to justify developing more of the hard-to-extract, energy-intensive, low-quality sludgy bitumen. "I think what people forget was that, in 1993, it wasn't clear what the future of the oil sands might be, and it wasn't clear it had a future for a whole lot of reasons," then Liberal Natural Resources Minister Anne McLellan acknowledged a few years ago, in an interview with an Oral History project housed at the Glenbow Museum in Calgary.

From the inception of the first tar sands projects in the 1970s, the governments of Alberta and Canada had been closely involved as partners—providing financing, funding research, and developing extraction technologies that had gotten the industry off the ground. But private companies and investors now wanted support to kickstart the next wave of expansion—and to ensure that government would leave environmental management, as well profits, to themselves.[45]

In the 1993 election, when Jean Chrétien made his lone Alberta MP the minister of natural resources, the aim was "to send a message to the Province of Alberta, and to the oil and gas industry, that things had changed," McLellan said.[46] It was exactly what tar sands companies wanted to hear. The oil and business lobby ramped up its lobbying efforts, putting forward a 25-year plan for what their desired shift would look like: much lower royalties, more tax giveaways, faster project approvals, and letting the companies regulate themselves. It also advocated rebranding what had been accurately described as tar sands to the more innocuous-sounding "oil sands".

Under newly elected right-wing Alberta Premier Ralph Klein, the provincial government "turned the process over to the industry," Kevin Taft writes.[47] Winning over the federal government required a bit more work. The lobby's next step, McLellan recalls, was their arrival in Ottawa to explain how they could "get that uplift that it needed."[48] Syncrude's chief lobbyist and the architect of the new plan, Al Hyndman, enjoyed a remarkable level of access and influence, McLellan remembered:

> I joke with Al Hyndman even now that Al practically lived in Ottawa at the time. He showed up at every Liberal event. He bought tickets for every Liberal reception. He'd even show up at the Liberal Christmas caucus parties. I'd say, 'How did you get in here?' He'd say, 'I know people'…and we would laugh. And wherever the Minister of Finance [Paul Martin] was, you'd find Al Hyndman not far behind.[49]

McLellan also gave Syncrude's President Eric Newell a piece of invaluable advice: if he wanted to gain the Liberal government's support for their tar sands proposals, he would need to "sell this as a national project." That's precisely what Newell did, inaugurating an exercise in bitumen-nationalism that we have been subjected to endlessly by the corporate elite over the subsequent 25 years. "He and I have often laughed," McLellan said, "because I think he visited every Chamber of Commerce he could possibly get an invitation to to talk about the benefits, the potential benefits for other parts of the country."[50]

Working together, the Alberta Progressive Conservatives and the federal Liberals soon gave the oil industry everything they wanted.[51] Ralph Klein introduced bargain-basement royalty rates: one percent until companies recovered their project costs (which could be creatively extended for years), and then 25 percent of profits. Alberta's future energy minister would describe the royalty structure in a straightforward manner: "we give it away."[52] A few months later, Paul Martin did his part too: he extended tax write-offs for capital investments to all tar sands projects, worth about $300 million a year, alongside other tax incentives.[53] (The corporate giveaway happened at the same time as the Liberal government were telling Canadians that the country was gripped by a debt crisis that could only be addressed through severe cuts to social programs.) As a token of their appreciation, the Canadian Association of Petroleum Producers invited Paul Martin as an honorary speaker to their annual gala in Calgary—it had been 15 years since they last invited a Liberal finance minister.

McLellan also entrenched a system of corporate self-regulation. Ever since Canada had signed on to the Rio accords in 1992—which committed the country to stabilize carbon emissions by 2000—Canada's oil lobby had pushed for it to be implemented through a voluntary emissions plan, with companies developing their own plans and recording the results in a voluntary database. McLellan ensured that any thoughts about a carbon tax were dropped. Ottawa also made huge cuts to the federal environment ministry and transferred regulatory responsibilities to the province—Klein quickly followed up by shutting down Alberta's relevant agencies. "I think I'm doing quite a good job of helping government get out of business," McLellan remarked at the time.[54]

The neoliberal makeover of the tar sands—with private companies taking full control of a publicly-owned resource—unleashed an unprecedented boom. Applications for new tar sands projects doubled in the next year. The tax and royalty giveaways spurred a frenzy of domestic and international investment and construction. In 1996, Jean Chrétien flew into Fort McMurray by helicopter to announce $5 billion in new investments in tar sands projects. "It's fantastic because we have more oil here than Saudi

Arabia," Chrétien told a curling rink packed with cheering Albertans. Corporate executives should have been cheering loudest. With oil prices increasing, production would triple by 2008, then double again by 2016, at which point production reached 2.4 million barrels a day. U.S. and Canadian companies would make astounding profits, larger than any that private firms have made in the history of the country. Over little more than the decade that followed, tar sands producers amassed the rights to extract and sell more than $205 billion worth of bitumen, while paying the Albertan government less than $20 billion in royalties and land sales.[55] On the heels of Chrétien's visit in 1996, the Pembina Institute issued a warning that would become dismally familiar: new expansion and investment "threatened to make a mockery of Canada's commitments to fight climate change."[56]

In order to protect the industry, d'Aquino led a charge against the Kyoto climate talks. He wielded so much clout with the Liberal government that, in 1997, when he gave a presentation laying out what he thought Canada's approach should be, deputy ministers from no less than 17 federal departments gathered to listen.[57] Over the summer of 2002, as it became likely that Chrétien might sign the Kyoto Protocol, the corporate offensive mounted. They blanketed television and newspapers with advertisements, and lobbied Liberal ministers and MPs at a summer caucus retreat in Chicoutimi, Quebec, where they coordinated joining a Liberal golf tournament open to outsiders.[58]

But Chrétien was determined to sign the Kyoto Protocol to prove Canada could outdo the Americans. He signed on to reduce emissions by six percent below 1990 levels by 2012. But companies were bound only by the voluntary corporate reporting requirements brought in previously by the Liberals. Five years on, a study found that many companies hadn't registered and most had failed to report their emissions. The day Canada signed the

Protocol, there were more than $20 billion in new investments in tar sands projects on the books for the next decade.[59] Trudeau was the heir to this brand of Liberal climate hypocrisy, not its inventor: Jean Chrétien triumphantly declared that Canada "should strive to be first" in championing the climate, while simultaneously backing the unregulated expansion of the Alberta tar sands.

By the time Paul Martin's government fell to Stephen Harper's Conservatives in 2006, emissions were spiralling out of control, 30 percent above Canada's Kyoto targets. It would be Harper, ironically, who phased out Martin's corporate tax giveaway to the tar sands in his budget the following year.[60] By that point, it was evident even to Harper that some forms of support were excessive.

But Anne McLellan looked back on the transformation she had overseen in the mid-1990s with pride. "We had done what was necessary to give the oil sands a chance," she said.[61]

The Grand Centrist Climate Bargain

Just a few days after the Liberals came to power in October 2015, a secret dinner between some of the country's most powerful political insiders took place in Ottawa's upscale Glebe Market. Gathered at the table were key members of Trudeau's government: Gerald Butts and Katie Telford, as well as the head of the federal public service. And there were equally key people tied to Rachel Notley's government in Alberta: her chief of staff Brian Topp, economist and government advisor Andrew Leach, who was then drafting Alberta's new climate plan, and the head of the provincial public service.

It proved to be a friendly meal, because the Albertans soon discovered that Trudeau not only approved of Notley's pledge to introduce a carbon tax and other measures, but that he wanted to work in alliance with her to "take it national." That national climate plan, in turn, would become a powerful justification for greenlighting the approval of the Kinder Morgan pipeline project, which Notley would soon stake her political life on.[62] What was being struck was not merely a bargain between Trudeau and Notley. It was the bargain that the oil industry and its sprawling lobby had long coveted striking with the two levels of government.

With this quiet pact in hand, Notley publicly announced her provincial climate plan the following month. There were some good steps in the right direction: phasing out coal by 2030, reducing methane emissions, and imposing a carbon tax that would rise to $30 per tonne by 2018. But there was also a huge step back: the plan put a limit of 100 megatonnes of emissions for the tar sands, which would still allow for a further 40 percent expansion of the tar sands. This was a cap so high you could drive a three-story tar sands truck through it. (At any rate, because there were no regulations to enforce it, the number of projects approved by Alberta soon exceeded even that limit.)

So it was little wonder that several CEOs of oil companies happily joined Notley at the press conference announcing the plan. "Beware environmental announcements that the old industry likes," *The Globe and Mail* business columnist Eric Reguly suggested. "And the Alberta oil industry certainly liked Alberta Premier Rachel Notley's response to her province's delinquent status on the climate file." The president of the Canadian Association of Petroleum Producers was candid about why they liked it so much: it would "further enhance the reputation of our sector and improve our province's environmental credibility as we seek to expand market access nationally and internationally."[63]

Notley having done her part, attention turned back to Trudeau. Speaking to a business forum in Alberta, John Manley reminded the prime minister that "acquiescence to a price on carbon really is looked at as one side of a grand bargain that would see pipelines built in return." When Trudeau promptly approved the Kinder Morgan and Line 3 pipelines, Manley applauded.[64] After negotiations with the provinces, a year later, Trudeau announced his full climate plan—named the Pan-Canadian Framework, to avoid any hint of his father's policies. The core elements of the national plan shared remarkable parallels with the Business Council of Canada's declaration from a decade before: weak emissions targets, promised investment in clean technologies, and a market-based carbon price.

This bargain set the terms for much of the Trudeau government moves that followed. Though the Trans Mountain pipeline was meant to be fairly assessed in Trudeau's supposedly rebooted review process, its approval was preordained. As Mike De Souza reported in *The National Observer*, senior officials in the office of the Minister of Natural Resources Jim Carr told the team of government civil servants working on this file to "give cabinet a legally-sound basis to say 'yes' to Trans Mountain."[65] This directive had come while the Trudeau government was supposed to be negotiating in good faith with First Nations.

But as resistance mounted to Kinder Morgan's pipeline, the U.S. company began looking for a way out. Indeed, it had been looking for one since 2012, when it tried to sell the pipeline to Alberta's Redford government. It issued an ultimatum to the Canadian government that it would walk away from the project at the end of May 2018. Trudeau had hung his entire climate plan on its success. The government quickly entered into negotiations. A parliamentary budget officer estimated that Canada overpaid by $1 billion for the pipeline. After construction costs, some estimates have the pipeline costing Canadians as much as $14 billion.

Although a coalition of Conservative politicians would eventually launch a concerted campaign riddled with untruths and distortions against the climate plan, the corporate world was initially quite pleased with the outcome. A carbon tax was, in itself, good policy: polluters should pay for what they pollute, as the basic environmental principle that the Liberals repeated goes. But on its own, it was woefully inadequate. The carbon tax would levy $20 per tonne of emissions in 2019, rising $10 every year to $50 per tonne by 2022. Canadians would pay a bit more at the pump, but under the system, the money would be returned to them through a tax rebate every year and 70 percent of families would get more money back from the carbon tax than what they paid. Simon Fraser University energy economist Mark Jaccard, an expert on carbon pricing, published a study that concluded that the combined federal and provincial carbon-pricing plans would reduce greenhouse gas emissions by up to 60 million tonnes in 2020—equivalent to only about 7-8 percent of the country's emissions in 2015. On its own, the federal policy would reduce emissions by only one or two percent from Canada's 2005 levels. And if the carbon policy were relied on as one of the primary policies, it would have to reach at least as high as $250 pertonne by 2030. The carbon tax could only be successful if it was conceived as one piece of a broad range of policies that could together achieve the sweeping and rapid scale of changes required. So it was no wonder the corporate and oil lobby had embraced a carbon tax.

The thing about bargains is that the stronger partners always clamour for more and more. When there was anything in the pan-Canadian climate framework they didn't like, the corporate lobby quickly went to work. After months of lobbying, the government granted the oil and gas industry, as well as other industrial sectors, an exemption on paying carbon tax on as much as 70 percent of their emissions. They weren't quite satisfied. After closed-door meetings with Environment Canada at the end of the summer in 2018, the government announced further exemptions of up to

80 percent of their emissions, with some industries like cement getting exempted on as much as 90 percent. Regularly echoing the corporate lobby, the Liberals would justify this as protecting "competitiveness."[66]

The framework also promised regulations to reduce methane, a highly potent greenhouse gas, by 40 to 45 percent in the oil and gas industry. According to a secret presentation, the Canadian Association of Petroleum Producers suggested that the costs of implementation were three times as high as calculated by Environment Canada. They also argued that the government should be "delaying the timing of regulatory implementation for existing equipment beyond the currently proposed 2020."[67] After months of consultation with the oil industry in 2017, the Liberals watered down their targets and implementation was pushed back by three years. Trudeau was supposed to have shone in Trump's shadow. But Trump's cancellation of Obama's methane policies became the rationale for delaying Canada's. "We have to keep a very close eye on what our American partners do because the economies are so interlinked," Minister of Natural Resources Jim Carr said.[68]

The oil lobby next turned their attention to the Clean Fuel Standard, which would reduce the carbon intensity of fuels and, among the policies included in Trudeau's climate plan, was touted as taking the biggest bite out of emissions. The lobby won an initial victory by ensuring that the measure would accept all oil as equivalent, even though tar sands oil is much more carbon-intensive. After more lobbying, the Liberals delayed the regulations until after the next election, with full implementation to be completed by 2023.

The Liberals' federal phase-out of coal remained full of loopholes, allowing Nova Scotia to continue burning the highly-polluting fossil fuel until after 2030.[69] Its promise to come up with a national strategy to ensure car manufacturers produce a certain number of electric vehicles every year never materialized, because of the intransigence of the car makers on a Liberal advisory group.[70] On major issues of housing energy efficiency, renewables, and public transportation, the government flipped the file to the provinces.

Bill C-69, the Liberals' legislation to overhaul environmental reviews, was a moderate improvement on the Harper government's process, but in many ways it was geared to creating more certainty and clarity for resource companies. Even this was too much for the oil industry, which was used to getting everything it wanted from governments. Industry lobbyists issued a long list of amendments they preferred, and between April 2017 and March 2018 they met with federal officials 139 times on Bill C-69, an average of more than once per workday.[71] Among their demands—which Minister McKenna indicated she would likely meet—was to exempt new *in situ* tar sands projects from the federal environmental assessments.[72]

A Catastrophically Constrained Debate

At the end of 2018, *Maclean's* published a feature story about the growing opposition to Trudeau's carbon tax from Conservative leaders across Canada. The magazine's cover photo displayed a quintet of white male politicians—Doug Ford, Andrew Scheer, Jason Kenney, Brad Pallister, and Scott Moe—dressed in drab suits, grimacing at the camera. Its headline? "The Resistance."

It quickly became the butt of jokes on Twitter, with people suggesting better captions. "Harry Rosen sales associates looking at you when you enter the store." "Siri, show me a box seat at a Steve Miller Band show." "Diversity is for tie colours." "The Tragically Unhip." "The Resistance? More like the First Order!"[73]

Comic relief aside, the story was a disturbing sign of the nature of the debate about the climate crisis in Canada. On one side, you have an emerging coalition of right-wingers, led by federal Conservative Leader Andrew Scheer and the premiers of Manitoba, Saskatchewan, Ontario, and New Brunswick, launching political and legal attacks against Trudeau's carbon pricing policy. They have spared no inanity in their fear-mongering, accusing it baselessly of killing jobs, plunging the country into recession, raising "the price of everything," and serving as a "cash grab."[74] In fact, most people in Canada are receiving more in tax rebates than they pay out—which is why the Chief Justice of Ontario's top court said it shouldn't even be described as a "tax," as he ruled against the Conservative premiers by declaring the policy constitutional.[75] Scheer has insisted the Conservatives have better ideas for how to reduce carbon emissions, but when he released his threadbare climate plan, a non-partisan environmental organization calculated it would not only raise emissions beyond the Liberals' own plan, but also cost households more.[76] And as the 2019 election approached, Scheer's deputy leader Lisa Raitt, even seemed to dabble in outright climate change denial.[77]

On the other side of the mainstream aisle are woefully insufficient policies promoted by Liberals, who confidently project themselves as the only adults in the room. Yet the range of conceivable options is drastically narrow: a "yes" or "no" to a feeble carbon tax, Tory- or Liberal-branded pipelines, and a corporate-backed climate plan that would not adequately reduce emissions or no climate plan at all. It was a choose-your-own-political-adventure with equally catastrophic consequences.

Worse still, the technocratic policies of the Liberal government made it very easy for the right-wing to paint the climate crisis as a concern of elites—and expose even marginally useful measures like the carbon tax to political defeat. Families who have not seen increases in their wages or standard of living in decades are, for good reason, sensitive to yet more increases in consumer costs—or susceptible to manipulation about increases that are merely perceived. The Doug Ford government in Ontario had used exactly this line of attack. "Supporting a carbon tax may win you brownie points in the faculty lounge or win the praise of jet-setting Hollywood elites, but it is not the only way to fight climate change," Ford's spokesperson said in early 2019. "Elite economists may sit in their ivory towers and lecture hard-working families about the need to make everything more expensive, but they will never understand the struggle of counting the pennies and living paycheque to paycheque."[78] Any hope of winning ambitious climate action depended on policies that would simultaneously and radically improve people's material lives—inspiring them to fight for them, rather than just to fear them.

What this narrow debate in Canada blocked from view was the emergence of precisely those types of ambitious and beneficial proposals around the world, where the debates about the climate crisis are far less constricted than here. New Zealand has banned any new offshore drilling. Spain is implementing ambitious just transitions for their workers. Many of the Scandinavian countries get most of their energy from renewables, including nearly 100 percent in Iceland. In the United States, many of the Democratic presidential candidates in 2019 put climate plans on the table that were far more ambitious than anything advocated by the mainstream parties in Canada—the NDP and Greens included.

But even within Canada, there was a sector that was already entertaining what radical changes would look like. Just as the major oil companies had been ahead of the curve in embracing the carbon tax as a strategic concession, they were reckoning with what a world beyond oil might look like. Suncor produced a report in which they envisioned what a precipitous drop in demand for oil might do to their business. International companies like Chevron, Shell, ConocoPhillips, Statoil, and BP sold their investments in the Alberta tar sands, after evaluating the poor economic case and climate liabilities. And perhaps most significantly, French oil giant Total announced that it would be bringing its investments in line with the upper-limit 2-degree temperature target in the Paris accord, and would "reduce our exposure to Canada's oil sands" and "not conduct oil exploration or production in the Arctic." It was the first time a major oil company had recognized the scientific imperative to keep any oil in the ground, yet no political party leader in Canada seemed ready to dare to utter the same.

Realism today means something different than it did two decades ago, when a modest carbon tax might have gotten the job done. These days, it isn't only the business model of oil companies that is at odds with a habitable climate. The governing philosophy of the Liberal Party is just as incompatible. Their attachment to incremental change, to market solutions, to seeking win-wins with corporations, in the face of laws of physics demanding that politics adapt, can no longer be described as pragmatic. It is better described as fanatical moderation. True pragmatism looks like the diverse crowds of ordinary people, willing to risk jail time, standing in the path of the Kinder Morgan pipeline. Just like the heroic grandmothers on Vancouver's Burnaby Mountain, we are all being called to rise to more radical measures—our only realistic path to safety and survival.

7

The Reconciliation Industry

Justin Trudeau's smiling face is being beamed from a giant screen into a cavernous conference hall, as he lauds the benefits of Canada's mineral and oil wealth to an audience of Indigenous youth. "I've said it before, and I promise I'll say it again, but as young people, you're not just the leaders of tomorrow, you're the leaders of today," he tells them. "We need your voices and vision to build a natural resources sector that is just, sustainable, and inclusive." Charming a crowd with earnestness is vintage Trudeau, but on this occasion, it isn't clicking. When he finishes his speech, the applause barely rises to a smattering. Most in the hall are focused on their cellphones or their lunches of salmon and wild rice.

It's the opening of "Our Land, Our Future," a national summit on resource extraction put on in November 2017 by the Conference Board of Canada, the business think tank and lobby group. They expected a friendlier audience: the $1,500 registration fee, which no resolute critic could possibly stomach, has been waived or steeply discounted for hundreds of young Indigenous people flown into the Grey Eagle resort and casino in the Tsuut'ina First Nation, on the outskirts of Calgary. Officials from industry and government mingle in the crowd. Above the stage, the names of corporate sponsors flash across the screen: Shell, Suncor, Enbridge, miner Teck Resources, SNC-Lavalin, and major hydro companies.

The response to Trudeau's speech is only the first hiccup of the summit. A vice-president of SNC-Lavalin, moderating a youth panel later that afternoon, is struggling to generate enthusiasm for questions about how to increase Indigenous involvement in resource projects. After consulting his notepad, he asks, "What is the good life to you?"

"Living the good life has nothing to do with money," replies Olivia Ikey, a member of the Qarjuit youth council in Nunavik. "We need clean rivers and clean energy and to be able to eat the moose and to live like we always have," adds Mitchell Case, who serves on the youth council of the Métis Nation of Ontario. The last to answer is Rosalie LaBillois, a cheerful 20-year-old Mi'kmaq student from New Brunswick. "It's about the healing and love that comes from our people," she says. "The connection that we have to land, no one should be able to take that away. We need to live our truths when we make decisions about resource development. The government has tried to tell us who we are. We are so much more than they think." As the young audience breaks into applause, the vice-president shifts in his seat. "That's very insightful," he says, looking deflated.

The clash of views on stage is a sign that the barely-veiled goal of the summit—ensuring young Indigenous peoples become partners, rather than opponents, to corporate Canada's resource rush—might be more elusive than hoped. And if the mood in the hall is an indication, "Our Land, Our Future," taken seriously as a principle rather than a PR slogan, may not include any place whatsoever for the likes of Shell and Suncor. By the time the summit concludes the next day with a session harvesting advice on how companies can "better approach" Indigenous communities, it is mostly older people remaining in the hall. They trade suggestions about offering cultural sensitivity trainings to employees, or wearing casual attire instead of suits. The youth have escaped back to the hotel.

A year and a half before, at this same venue, Justin Trudeau had received a much warmer reception. During a public ceremony in the spring of 2016, not long after his election, the leaders of the Tsuut'ina First Nation thanked Trudeau for his commitment to Indigenous peoples. They gifted him a ceremonial headdress and an Indigenous name, Gumistiyi, "the one that keeps trying." As cameras flickered, he locked arms with Assembly of First Nations (AFN) National Chief Perry Bellegarde and danced energetically around the hall.

A painting of Trudeau in his new headdress now hangs in the foyer of the resort's hotel. It isn't the most flattering portrait: his chin is upturned in pomp, his lips pursed in a look of pride. On the last night, a crowd of young summit participants hang around it, joking about alternate translations of Trudeau's new Indigenous name. "The one that keeps trying to fool you" elicits the most laughter.

The New, Most Important Relationship

That Canada's most powerful business think tank would lavish such energy and expense on this initiative is a new development. Until very recently, Indigenous peoples were not a public preoccupation of the country's political and corporate elite. In 2004, under the last Liberal government, Minister of Indigenous Affairs Andy Mitchell was advised to keep a lid on their media profile. "Low public awareness of aboriginal issues may in fact lead to a more stable and relaxed public environment, which is more conducive to reasoned policy approaches to the file," a secret government memo suggested.[1] It was bureaucratese for an old, straightforward dictum: keep the Indians out of sight and out of mind. The Ministry of Indigenous Affairs preferred to manage the affairs of Indigenous peoples as they saw fit, hidden from the scrutiny of potentially sympathetic non-Indigenous Canadians by distance and official jargon. While other government departments issued a press release practically every day, they published barely two or three a month. What media coverage did occur, in any case, was rarely well-informed: ten years ago, you would not have found a single Indigenous person granted regular space in the mainstream media.

The Idle No More movement changed this, forever. The effusion of activism that began in December 2012 cracked the country's cold, placid political surface. Led by Indigenous women, the most marginalized of a marginalized population, the movement showed an unparalleled spirit of generosity toward non-native people. Anyone who accepted an outstretched hand, inviting them into a round-dance, will remember the astonishing feeling of connection and friendship. The story captivated even the corporate media, which, breaking with a long pattern of disparaging reporting, was often uncharacteristically supportive. The attention that Indigenous peoples had gained with their organizing, much to the government's chagrin, had obliterated a "stable and relaxed public environment."

During those winter months, the movement's activists didn't just occupy malls and legislatures, city squares, and highways. They occupied the public imagination—and they stayed put. When Idle No More's organizational activities began to wane, it had not achieved any reforms to the institutions or policies of the Canadian government. But its cultural and social impact was profound. In the years since, Indigenous peoples have become an increasing presence in multiple spheres: as op-ed writers in newspapers and commentators on radio, television, and social media; as professors in new university programs; and as leaders of legal firms, think tanks and environmental organizations. Canadians are listening to Tanya Tagaq and Jeremy Dutcher, reading Eden Robinson and Leanne Simpson, viewing the art of Christi Belcourt and Kent Monkman, watching the films of Tasha Hubbard and Alethea Arnaquq-Baril—the dazzling cultural constellation of a rising social movement. And were it not for Idle No More, the release of the Truth and Reconciliation Commission in 2015 could not have had the impact it did. Rather than being ignored, like the Royal Commission on Aboriginal Peoples in the mid-1990s, it was carried into broader consciousness by the catalytic force of a social movement.

This new era—with "reconciliation" increasingly as its byword—raised the expectations by which we judged politicians. Conservative Prime Minister Stephen Harper had apologized in 2008 for residential schools, legally obligated by an agreement between the Assembly of First Nations and Paul Martin's Liberals, who were themselves trying to head off a costly lawsuit launched by survivors. All of Harper's other gestures, however, communicated contempt. He suggested that Canada had "no history of colonialism" at a G20 gathering in Pittsburgh. He shrugged off calls for an inquiry into thousands of missing and murdered Indigenous women. He spurred Idle No More's growth by refusing to agree to the reasonable demands of hunger-striking Chief Theresa Spence. One image summed up his aloof and dismissive approach: when Justice Murray Sinclair delivered the Truth and Reconciliation Commission on Parliament Hill to a standing ovation, Harper's Indigenous Affairs Minister was the lone person in the room stuck to his seat.

In style, Justin Trudeau was to grandiloquently reverse this approach. While running for the Liberal leadership, Trudeau had been among the first politicians to visit Theresa Spence in her teepee near Parliament, an indication of his team's exceptional ability to read shifting political currents. When it came time to launch his campaign for federal office, his team decided to not simply wait to react to the changing balance of forces heralded by Idle No More. While Harper had stonewalled the movement, Trudeau would harness its hope and promise and ride it to power.

His election in 2015 marked an explosion in the politics of reconciliation. The "nation-to-nation" relationship with Indigenous peoples, Trudeau told us, was his most important. An inquiry was launched for missing and murdered Indigenous women. The name of residential schools architect Hector-Louis Langevin was removed from the Prime Minister's Office and National Aboriginal Day renamed National Indigenous Peoples Day. The old, long-vacated U.S. embassy in Ottawa was slated to be given over to Inuit, Métis, and First Nations people. Jody Wilson-Raybould was appointed Minister of Justice, the most powerful cabinet position ever held by an Indigenous person. Harper's government had voted against the Declaration on the Rights of Indigenous Peoples at the United Nations, but Trudeau pledged to implement it unconditionally.

Visitors to the Ministry of Indigenous Affairs in Gatineau, across the river from Ottawa, were now greeted by the smell of sweetgrass wafting from a daily smudge in an Elder's Lodge. "It's a historic time," Senior Assistant Deputy Minister Joe Wild declared in a video on their website that featured interviews with the first bureaucrats in Canadian history to casually use the word "decolonization." Cities, universities, and corporations got in on the action too: UBC raised a reconciliation-themed totem pole; RCMP vehicles in Vancouver were splashed with new logos; Suncor and Teck Resources developed reconciliation plans; and even steakhouses opened Gord Downie reconciliation awareness rooms.[2] Tears, public money, and proclamations of a new sensitivity flowed. Resetting the relationship, we heard from Wilson-Raybould and Minister of Indigenous Affairs Carolyn Bennett, would complete the "unfinished business of confederation."

But the transformation underway among the Liberal Party, government institutions, and the broader establishment was less

a sea change than a shape-shift. Faced with an Indigenous uprising unlike anything in Canadian history, they were prepared
to accept, and even help construct, a new public consensus—
making a taboo of overt racism, cleansing our public squares of
ugly tokens of our past, embracing the resurgence in Indigenous
cultural expression, and adopting the language of Indigenous
liberation. But within this consensus, there were several great
unmentionables: land, resources, and power, and the sharing of
any of it. Such a consensus would serve to contain and silence
the transformative potential of Indigenous rights—held over vast
territories, posing a barrier to reckless extraction, and grounded
in a vision of a different relationship to each other and the natural
world. Among the "radical options" that Trudeau had forebod-
ingly suggested Canadians might begin to consider in his speech
to a Bay Street audience in 2015, there was scarcely a more profound one than this.

In the "Our Land, Our Future" summit in Calgary, in legislation rolled out by the Liberals, and in conflicts on the land across
Canada, you could trace the outlines of the real agenda behind
reconciliation. It was not in fact a new agenda, but a modification of one that—mostly quietly and without fanfare—had for
decades been overseen by all federal parties in power, driven and
implemented by the state's bureaucracy, and supported by the
corporate elite. In many ways, it was an agenda as old as Canada
itself, a project of remaking the northern half of a continent into
a liberal political order—based on private property and indi-
vidualism, geared to the accumulation of profit and wealth, and
dependent on the assimilation of Indigenous peoples as nations.
This required, above all, the maintenance of control and jurisdiction over the lands, governments, and bodies of Indigenous
peoples. Harper had presided over this agenda with belligerence,
provoking incredible resistance. It was a testament to the beguiling charms of the new prime minister that his own efforts to steer

it could be repackaged as a spectacular break with the past—and be advanced further than they ever had under Harper. Reconciliation wasn't the unfinished business of confederation. It was the unfinished business of colonization.

In this late stage of colonialism, the most valuable resources to be extracted were no longer merely copper, oil, or timber. As was evident at the "Our Land, Our Future" summit, the country's elite needed to extract something else: the consent of Indigenous peoples themselves. As the power of Indigenous peoples grew, in the law and on the land, in social movements and in cultural arenas, it was becoming ever more difficult to implement any agenda without their buy-in. To complete their unfinished business, the elite would thus have to win the hearts and minds of Indigenous peoples. But they would have to win those as well of non-Indigenous people, many of whom increasingly saw their interests, and the interests of our living planet, represented in the fundamental change sought by an Indigenous rights movement. Some were even starting to call this elite mission by a specific name: the Reconciliation Industry.

Three Hundred Years of Dispossession

A megaphone slung over her shoulder, Ellen Gabriel walks at the front of a march as it moves through Oka Village, a 45-minute drive west of Montreal. On an overcast Saturday in August 2017, nearly 200 people proceed slowly behind her and several elders, down the road from the Mohawk First Nation of Kanehsatake.

Gabriel—an artist with a youthful face and penetrating eyes— became widely known for her poise and eloquence during the "Oka Crisis" in 1990. That's when this road was crisscrossed by barricades and barbed wire, and Mohawk residents on one side stared down the Canadian army on the other. The images of camouflaged, rifle-toting Warriors became iconic symbols, either of menacing lawlessness or courageous defiance.

Far less remembered is what started the conflict. The Mayor of Oka decided to raze a revered patch of forest called The Pines, the last of the Mohawk's collectively-held lands, in order to add nine holes to an exclusive, whites-only golf course. A Mohawk graveyard would be paved over for a parking lot.

For months, local Mohawk residents tried peacefully to avert a crisis, then eventually erected a blockade—a mound of dirt piled on a sandy road in the woods. When the mayor appealed to Quebec's police to crack down aggressively on their protest, some Mohawk traditionalists took up arms in self-defense. Gabriel, barely 30 years old, became their spokesperson. Not long after, a raid by Quebec police ended in a shoot-out and left an officer dead—it's unclear to this day whether from Mohawk or police fire. When the Canadian military invaded with troops and tanks, it unleashed a hot summer of discontent and rage across the country.

Nearly 30 years later, the community is marching again, this time against a non-native housing development that could eat into the same forest. Rain begins to fall. We pass by signs that Mohawk have stapled to hydro posts. *Saviez vous c'est un terre contestée? Do you know this is contested land?* "It's no exaggeration to say we've been repeating this for 300 years," Gabriel tells me, as I walk alongside her.

Gabriel long ago traded in her camouflage for floral shirts, but her fierceness is undiminished. She tells me how the British Crown granted their land in 1717 to French Catholic priests, the Sulpician Blackrobes. Through the 1800s, the Blackrobes had Mohawk arrested for cutting wood without their permission, and when Mohawk were away on hunting or work trips, they sold their property from under them to French-Canadian settlers. Chief Joseph Gabriel—her great-great-uncle—rebuilt the traditional seat of Mohawk religion and governance, the Longhouse. In 1911, he helped block a railway from coming through their lands; its unfinished tracks, overgrown with wild grass, can still be found at the edge of the community. The government branded him a "ringleader of Mohawk rebelliousness." Hunted by police, he was forced underground.

Re-emerging a decade and a half later, he was arrested for hiding his children from residential schools. After a sympathetic lawyer demanded compensation for him, the Federal Minister of Indian Affairs agreed. But it was the head of the bureaucracy— Deputy Minister Duncan Campbell Scott—who had the final say. He rejected the idea, writing: "The Indians of Oka have always been treated most generously by the Department, and you are quite at liberty to take any action in the courts that you may consider necessary on Gabriel's behalf."[3] The Sulpician priests eventually sold most of what remained of Mohawk land to the town of Oka. Years later, the relentless creep of encroachment exploded into a standoff over a golf course.

When Ellen Gabriel and the Mohawk warriors buried their weapons and walked out from behind the barricades, Progressive Conservative Prime Minister Brian Mulroney tasked a Royal Commission to "make recommendations promoting reconciliation between aboriginal peoples and Canadian society as a whole"—the first time the term "reconciliation" was ever invoked in Canada.[4] Among the central arguments of the Commission's five-volume report, backed up by reams of evidence, was that the poverty, dependency, and social ills experienced by Indigenous peoples had a root cause: the continuing dispossession of their lands. Providing an adequate land and resource base wasn't an optional measure that would complement self-government, economic self-sufficiency, and healthy communities. It was their precondition. This was a lesson Canada's elite have been loathe to accept: land restitution, the key to everything.

The responsibility for responding to the Royal Commission fell to the Liberal government of Jean Chrétien. But by 1998, the images of tanks rolling down Quebec streets toward a small, out-gunned First Nation were receding in memory. Some joked bitterly that the document the Liberal government released, Gathering Strength, would have been better titled "Gathering Dust." Little action would be taken on its 400 recommendations.

Yet it was in this document that the seeds of the Reconciliation Industry were planted. Funding was allocated for an Aboriginal Healing Foundation, which focussed on repairing the harm suffered by residential school survivors. This would be a pillar of the new reconciliation politics: stress the injury done to individuals, instead of the injury done to nations. And even though the Royal Commission had criticized the current policies of the government, Gathering Strength only clumsily acknowledged mistakes made in the past: it wrote of Canadian society being "burdened by past actions" or "historic injustices," dealing with the "negative impacts that certain historical decisions continue to have."[5] This convenient neglect of the present would become another pillar of reconciliation politics. "If there is no colonial present," Indigenous Dene scholar Glen Coulthard writes in his book *Red Skin, White Masks*, "but only a colonial past that continues to have adverse effects on Indigenous peoples and communities, then the federal government need not undertake the actions required to transform the current institutional and social relationships."[6] There may have been a crime, but the criminal had vanished.

As the march in August arrives at the site of the new residential development, the Domaine des Collines d'Oka, we can see The Pines in the near distance. Gabriel remembers riding horses here when she was a child, and picking plant medicines in the forest. Three-quarters of 400 new multi-level detached homes, attracting new residents to Oka, are already constructed. Others are still holes in the ground. The developer has claimed no trees will be touched, but there are signs of clear-cutting at the edge of the forest. And Gabriel recently found properties advertised on a real estate website. "A big lot with mature trees," the listing promised.[7] There were photos of The Pines in the background.

A month before the march, Gabriel is captured on camera by a reporter from Indigenous broadcaster APTN confronting Oka's mayor at the housing site. "You know you are committing fraud by selling land that is contested," she tells him, surrounded by a group of Mohawk women.[8] The Mayor shrugs, saying it is out of his hands. She switches between speaking English and French, but his position doesn't budge, as if to show the folly of Indigenous attempts at accommodation.

The developer builds the homes. The municipality issues the permits. The federal government looks the other way.

"The government's dealings are at the root of the problem but they seem to have little will to even deal with its symptoms," Gabriel tells me. The federal government negotiates only with the band council, refusing to deal with the Longhouse that Gabriel and many community members belong to. Communication with Indigenous Affairs Minister Carolyn Bennettt has netted her only canned statements about "seeking to facilitate solutions."[9] When Gabriel ran into Bennett at a university conference in 2017 in Montreal, she reminded her they wanted the government to step in and impose a moratorium on housing development. At the end of a long argument, Bennett gave her a line that Mohawks have become used to hearing: "If you don't like it, you can take it to the courts."

In 2019, the campaign led by Gabriel finally has an impact. The housing developer, feeling the pressure of the protests, contacts her to to say there will no further developments on the site, for now. Nothing will change about those houses already built, but it is a respite, a small victory. All tentative victories for the

Mohawk have come about this way. Working with local farmers, they've blocked a company from mining for niobium on their land for more than a decade. Three summers ago, Gabriel greeted scores of young Quebecois activists who walked hundreds of kilometres in a "March for Mother Earth" along the proposed route of the Energy East tar sands pipeline, ending their walk in Kanehsatake. That pipeline has also been defeated.

Gabriel is heartened by this new activism that, more than ever, embraces Indigenous perspectives. But she is impatient. "Three decades ago, we were talking about the same things," she says. "There is greater awareness today, and politicians have started talking differently, but the laws are still the same. We are still being criminalized. Still being killed. You are telling me this is reconciliation? What community should more be an example of reconciliation than Kanehsatake?"

When she is not traveling the country doing public speaking, Gabriel works at the cultural centre in the community. If she can find the time, she paints vivid portraits of her Mohawk ancestors and glowing landscapes where The Pines are ever-present. "What makes art such a powerful tool is that it seems like everything can be absolutely transformed," she says. "Reality is harder."

By the time the speeches start at the housing development demonstration in August, the few media cameras have left. "We're not asking for the keys to the houses, but we want you to know this is disputed territory," Gabriel tells the crowd. "The Mohawks have never had problems living with their neighbours—but we do not take to laying down in front of them." Gabriel's voice, even projected by a megaphone, is faint. I cup my ears to hear. She's not hoarse from shouting. She just sounds tired.

The Weeper-in-Chief

When Justin Trudeau is about to deal with an especially sensitive situation, there is one sure way to tell: he has donned a jean jacket. Like in the lead-up to the nation's 150th birthday party in the summer of 2017, when young Indigenous activists attempted to erect a protest teepee on Parliament Hill. Following tense confrontations with security, the group was allowed to set up in the corner of the parliament's giant lawn. The situation was being monitored closely; half a million people were expected for celebrations in two days' time.

The next morning, a denim-outfitted Trudeau surprised onlookers with a visit. Stepping shoeless into the teepee, sitting cross-legged with the youth, holding a feather offered to him: it was the image of authenticity and openness, the shedding of the trappings of power. "You have a prime minister who is listening to you and who is looking forward to working with you," he said in the teepee, "and you have an entire government who is interested in moving forward, hand in hand, in true partnership." His shoulders shrugged, rising and falling more than once, a habitual tic when he is nervous and unsure about the outcome of an exchange. But when one of the young women responded, you could hear in her voice, despite her skeptical instincts, that she believed him: she'd been disarmed. All that remained was for Gerald Butts to tweet a photo of Trudeau stepping out of the teepee, adding the #reoccupation hashtag used by the young Indigenous group. "We are on a journey of many steps," Butts wrote. "This is just one of them." The tweet was widely shared.

As with his teepee visit, each step of Trudeau's journey became a clip in a heartwarming reel. We watched him paddling down the Ottawa river in a canoe with Indigenous youth. Or conducting a sunrise ceremony at dawn on the steps of Parliament Hill. Or carrying water from house to house in the Manitoba First

Nation of Shoal Lake 40, a community lacking potable water. Or ice-fishing in Northern Ontario's Pikangikum, becoming the first prime minister to visit a fly-in remote reserve. All of it a walking, talking advertisement for reconciliation, offering the possibility of redemption from Canada's long and brutal legacy of colonialism.

The public was meant to draw an obvious lesson: Trudeau was demonstrating that a government could act as graciously as he does, that a powerful state could relinquish its long-held control over Indigenous peoples as readily as he showed up to a teepee for a heart-to-heart. Reducing politics to the posture of an individual—the art of symbolic statecraft—is a skill that Trudeau and his Liberal team have mastered. He has mastered it, in part, because it comes naturally: Trudeau is not only likeable, but he clearly has a deep, abiding desire to be liked, even loved. He wants Indigenous peoples as his friends.

In this, he had a prior model in Liberal politics. When I interviewed Paul Martin in the spring of 2018, he reminded me proudly that he was the first incoming prime minister to conduct a smudging ceremony at his swearing-in. He counts Indigenous people like former AFN National Chief Phil Fontaine among his best friends. Other figures at the centre of reconciliation politics have encouraged this notion that friendship is the basis for social transformation. "Reconciliation turns on this concept," former Chief Justice Murray Sinclair told an audience in 2015. "I want to be your friend and I want you to be mine, and if we are friends then I'll have your back when you need it and you'll have mine."

But colonial states make for poor friends. This is what Indigenous Secwepemc writer and activist Arthur Manuel had in mind when, in a posthumously published book of essays, he left a warning about Justin Trudeau. "Colonialism is not a 'behaviour' that can be superficially changed by a prime minister professing 'sunny ways,'" he wrote. "It is the foundational system in

Canada."[10] Manuel knew this as a matter of intergenerational struggle. His father George Manuel had been a leader of the National Indian Brotherhood—which later became the Assembly of First Nations—and an adversary of Pierre Elliott Trudeau's policies, just as Arthur was to become one of the most prominent critics of his son. Manuel knew from hard experience that a pique of conscience isn't a sign of a policy shift. That personal comportment was no substitute for political change. That new friendships could form, indeed flourish, alongside an unreconstructed power structure.

But under Trudeau, statements of moral feeling have been elevated to a governing strategy. Canadians learned to expect a formal apology from him practically every few months: for residential schools in Newfoundland and Labrador, the hanging of six BC Tsilhqot'in chiefs in the late 1800s, the relocation of the Sayisi Dene in Manitoba, the mistreatment of Inuit during tuberculosis outbreaks in the 1950s and 1960s, and the conviction of Cree Chief Poundmaker on charges of treason-felony. The apologies were so often delivered with Trudeau dabbing his eyes that Mohawk scholar Audra Simpson began calling him the Weeper-in-Chief. It reminded me of a Hebrew expression used to describe the behaviour of Israeli soldiers in the occupied Palestinian territories: "yorim ve'bochim," or shooting and crying. In this exercise of government myth-making, the reality of systematic abuses and human rights violations of the Palestinians were explained away. Because these soldiers were said to cry, demonstrating the moral depth of what the Israeli state likes to describe as the "most ethical army in the world," the charges against them couldn't be true. In Canada, too, the government was colonizing and crying, with Trudeau's tears over past actions, no matter how sincere, bathing us in a renewed innocence about present policies.

It's a new era of reconciliation. It's a continuing era of colonization. And Justin Trudeau may be its perfect politician: woke, teary, and sympathetic, presiding over a project of dispossession that proceeds unabated.

The Extinguishment Business

When she was nine years old, Josey Willier's overbite began causing her chronic tooth pain. By the time she was 13, the Cree girl from Calgary was unable to chew properly and had to take pain medication daily. A dentist strongly advised braces. Without them, her overbite would worsen, until her jaw could only be fixed by breaking it and screwing it back together.

But when her mother applied to a federal government program that covers medically necessary treatment for Indigenous peoples, the request was denied. The case went to court in 2017, and over the next year the Liberal government spent more than $110,000 in legal fees fighting the claim—over a dental bill that amounted to $6,000.[11]

It didn't seem to matter that Indigenous Affairs Minister Carolyn Bennett had, as opposition critic, said a "'see you in court' mentality is absolutely destroying the relationships with First Nations in Canada." Nor that former Justice Minister Jody Wilson-Raybould had in 2017 issued an internal directive, released publicly in early 2019, promoting litigation as a "last resort" within the Ministry. "Litigation is by its nature an adversarial process," the directive stated, "and cannot be the primary forum for broad reconciliation and the renewal of the Crown-Indigenous relationship."[12]

Since their election in 2015, the Liberal government turned to the courts over and over again. With the Ministry of Indigenous Affairs setting the direction, they refused to release documents detailing the abuse of survivors of a residential school in St. Albany, Ontario, where young students had been tortured with a homemade electric chair in the 1950s and 1960s. They attempted to deny compensation to thousands of Indigenous people snatched from their homes and adopted by non-Indigenous families in the Sixties Scoop. They supported the Yukon government in trying to scrap a binding conservation agreement to protect large parts of the pristine Peel watershed region. They tried to ensure an Inuit community couldn't stop seismic blasting during oil exploration in Nunavut, which was causing debilitating disturbances to whales. They ignored four consecutive orders of the Canadian Human Rights Tribunal directing the government to end discrimination against First Nations children, who receive substantially less funding for child welfare services on reserves than non-native children. They tried to deny a woman her Indian status because she didn't know her paternal grandfather's identity, despite tracing her Indigenous ancestry back five generations. They backed the dismissal of a First Nation's attempt to prevent the construction, on religious charter grounds, of a ski resort on their territory in British Columbia.[13] Whether over a sacred mountain or a child's jaws, an Indigenous territory or Indigenous body, there was an inescapable and relentless logic propelling these cases forward: a legal war of attrition to contain, minimize, or dismiss Indigenous rights.

Though it has gone unreported, in 2018 the two federal Indigenous ministries spent an astonishing $70 million on legal battles, according to the Public Accounts registry.[14] While such legal spending under Harper had reached as much as $110 million in 2012, both his and Trudeau's government have spent more money in the courts fighting Indigenous peoples than fighting tax frauds.

But the legal battle that has most concerned the Ministry of Indigenous Affairs has played out well beyond the media headlines. In British Columbia, Quebec, the Atlantic provinces, and in areas elsewhere throughout Canada, there are hundreds of First Nations who have never signed away their land rights through treaties. A century of government denial has been slowly but dramatically punctured by major Supreme Court rulings. In 1973, when George Manuel hailed the historic Calder decision acknowledging that Aboriginal title still existed in Canadian law, Prime Minister Pierre Elliott Trudeau responded, "maybe you have more rights than we thought."[15] When the highest court in the land handed down the 1997 Delgamuukw and 2014 Tsilhqot'in decisions, it established the continuing existence of a form of land ownership, Aboriginal Title, which it directed the Canadian government to recognize and implement. The Royal Commission on Aboriginal Peoples added its voice: these lands should move toward shared sovereignty or co-management.

But rather than embrace these court-recognized land rights, the government changed its strategy in how it sought to eliminate them. Established under Trudeau in the aftermath of the Calder decision, the Comprehensive Land Claims policy was designed to bring the land securely back under legal control of the Canadian government. The policy would offer First Nations cash-for-land deals, taking advantage of their poverty and the duress they felt as resource companies moved unhindered into their territories. Since the 1970s, this policy has undergone small alterations, but its core purpose has remained the same: land rights "extinguishment," the ugliest term in the linguistic arsenal of the state.

As a precondition for signing one of these modern treaties, the government demands that First Nations trade away their rights to nine out of ten parts of their traditional territory—rivers, forests, mountains, farmland, and everything underneath. In exchange, they receive money and small parcels of land in the form of private property, rather than in the collective way Indigenous peoples have long held and stewarded it. And the onus to show who has used and occupied the land is not on the government but on First Nations, who are required to provide exhaustive and costly research proof, which has forced them to amass a stunning $1.4 billion in government debt. The Ministry of Indigenous Affairs holds these loans over the heads of First Nations to induce them to sign agreements (the deal's cash settlement is the only way they can hope to pay off their debts). This is Canada's preferred method of dispossession: achieved by orderly negotiation, rather than outright force.

The outcome of these treaties is to achieve what the Ministry of Indigenous Affairs calls "certainty." By settling the question of jurisdiction over these lands, it creates stability for corporate investment, the extraction of resources, and the accumulation of profits. Enduring uncertainty, on the other hand, makes corporate life difficult: "native land claims scare the hell out of investors," noted risk consultancy firm Eurasia Group in 2012.[16] And these days, what's at stake is $650 billion of investment in mining, forestry, gas, and oil projects, trumpeted as much by the Liberals as the Conservatives, much of it on or near traditional Indigenous lands.

But when Harper helped provoke the rise of Idle No More, the uncertainty over these lands only deepened. In 2014, Arthur Manuel and Ryerson professor Shiri Pasternak uncovered reports from a federal government program monitoring the increasing risks that an empowered Indigenous rights movement posed to the extinguishment agenda. When I questioned the Ministry of Indigenous Affairs, their officials insisted that "a good deal of [its] content would only be understandable to those working for the department as it speaks to the details of the operations of specific programs." It was that familiar old dictum: best let us look after the Indians. But the reports in fact were refreshing in their candour. They calculated, along a spectrum, the level of risk posed to each aspect of the government's approach. The government's "Indigenous relationship" had reached a risk level of "very high."

The legal situation was troubling, too. "There is a risk that the legal landscape can undermine the ability of the department to move forward in its policy agenda," admitted one report from 2013. "There is a tension between the rights-based agenda of Aboriginal groups and the non-rights based policy approaches" of the federal government.[17]

That tension over the government's refusal to recognize and implement Supreme Court-recognized rights has meant that, for years, negotiations with First Nations had dragged on, failing to achieve the desired certainty. Between 1992 and 2015, the government had managed to sign only three new modern treaties in British Columbia. But the arrival of Justin Trudeau offered new hope to the ministry. If Harper had failed to move the dial, Trudeau's reconciliation politics might serve as an effective insurance policy, mitigating against the risks posed by Indigenous rights, even removing them as an obstacle. Senior Assistant Deputy Minister Joe Wild began insisting that the policies were changing. "I am not in the business of extinguishing rights," he told a parliamentary committee hearing in November 2017. "I am not in the business of rights termination."[18] Semantically, this doubled down on an old strategy. For years, officials had begun coyly replacing "extinguishment" with terms like "non-assertion" or the "modification of rights." But Indigenous peoples signing an agreement to not claim or "assert" their land rights in perpetuity still amounted to their being stripped of them.

Faced with a wall of Indigenous resistance to pipelines and resource projects in Western Canada, Stephen Harper had appointed lawyer Douglas Eyford as an envoy to chart a better approach. Working off his recommendations, the Liberals gave government negotiators new marching orders: while their mandates might not change, the dialogue would intensify. When I obtained the government's much-sanitized 2018 risk report, it showed that this new approach was helping—risk levels had dropped under Trudeau. The legal risks remained "high," but "Indigenous relationship risk" had dipped from "very high" to a more manageable "high." The BC Treaty Commission, which has overseen the push for modern extinguishment treaties in British Columbia for more than 25 years, launched a campaign announcing that their work now embodied the "highest expression of reconciliation."[19] Moving ahead with these treaties would be an "opportunity for the Governments of Canada, BC, and First Nations to lead the world in reconciliation." Following Trudeau's example, the status quo had been rebranded.

The ABCs of Reconciliation— Anything But Consent

It sounds like a phrase hatched deep in a strategic vault of Liberal spin-doctors: "collaborative consent." It is blandly positive, ambiguously open to interpretation, and just technical enough to make us flinch and hope their experts have it covered.

Like all Liberal coinages, it was intended to solve a nagging problem. Having endorsed the United Nations Declaration on the Rights of Indigenous Peoples (UNDRIP) to rapturous global praise, the Liberal government now had to contend with one of its central principles: Indigenous peoples' right to "free, prior and informed consent" over resource developments on their territories. They are deeply averse to implementing it.

On Trudeau's campaign trail in 2015, it certainly didn't appear that way. Whether in flip-flops speaking to families barbecuing on the BC coast or in suit-and-tie addressing the Board of Trade in Calgary, he repeated one of his favourite slogans: "Governments may be able to issue permits, but only communities can grant permission." APTN settled any lingering confusion by asking

Trudeau during a town hall, "Would 'no' mean 'no' under your government?" His response was clear: "Absolutely!"[20]

The country's two largest resource lobby groups soon jumped on board, suggesting that the Liberal reversal of a Conservative stance was in line with their policies. "A lot of our companies feel they already achieve a lot of what's required by UNDRIP," said the manager of Aboriginal Policy for the Canadian Association of Petroleum Producers. "This move really puts us back where we properly belong and also where I think, in practice, we have largely been," added the president of the Mining Association of Canada.[21] This was savvy public relations. In truth, free, prior, and informed consent is nothing like the impact-benefit agreements that resource companies currently sign with First Nations, offering them some jobs, a dribble of revenue, and a few university scholarships. It is a simple and straightforward sundering of a century-and-a-half-long colonial arrangement: the hoarding by the federal and provincial governments of all decision-making power over lands and resources, to the engorgement of extractive corporations and exclusion of Indigenous peoples. So while championing the right of consent made for a great slogan on the campaign trail and a key part of the Reconciliation Industry's allure, the Liberals have ever since sought to turn it into a feeble simulation of itself. And this is where "collaborative consent" came in: a conceptual ace-up-the-sleeve to resolve the problem of heightened expectations and preserve a deeply unequal power imbalance.

The concept has been spearheaded by a group of Liberal and Liberal-friendly politicians, lawyers, and environmentalists, including former AFN National Chief Phil Fontaine and a former minister in the Northwest Territories. Through Fontaine's ties to the Liberal Party, a report was produced for Minister of Natural Resources Jim Carr in late 2015. Titled "Collaborative Consent," it suggested that the NWT already offered a nationally-scalable model for "consent-based discussions" (another warm, fuzzy coinage). The report then made its way onto Justin Trudeau's desk. He loved it, I was told by someone familiar with the lobbying. A few weeks later, in April 2016, while on a high-profile visit to the Manitoba First Nation of Shoal Lake 40, Trudeau invoked the concept in an interview with VICE. "In the NWT they have boards that examine the projects from the very beginning with Indigenous voices," he said. "The talk of veto or not veto is highlighting the failure of the process as it exists right now. It shouldn't ever even come to the decision, is it a veto or not a veto. We should be working together from the very beginning."[22]

When I asked the person familiar with the lobbying how this would in fact work, I didn't gain any clarity. "It's like reciprocal consent," they said. "Both parties have veto. Or neither do. It's about staying at the table." But when I obtained a slideshow used by the proponents, I found the answer I was looking for. They explicitly mentioned "no veto," denying the principle of rejecting unwanted resource developments.[23] Indigenous feminists have made a brilliant analogy here: whether it's bodies or territories, if you don't have the actual power to say "no," then consent is meaningless.[24]

The Trudeau government began to lower expectations about his promise that communities would "grant permission" for resource projects. On his first trip to British Columbia after having approved the Kinder Morgan Trans Mountain pipeline, at the end of 2016, Trudeau was questioned about whether First Nations near Vancouver—the Musqueam, Squamish, and Tsleil-Waututh, all of whom have unceded land rights—could block the project. "No, they don't have a veto," Trudeau said.[25] A month later, a senior Liberal official told journalist Peter O'Neil that this expectation had been an "unreasonable" interpretation. "The intent was to say, 'We'll consult communities more seriously [than the Harper government],'" the official said. "If we wanted to say community support was mandatory and that communities had a veto, we would have said that."[26] It was a convenient answer: this version didn't exactly have the same ring as what Trudeau had said on the campaign trail.

Meanwhile, the more pliable notion of collaborative consent was promoted in op-eds, reports, and small-scale governance initiatives as part of an "on-the-ground-offensive"—trying to build its popularity and bring the UN declaration's "high fluffy goals down to earth," as was explained to me by the lobbyist. It soon appeared in the interim changes to the new environmental review process proposed by the Ministries of Natural Resources and Environment. In the fall of 2017, an environmental lawyer met with Marlo Reynolds, the chief of staff of Environment Minister Catherine McKenna, to push for this new review process to include the UN Declaration. Its inclusion would be "unworkable," Reynolds told them. "Name me a project that could get approved," Reynolds said. In the final legislation for the review process, Bill C-69, free prior and informed consent and UN Declaration are not mentioned anywhere.

The manufactured fear of Indigenous peoples pervades every settler colony whose foundation is the theft of their lands and whose heritage is the disregard of their lives. Even the term "veto" itself—deployed by right wing politicians, the media, and the Liberal government—plays on this fear. Unlike the word "consent," which means the equivalent, it evokes an unyielding Indigenous obstinacy, the foolish stalling of great works, the obstruction of a march of progress.[27] But most Canadians seem to know something the Liberal government does not: the economy would not be befallen by disaster. Bad projects might be blocked, but good ones would proceed. Ellen Gabriel's community could have the right to say "no" to yet more houses built on Mohawk lands. Endless taking might become caretaking, and the frontier would finally close.

Governments Who Promise So Much

It was April 2018, and the Liberal Indigenous Peoples' Commission was gathering at the party's convention in Halifax. Minister Carolyn Bennett was doling out gifts at the front of the room. The mood was upbeat. Co-chair Chad Cowie, from the Mississaugas of Rice Lake First Nation, was invited up to receive a framed art print. He had been instrumental, Bennett told everyone, to the Liberals' electoral success in 2015. "Chad's master's thesis and his work was crucial in helping us identify the ridings we could flip if we could get out the Indigenous vote," she said. "It was a make-or-break moment for us."

When I chatted after the meeting with Cowie—a university lecturer wearing a fashionable baby blue blazer—he admitted to being surprised about his impact. "I had made the argument that the party should do outreach and not just show up during election time," he said. "I guess some of that stuff reverberated through the party structure." His thesis, published in 2013, had mapped out "influential" or "decisive" ridings where Indigenous populations represented a significant or majority voting block. The Liberals' extra efforts in these places paid off: they defeated both Conservatives and New Democrats in Kenora, Winnipeg, Nunavut, and the Northwest Territories. Indigenous peoples had not only voted overwhelmingly for Liberals, but like Cowie, had joined the party in record numbers. In 2012, the Liberals had just 350 registered Indigenous members. By 2018, he said, they had over 5,000.

At the time, there were plenty of other reasons for the Liberals to be confident. Media coverage about their "most important relationship" was reliably glowing. To cultivate political support, key members of the Liberal cabinet and the prime minister were involved in secretive half-day "learning sessions" with select establishment-friendly Indigenous leaders, including Phil Fontaine, Ed John, and Willie Littlechild. AFN National Chief Perry Bellegarde, chummy with Trudeau, looked like he would comfortably win re-election. The AFN's funding, following cuts under Stephen Harper, had also been increased from $10 million to $34 million in 2018. Justice Minister Jody Wilson-Raybould received huge applause at the convention, second only to the prime minister's reception. She cast a powerful symbolic spell on party members and the public. The reconciliation agenda, by any measure, was humming along smoothly.

Through the spring of 2018, the Liberals were buoyed by the success of Trudeau's Valentine's Day address in parliament announcing "historic" Indigenous rights legislation. It was perhaps Trudeau's best speech ever—eloquent, critical of his own party's history, and politically very slippery. "If you look at how things have been handled in the past, it's hard to say that [Indigenous] skepticism is misplaced," he said. What gains had been made, like the affirmation of aboriginal rights in Section 35 of the Constitution in 1982, had not been handed down from on high by a prime minister, he acknowledged, but won through Indigenous struggle from below. "You might recall," Trudeau admitted, "that the government of the day—led by my father—did not intend to include these rights at the outset. It was the outspoken advocacy of First Nations, Inuit, and Métis peoples, supported by non-Indigenous Canadians, that forced the government to reconsider." He talked empathically of "mounting disappointment—the unsurprising and familiar heartache, and the rising tide of anger—when governments that had promised so much did so little to keep their word." He was accurate in describing the problem "that while Section 35 recognizes and affirms Aboriginal and treaty rights, those rights have not been implemented by our governments." And he conceded that the federal government must relinquish their clench-hold on the affairs of Indigenous peoples: "No matter how responsible or well-meaning or thoughtful a solution that comes out of Ottawa might be, it cannot be the solution if it comes out of Ottawa alone."

By the end of 2018, Trudeau promised, they would introduce legislation that would make "the recognition and implementation of rights the basis for all relations" moving forward. This framework would pass into law before the next election, laying "the foundation for real and lasting change—the kind of change that can only come when we fully recognize and implement Indigenous rights." Previous governments had sometimes mouthed the right words. But never before had the government sounded exactly like Indigenous peoples hoped they would.

While waiting on the plenary floor at the Liberal convention, I bumped into Leroy Denny, Chief of the Mi'kmaq Eskasoni First Nation. "They are definitely not the Harper government," he told me when I asked him about Trudeau. "They talk with us, they listen, they are respectful, and they seem committed to a transformation." That impression would soon become much harder to defend.

Shock and Awe

In Vancouver three months later, Russell Diabo was on stage giving an unusual concession speech. He had just finished in fourth place in the race for National Chief of the AFN, and he was using his final minutes at the microphone to blast certain Indigenous leaders, who he accused of leading First Nations like cattle to slaughter. In the audience, supporters of re-elected Perry Bellegarde began booing him. "Are those status quo moos I hear?" Diabo retorted.

It wasn't a typical concession speech, but then, Diabo wasn't a typical politician. It was his first foray out of the backrooms, after a 40-year career as a policy analyst, including advisor to former National Chiefs Ovide Mercredi and David Ahenakew. A Mohawk from Kahnawake First Nation, he wears a ponytail, silver moustache, and thick glasses that slip to the edge of his nose, giving him the look of a librarian. What makes it even easier to imagine him shuffling around an archive is that his knowledge of Canada's history with Indigenous peoples is encyclopedic and instantly recallable. Diabo speaks, a friend of his once joked, in 100-word footnotes.

Just before the emergence of Idle No More in the fall of 2012, Diabo had written a long, technical analysis of Stephen Harper's agenda on Indigenous rights—what he considered a particularly aggressive version of the long-standing policies of the Ministry of Indigenous Affairs. The article was so widely-read and influential that it turned him into a kind of policy godfather of the movement. So when Justin Trudeau announced his "historic" legislation, Diabo applied his forensic lenses. He soon shared his critical commentary to 16,000 Twitter followers. Yet he seemed a lonely voice. On social media, prominent Indigenous commentators even suggested he cool it and give Trudeau a chance.

That wasn't Diabo's style. His father had been an iron-worker on the highrises of New York, his grandmother a tough traditionalist who taught him the importance of standing by what you believe. Diabo also had the benefit of an experience shared by few other Indigenous activists: he was once a ranking Liberal official. In the early 1990s, he and his friends, lawyers David Naweghabow and Marilyn Buffalo, had joined the party as an "experiment," Diabo recalls. During the Oka Crisis, Diabo used his connections to get then-opposition leader Jean Chrétien smuggled into a motorboat, sped across the St. Lawrence river, and dashed into a meeting with Mohawk traditionalists behind the barricades in Kanehsatake. Later, he co-founded the Liberals' Indigenous Peoples' Commission and served as its vice-president of policy, helping write a section of Chrétien's Red Book. At the time, it was the boldest declaration of support for Indigenous rights from any Canadian political party.

Rubbing shoulders with Liberal politicians and government officials, Diabo soon learned that the party was comfortable letting the Ministry of Indigenous Affairs run the show. "Chrétien's advisor Eddie Goldenberg handed the Red Book to the bureaucrats and they told him, 'yeah, we can work with this,'" Diabo says. Any pretense of following through on Liberal commitments was abandoned, as the age-old agenda of the Ministry asserted itself. By 1996, Diabo had left the party and was working for Ovide Mercredi. That year, they split with the Liberals in dramatic fashion: outside the party's convention in Winnipeg and in front of the media, Mercredi burned a copy of the Red Book. Diabo's experiment with the Liberal Party had gone disastrously wrong, but it had dispelled illusions that he would later watch others succumb to.

As Diabo evaluated the dizzying array of initiatives that were being quickly rolled out by the Trudeau Liberals, he grew more worried. Alongside the promised new framework, there were several other new pieces of legislation, a new cabinet committee to review Canada's laws, ten new federal principles for dealing with Indigenous peoples, new fiscal policies, two new ministries of Indigenous Affairs, and new political accords with the AFN. Guiding the direction was a special cabinet committee on reconciliation that met regularly, as well as a committee of deputy ministers from several government departments. The Yellowhead Institute, an Indigenous think tank based at Ryerson University, produced a report that tallied up this staggering amount of activity: if the Liberals succeeded in bringing their bills into law, they would be responsible for 40 percent of all legislation related to Indigenous peoples passed by governments since 1867.[28] On top of that, hundreds of First Nations had begun negotiations at tables created under the Liberals that were supported with hundreds of millions of dollars, which flowed into band council offices, paying the salaries of chiefs, staff, advisors, and lawyers. "That kind of money was buying a lot of silence and consent," Diabo says. It was a "deliberate shock and awe strategy," and it was lulling people into complacency.

As more details dribbled out about the legislation—soon named the Recognition and Implementation of Indigenous Rights Framework—Diabo and others began to see in it distinct echoes of the notorious White Paper of 1969. At the time, Pierre Elliott Trudeau's Liberal government had put forward major legislation that he said would give Indigenous peoples "full equality." Trudeau drew on the language of social movements, repeating the U.S. civil rights call for an end to legal discrimination. But the legislation's promise of equality was merely a weapon. It was in fact a culmination of the longstanding assimilationist aims of the Canadian government: municipalizing and privatizing reserves, abandoning the treaties, getting rid of Indian Status, and absorbing Indigenous peoples into Canadian society. A few decades later, Ovide Mercredi would offer a timeless critique. "They talk of equality, after they've taken our land," he said. "They talk of equality, after they've taken our resources." Indigenous peoples wanted out from the prison of the discriminatory Indian Act, but not for a fate they described as cultural genocide.

As the 50th anniversary of the successful Indigenous efforts to defeat the White Paper neared, Diabo issued a warning that Justin Trudeau's legislation would itself undermine and terminate Indigenous peoples' rights, with consequences stretching generations into the future. The legislation would function, he argued,

as an assembly line: those First Nations that agreed to enter the
process would get packaged into a small legal box, with their
rights strictly limited. All powers of sovereign decision-making
and jurisdiction would remain with the federal and provincial
governments. At the end, First Nations would not gain any powers of major commerce, international trade, or criminal law.
They would have delegated authority only over local matters, like
marriages, service delivery, and education. Provinces would have
vetoes over any matter that concerned them, and the federal government remained the unilateral decision-maker. The framework
even introduced a new euphemism for the extinguishment of land
rights: agreements signed by First Nations would now "enable the
continuation of rights (rather than extinguishing rights) through
evolutionary provisions and periodic review processes," a Liberal statement to a parliamentary committee read.[29] The cattle
analogy Diabo was to later use at the AFN election wasn't a glib
remark—First Nations, he believed, were letting themselves be
corralled and domesticated. The permanent disempowerment of
Indigenous peoples as second-class citizens within Canada would
be achieved through their self-surrender.

What appeared to be a sweeping transformation was in fact a
skillful technique for managing the status quo: everything would
appear to change, in order for things to remain the same. It was the
changeless change that the Liberals so excelled in. The outcome
would be stamped as reconciliation, but would in fact be what
Indigenous peoples had been fighting in each generation: being
consigned to small land bases, shorn of any say over developments
in their traditional territories, with the right to administer their
own poverty. This relationship wouldn't be nation-to-nation. It
would be nation-to-municipalization. Nation-to-glorified-reser-
vation. Nation-to-dressed-up-subjugation.

In all of the legislation, Trudeau's speeches, and Liberal Party
declarations, there was one word that always went unmentioned:

land. There was no talk of power-sharing, of access to resources, and certainly none of land restitution. But the concerns of certain quarters were being taken care of. In a speech delivered to the Business Council of British Columbia in April 2018, Justice Minister Jody Wilson-Raybould assured the corporate audience their interests would be looked after. If the legislation passed, she said, a "new, inclusive level of clarity and predictability will be brought to land and resource decision-making."[30] In a short speech, she mentioned certainty—"which we all desire," she told her listeners—no less than 24 times. It was the much-coveted certainty over jurisdiction that would smooth the way for corporate investment, extraction, and accumulation. This was not any sort of decolonization. It was, Diabo concluded, Justin Trudeau trying to finish the work his father had started.

The White Paper 2.0

Urged on by several Idle No More activists, Diabo launched a campaign for leadership of the AFN, to fight what he had now started calling the White Paper 2.0. He crisscrossed the country, with his wife as his manager, visiting cities and reserves on a low-budget "Bannock and Baloney tour." Friends of his questioned whether the wonky intellectual could pull off a stump speech. But the campaign was a spark. National media began regularly quoting Diabo excoriating Trudeau and AFN Chief Perry Bellegarde—the first sustained, critical coverage of the Liberals on Indigenous issues since their election.

Momentum began to build against the legislation. At the AFN election in July 2018, where Diabo finished fourth, a resolution was nevertheless introduced from the convention floor demanding the federal government halt their legislative initiative, replacing it with a First Nations-led process. Minister Bennett made phone calls to some Chiefs, lobbying them to vote against the resolution. She also took the uncommon step of making an appearance in the private caucuses of regional Chiefs, including the Alberta Chiefs, who she encouraged to "stay the course." The resolution still passed overwhelmingly.

A few months later, on September 12, 2018, I stood at the back of an Ottawa ballroom at a special AFN forum devoted to Trudeau's legislation. The anger among many First Nations chiefs was now flaring openly. That morning, there was a leak of a private letter to the prime minister from some of the same establishment Indigenous figures—Willie Littlechild, Ed John, Mary Ellen Turpel-Lafond—whose alliance the Liberals had carefully cultivated. But they too were distancing themselves from the legislation, suggesting it be put on pause. National Chief Bellegarde had clearly also read the room. His speech, which invoked the need to resist any "termination" of Indigenous rights, sounded remarkably like Diabo's commentary. I sent a text to Diabo, who was sitting near the stage. "You should ask for a writing credit," I wrote. "LOL," he texted back.

Crown and Indigenous Affairs Minister Carolyn Bennett, in her own speech to the forum, was forced to respond directly to arguments Diabo and others had advanced about the legislation. "No, we would not impose it on Indigenous peoples," she protested. "This is not the White Paper 2.0. Really, it's the opposite." She didn't stop there. "The framework will not define and limit the rights of Indigenous people," she maintained. "We have no interest or desire in making proud First Nations into municipalities that remain under the thumb of the federal government, with only limited authority and power, delegated by the federal government." The cool reception to her remarks made me think others might have journalist Claud Cockburn's motto on their minds: never believe anything until the government denies it.

The MC announced that Bennett, along with top-ranking Ministry of Indigenous Affairs official Joe Wild, could stay only for a five-minute Q&A. She had a flight to catch, her aides insisted. But the line of chiefs at the microphones was already coiling through the room. They may be some of the most conservative voices among Indigenous peoples, but many of them were bubbling toward a revolt. The Liberal government's attempt to manufacture their consent had failed. It reminded me of December 2012, when at the end of another AFN assembly the chiefs had vacated the hall and marched to Parliament Hill. Between a hunger strike by Theresa Spence, rallies in the Prairies, and Indigenous leaders pounding on parliament's doors, it was the day the media recognized that Idle No More had become a national movement. When Minister Bennett finally left the stage with Wild trailing behind her, nearly two hours later, I caught a glimpse of Diabo's smiling face. He knew something had shifted.

A few weeks later, the federal government announced the obvious: the legislation would be delayed and taken back to the drawing board. It could now not be passed before the 2019 election, and perhaps never resurrected. It was a victory for Diabo and the Indigenous rights movement, and a major defeat for the Reconciliation Industry.

Diabo's fears, however, were not completely alleviated. What was transpiring was much like what had happened after the defeat of the 1969 White Paper, when the proposed policies had gone underground, only to be implemented by stealth by the federal Ministry of Indigenous Affairs. Over half the band councils across the country remained involved in negotiations established by the Liberals, which Diabo had branded "termination tables." Money continued to flow. In the March 2019 budget, the Liberal government would write off $1.4 billion in loans that First Nations had accumulated while preparing their Aboriginal title cases over the last 25 years.[31] This built off a 2018 Liberal move to replace new loans with contributions that didn't need to be paid back. By forgiving the debts, the federal government was abandoning one of their hardball pressure tactics. But it was hardly a benevolent gesture. It was a calculated attempt to smooth over and accelerate the slow-moving negotiations, which would ultimately still lead to the extinguishment of Indigenous peoples' land rights.

In Diabo's view, First Nations needed to walk away from these dead-end negotiations, and use the uncertainty over their lands as leverage to force the government to finally recognize their rights. He put his hope in the grassroots movement of Indigenous peoples, who had now beaten back the plans of the Ministry of Indigenous Affairs under both Harper and Trudeau. "The Liberals may have bought some of the chiefs, but they haven't bought the people," he said.

The Loneliness of Jody Wilson-Raybould

At the special AFN assembly in September 2018, there were murmurs about the conspicuous absence of one person: Justice Minister Jody Wilson-Raybould. By that point, it was an open secret that she was a primary architect of the legislation whose fate had come to a head that day. Was it a sign that she herself was having second thoughts?

Wilson-Raybould, from the We Wai Ka Nation on Vancouver Island, had been front and centre in the Trudeau government's reconciliation politics, but rarely in a way that Indigenous activists praised. More often than not, she seemed tasked with being a credible delivery-person for harsh news. In 2016, for instance, she had stood on stage at an AFN meeting and told the audience that they should forget about seeing the implementation of the United Nations Declaration on the Rights of Indigenous Peoples. "Simplistic approaches such as adopting the United Nations declaration as being Canadian law are unworkable and, respectfully, a political distraction to undertaking the hard work actually required to implement it back home in communities," she had told the group of shocked chiefs.[32] During her time as Justice Minister, the prison rates of Indigenous peoples skyrocketed. As of 2018, Indigenous peoples made up just four percent of the population in Canada, but 26 percent of prisoners. (For Indigenous women, it was even worse: they represented 37 percent of female prisoners.)[33]

To some, it wasn't altogether surprising that Wilson-Raybould was playing this role. She had started her career in the employ of a state that many viewed as an enemy of Indigenous peoples, working as a Crown prosecutor in Vancouver's Downtown Eastside. In that position, she was responsible for putting young Indigenous defendants behind bars, often for poverty-related crimes like stealing food from grocery stores.[34] From there, she moved onto the BC Treaty Commission, eventually chairing the body that works closely with the federal and provincial governments, advancing a model of negotiations with First Nations that extinguishes their land rights.

After being elected to BC Assembly of First Nations Regional Chief, she squared off against Indigenous leaders like Arthur Manuel. In 2012, the AFN had created a committee to fight for a change to the government's extinguishment policies. Both Wilson-Raybould and Manuel participated in the committee as it deliberated between two strategic options. Plan A would bank on negotiation and cooperation with the government; Plan B would rely on education, lobbying, protest, and coalition-building with non-native organizations. Wilson-Raybould, who by then had been scouted for the Liberal Party by Paul Martin and was being mentored by him, made the case for the first. Manuel argued for the latter.

At the height of Idle No More's protests a few months later, Wilson-Raybould and a minority of chiefs would controversially defy the Indigenous rights movement and walk into a meeting with Prime Minister Stephen Harper. Those leaders behind Plan A negotiated a process with the Conservative government, sidelining Manuel and others. By the end of the year, as Manuel predicted, their plan had borne no fruit. But meanwhile, Wilson-Raybould had published a sprawling book, *Governance Toolkit: A Guide to Nation Building*, that would have a greater impact than anyone could have known at the time. In a presentation to the AFN at the end of 2013, she outlined its blueprint for reconciliation, which she believed the federal government could adopt. It included a plan for a new legislative framework, ten principles for dealing with Indigenous peoples, political accords with the AFN, and a review of existing laws. Harper would ignore the recommendations, miffed when he got wind that Justin Trudeau was set on recruiting Wilson-Raybould for the Liberals. But a few years later, with Wilson-Raybould serving as the Justice Minister, the Liberal government would roll out several initiatives that were, in almost exact wording and approach, lifted wholesale from her blueprint.

While she was one of the architects of the Trudeau government's reconciliation framework, she would not be its implementer. Through 2017, a power struggle within cabinet ensued between Wilson-Raybould and Carolyn Bennett, who believed that it was her prerogative as Indigenous Affairs Minister to roll out the legislation. Trudeau ultimately sided with Bennett. In 2018, as the Prime Minister's Office focussed on North American Free Trade Agreement negotiations, the legislation was guided by the clerk of the Privy Council, Michael Wernick, Canada's top civil servant. He had been the Deputy Minister of the Ministry of Indigenous Affairs under Harper, and was notorious among Indigenous peoples—though when he testified during the justice committee's hearings into the SNC-Lavalin affair, he claimed

Wilson-Raybould had been a "partner, ally and friend" for years. Wilson-Raybould reportedly wrote a 60-page paper laying out her concerns with the direction the legislation had taken. While she had lost control, she was still taking heat over it from Indigenous peoples, including from elders in her community.

On September 12, 2018, as Russ Diabo and hundreds of Indigenous leaders and activists stood united against the Trudeau's government's legislation, it was likely a lonely day for Wilson-Raybould. She appeared to be the last prominent Indigenous figure standing alongside the government. Many months later, as the SNC-Lavalin scandal broke, the corporate media would trawl through her public commentary, looking for signs of discontent over the prime minister's handling of that affair. They pointed out that through the fall of 2018, Wilson-Raybould began issuing thinly-veiled statements criticizing her own government. But no one noticed that her first critical salvo came on September 13, the day after a hall full of chiefs had dealt a unanimous, dramatic death blow to her blueprint.

In a speech in Saskatoon given to a conference on Indigenous women and the law, she seemed keen to distance herself from the Liberals. She defended her own record, stressing her "life-long commitment" and "consistent and considered" promotion of Indigenous rights.[35] In another speech a month later, she would say more: "I have unfortunately had it reinforced that when addressing Indigenous issues, no matter what table one sits around, or in what position, or with what title and appearance of influence and power, the experience of marginalization can still carry with you." Had the legislation's unravelling and defeat at the hands of a grassroots Indigenous opposition liberated her to take a new stand? It was impossible to know. But it seemed evident that the politics of reconciliation were not merely a sideshow, but a central factor, in her decision to defy Justin Trudeau over SNC-

Lavalin and eventually break with the Liberal government. And what was clear was that the criticisms she voiced in September were starkly at odds with anything she had said before:

> Too often we see the tendency—especially in politics—to use important words that have real meaning and importance, carelessly. We see them being applied to ideas and actions that in truth do not reflect their actual meaning—even, sometimes, their opposite. We see "recognition" applied to ideas that actually maintain "denial". We see "self-government" used to refer to ideas or processes that actually maintain control over others. We see "self-determination" applied to actions that actually interfere with the work of Nations rebuilding their governments and communities... Words, in the work of reconciliation, are also cheap without real action—action that goes to the core of undoing the colonial laws, policies, and practices, and that is based on the real meaning of reconciliation. The path of justice and equality is not advanced or achieved through half-measures, good intentions, or lofty rhetoric.

It was as damning an indictment of the Liberal government as anyone had made.

The Indigenous Irreconcilables

If the rise of the Reconciliation Industry has an accompanying downfall, it started somewhere along an icy, snow-swept winter road in northwest British Columbia. In the land of the Wet'suwet'en First Nation, during a blisteringly cold early morning in mid-January 2019, a group of community members and hereditary chiefs huddled around a fire near a makeshift blockade.

For nearly ten years, they had maintained an organized presence in the pathway of a proposed pipeline, which would carry fracked gas from Dawson Creek, BC, to the coastal town of Kitimat. In that time, a ramshackle camp turned into a mini-village, with a traditional pit lodge and a healing centre offering land-based education that drew Indigenous and non-Indigenous people from across the province. In December 2018, the company behind the pipeline project, Coastal GasLink, had sought an injunction to remove the camp—suspiciously timed for when one of its main leaders, Hereditary Chief Smogelgem, had received news of his mother's passing. It was granted by a lower provincial court, dubiously ignoring Supreme Court precedents recognizing the authority of the Wet'suwet'en in their territory, as well as the fact that the pipeline had yet to gain regulatory approval from National Energy Board hearings set for later in 2019.

Just a few months earlier, the Liberal government's efforts to manufacture the consent of First Nations for its major piece of legislation—its hoped-for crowning achievement—had faltered. But if there was anything to demonstrate that, no matter the means, a colonial state would get its way, it was what came next: heavily-armed RCMP moving in on a makeshift wooden gate the Wet'suwet'en had erected on the winter road. The Trudeau government could have intervened, imposed an approach of meditation or de-escalation. It didn't. Images of the police aggressively arresting a group of unarmed land defenders were soon carried by media globally, inspiring sympathy and anger.

Over the next days, hundreds of Vancouver students walked out of their high schools, taking their message to the downtown office of Coastal GasLink. Some 1,500 rallied in Victoria, others round-danced and blocked a bridge in Toronto, and a large march in Ottawa occupied a building where Justin Trudeau was intending to give a speech. In the speed of response, in size and scope, in online interest, it was an outpouring of support for Indigenous rights unlike anything ever seen in Canada.

A week later, Trudeau met with regional chiefs from the Assembly of First Nations in a closed-door meeting in Ottawa. According to a memo written by Gord Peters, Deputy Grand Chief of the Association of Iroquois and Allied Indians, Trudeau was pointedly asked why the RCMP had intervened this way on unceded lands. The chief reminded him of the country's most important land rights case, the 1997 Delgamuukw Supreme Court decision, that had established the existence of Aboriginal title—and which had involved the Wet'suwet'en and the very land in question.

In response, Trudeau surprised the chiefs by recounting the story of Aesop's Fable about the sun and wind, and their competition to disrobe a traveler of his jacket. Trudeau reminded his audience that his approach was that of the warm, positive sun. "He said that his government was doing something totally new," Peters wrote.[36] It was like a broken record, a Reconciliation Industry tune twisting and screeching on its tracks, insisting on its commitment to consent when all could see that coercion had become the order of the day.

A few months before, I had spoken over the phone with Kanahus Manuel, who had predicted such an unravelling would come to pass. No stranger herself to blockades and government violence, Manuel is a Secwepemc activist, tattoo artist, birthkeeper, mother of four children, and the daughter of Arthur Manuel.

Since the summer of 2018, she had been living in a solar-powered tiny house in Blue River, three hours north of Kamloops, British Columbia. The structure was one of more than a dozen that had been built as part of a crowd-funded project called the Tiny House Warriors. Intended to alleviate poverty and homelessness in her community of Neskonlith, the houses also doubled as roving blockades: they could be hitched to a truck and placed anywhere in Secwepemc traditional territory, in the path of the Kinder Morgan pipeline expansion.

A black bear visited their camp every day, she told me. Not far from the highway, they could see trucks carrying pipes and heavy machinery north. Kinder Morgan security kept close watch on the nearby pumping station. "Some of the local restaurants won't serve us," Manuel said. "Blue River is not used to having natives around." But she planned to stay put all winter. When we spoke, she was making a brief return to Neskonlith, to pick up winter gear for her children, aged seven to 16. In the spring, she hoped to return to Europe, which she had visited in 2017, to spread awareness at corporate AGMs about the risks of investing in pipelines and the Canadian tar sands. If Trudeau had, in his own way, sought to complete his father's work, Manuel intended to do the same.

"I'm the type who walks into a room looking for a confrontation," she told me, laughing. It was among the lessons Manuel had taken to heart from her father: conflict is the force that brings life to politics. Earlier in 2018, her sister and others had set up a similar camp in the North Thompson River Provincial Park, the site of an ancient Secwepemc village and not far from where the Kinder Morgan pipeline passes. They held a tattoo gathering with artists from across the country, part of their efforts to revive a traditional practice (Manuel herself has a striking tattoo across her chin). When RCMP officers moved in to enforce an eviction notice, she streamed her arrest live on a Facebook video that was watched by hundreds of thousands of people around the world. Later, when the Federal court ruled that consultation on the Kinder Morgan pipeline had been inadequate, the RCMP dropped the charges.[37]

"You may just see a little house on wheels, but as part of an occupation of our own lands, it stands as a powerful symbol," Manuel said. "The government is scared of that, because they know they look terrible in front of the world when they bust down the doors of people living in their homeland. Whose side will people want to choose?"

I think of Manuel, the Wet'suwet'en, and others like them, as Canada's irreconcilables: Indigenous peoples who know that to live as self-determining nations with a thriving connection to their land they have to become, by necessity, outlaws. The irony did not escape her that she was being treated like a criminal for doing a job that served the needs of everyone in the country: protecting the forests, valleys, waters, and climate that all life depends on.

Justin Trudeau and the Liberals had tried to use their style of sunny, consensual politics as cover for the most enduring, profound conflict in the country: the clash of political orders involved in shunting Indigenous peoples aside. But there was no fable, photo-op, or lofty speech that could gloss over a machinery of dispossession in motion, as it resorted to uniformed men with guns, taking land by force, on a British Columbian frontier. "People's eyes are opening," Manuel said. "And what is happening to us, what is happening to land defenders everywhere, shows them more clearly than anything the true nature of Justin Trudeau's Liberal government."

What Manuel said made me think again of the portrait of Trudeau hanging in the Grey Eagle casino resort outside Calgary. A headdress lush with feathers perched on his forehead, red paint dabbed on his cheeks, stage light illuminating his face, it was a mask Trudeau had worn better than any prime minister. It was a mask promising a desperately and urgently-needed new path. And it was a mask donned by the defender of a colonial society in front of those he robbed. The mask had slipped.

8

Stakeholders, Transparency, Democracy, and Other Obstacles

Chrystia Freeland was fighting back tears. It was October 2016, and as Canadian Minister of International Trade, she had just emerged from a parliament building in Namur, Belgium, to tell journalists that she was "very disappointed" and "very, very sad" that the European Union (EU) couldn't sign an agreement with her government. "Even with a country as nice and with as much patience as Canada," she said, her voice quaking with emotion.

The "most progressive free trade agreement in history," as she would later hail it, a "gold standard" that she said would "advance environmental protections, transparent investment rules, workers' rights and world-class public services," had hit a major roadblock. Most EU countries were ready to finalize the Canada-European Union Comprehensive Economic and Trade Agreement (CETA), but in Belgium's constitution, all five regional parliaments were required to give assent—and one was holding out.

The man who had brought Freeland to this state was a scruffy former constitutional law professor, Paul Magnette, the president of Wallonia, a Belgian region of 3.5 million people. The scorn soon heaped on this social democratic leader by Europe's media was relentless: to them, he was a dangerous, ill-informed ideologue.

Magnette, in fact, had become the inspired spokesperson of an insurgent, pan-European citizens' movement that was standing up to the reign of corporate supremacy enshrined in the architecture of global trade law. The agreement, negotiated in secret by the Harper government and the EU in 2014, had been leaked by German media only after its completion. Major protests in Belgium and France had followed, holding up its ratification for the next two years. Now, in 2016, after a few slight changes, the EU and the new Trudeau government were trying again to push through the contested deal. "Chrystia's tears," a title Magnette would give to a chapter in his memoir of the confrontation, were only the latest tactic in an escalating campaign to pressure him into standing down.

There was nothing ill-informed or ideological about how the government of Wallonia had arrived at their position. While their parliamentary chamber, under the flag of a strutting rooster, is a throwback to a grand medieval hall, the parliamentarians' examination of the trade agreement had been profoundly modern and democratic.[1] When the draft text of CETA was leaked, they had initiated extensive hearings. They deliberated for more than two years, pored over the agreement's almost impenetrable 1,600 pages, and heard the concerns of labour unions, consumer groups, and environmentalists. They were startled by what they found.

It claimed to be a trade pact, but many of CETA's features had little in fact to do with trade. It granted any corporation with headquarters in Canada the right to sue European governments before private international tribunals, allowing them to overturn any regulations passed in those countries that impacted their bottom line. This threat would have a chilling effect on any policies intended to protect the environment, public health, or workers' rights. It also risked locking in privatization—of utilities, railways, roads, or water systems—because attempts to put these services back into public control could trigger a claim that they threatened "future anticipated profits."[2] And it severely restricted "buy local" provisions of provincial or municipal governments, prohibiting the use of public funds to stimulate local economic activity. This trade deal was indeed a gold standard—for evading democratic sovereignty on behalf of corporate power.

In October 2016, Freeland's parliamentary secretary David Lametti was summoned to testify before the Wallonia parliament. When parliamentarians asked Lametti if a multinational corporation would be able to sue their government simply for enacting beneficial social or environmental policies, they were shocked by his response. "It is true that you have to pay, from time to time, when imposing regulations or passing laws," Lametti plainly stated. For Wallonia, Magnette writes, this was "the heart of the confrontation." The next day, Wallonia announced that it could not possibly support the deal, triggering a diplomatic crisis.

In his memoir, Magnette writes that he believed Canadians would understand their position. After all, thanks to the existence in other trade agreements of these so-called Investor-State Dispute Settlement (ISDS) tribunals that allowed corporate investors to hijack national laws, Canada had become the most sued industrialized country in the world. Through a section in the North American Free Trade Agreement (NAFTA), foreign corporations had filed $2.6 billion in ongoing challenges and 37 lawsuits against Canada. For instance, when Quebec had responded to widespread demands to halt fracking underneath the St. Lawrence River by passing a moratorium on shale gas, it was sued by American energy company Lone Pine Resources. The company demanded $250 million in compensation from the provincial government, claiming that its "potential profits" had been harmed.[3]

But you wouldn't have known this from corporate media coverage of the standoff with Wallonia. "The Europeans want Canada to compromise on the investor-state resolution process that allows companies to recover damages from arbitrary government decisions," reported *The Globe and Mail*, testing the outer limits of creative euphemism.[4]

Besides also becoming exposed to legal challenge from European corporations, Canada would be harmed in other ways. Changes to Canada's patent protection system required by the deal would add nearly one billion dollars annually to the cost of medication in Canada, which already had the second highest rates in the world. As trade experts Staurt Trew and Scott Sinclair pointed out, any savings from the reductions of the minimal tariffs that existed between Canada and Europe would be completely erased by these extra costs to medicine (yet supposed tariff reductions were one of the main justifications of trade deals).[5] And to top it off, CETA carried no binding targets on carbon emissions, and its labour, environment, and sustainable development clauses, despite being proudly brandished by Freeland, were just shiny words: unlike the robust protections for investors' profits, nothing in the agreement made them enforceable.

Once a prosperous region with a strong industrial base, Wallonia had experienced firsthand how corporate globalization could hollow out middle-class jobs and the economy. But rather than respond to the substance of Magnette's concerns, the Liberal government launched a charm offensive. Its officials repeatedly stressed the shared history and culture of the French-speaking Wallonia and Canada, and insisted that they were motivated by the same "progressive" and "social democratic" principles as Magnette's governing *Parti socialiste*—emotional appeals that Magnette described as "the trademark of the new progressive Canadian diplomacy."[6] And yet, at the negotiating table, Canadian officials did not budge. "The incomprehension of our Canadian partners is total," writes Magnette.[7] Magnette found that the Trudeau government was driven by the same "ideological fascination with free trade" as its Conservative predecessors:

> When we ask them where they will create jobs, they never respond. In what sectors? Where will it destroy them? How many? They don't respond... They say it will create thousands of jobs because we get rid of border tariffs. This is pure neoliberal ideology. In the end, it is an economic treaty where the real goal is to protect investments. And under the pretext of protecting investments, we want to erode a series of laws on public health, the environment and the exchange of financial data. That is the real problem.[8]

When it became apparent that Canada's entreaties weren't working, former International Trade Minister Pierre Pettigrew was dispatched as an envoy. Pettigrew, describing himself to Magnette as Justin Trudeau's "mentor," grew less and less cordial. His tone was "direct, almost brutal," softened just a little by what Magnette called the "soft musicality" of his Quebecois accent. "You must understand, he told me, that Justin Trudeau is a Prime Minister of great talent, that he is becoming a global leader and that he will be in place for over a decade," Magnette writes. "The failure of such a treaty would be a first defeat and 'a veritable slap in the face', and that all this would inevitably have serious repercussions on relations between Canada and Wallonia."[9]

A day later, Pettigrew received Magnette in a luxurious hotel furnished with Louis XV-era *fauteuils*. There would be no second chance to sign CETA, he was told. If the upcoming summit at which Justin Trudeau was scheduled to arrive to sign the treaty was cancelled, there "will be consequences." It was a "diplomatic expression I would hear hundreds of times over the course of these several days," Magnette writes, as pressure mounted, not just from Canada but from officials across the EU.[10] An ambassador told him that, unless Wallonia approved CETA, a large company in his country that had planned to invest in Wallonia would pull out.

When Pettigrew got nowhere, Chyrstia Freeland arrived for emergency negotiations. Freeland alternated between melodrama and flattery, ultimatums and enticements. A failure to reach an agreement would be "the end of the world for us," she told Magnette. Rebuffing Canada and its new prime minister, "who is very young and is destined to remain in office for many years to come," would also mark "the end of a page of shared history between Europe and Canada."[11]

Freeland dangled an offer: Magnette could fly out to Ottawa the next morning for a snap press conference with Justin Trudeau on Parliament Hill, which would make him "one of the heroes of European social democracy." But the moment he stepped out of the plane, Magnette replied, "I would be seen as a traitor or an opportunist who had abandoned a political struggle waged for over two years for the sake of 15 minutes of glory in the international media."[12] Soon after this photo-op gambit failed, Freeland called off the talks and emerged, sniffling, to proclaim to waiting journalists that it had proven "impossible" to sign a deal with Europe.

The diplomatic isolation, the relentless pressure, the threats and ultimatums that Wallonia had been subjected to, Magnette wrote, were like the European bullying that had forced the Syriza government of Greek Prime Minister Alex Tsipras to accept harsh austerity measures that it had been elected to overturn.[13] The difference was that, ultimately, Canada and the EU did not have the leverage of a desperately-needed bailout to exert over Wallonia. In the end, Magnette did sign, but not because, as many in the Canadian media suggested, Freeland's tears had an effect (which she had by then admitted were a tactic: "we wanted the Wallons to feel guilty").[14] Instead, he had been given a guarantee by the EU that Wallonia's concerns about corporations overriding progressive policy-making would be heard at the highest European court.

None of these events stopped Freeland and the Trudeau government from taking credit for their supposed achievement—a victory for "progressive trade."[15] And in 2017, they would re-deploy the branding exercise that had been so successful, when Trudeau signed on to another major trade agreement, the Trans-Pacific Partnership. Though the trade pact would add the corporations of seven more countries to the list of those able to sue Canada over potential profits, Trudeau asked for merely one change before he ratified it: that it be renamed the Trans Pacific and Progressive Partnership.

The Liberals would bring this approach to the renegotiation of the United States–Mexico–Canada Agreement (USMCA), the successor to NAFTA. The final deal eliminated Chapter 11—which enshrined corporate rights to override national laws—and Freeland depicted it as a win for Canada at the bargaining table. "It has cost Canadian taxpayers more than $300 million in penalties and legal fees," she said, sounding for a moment like Paul Magnette from just two years before. "[It] elevates the rights of corporations over those of sovereign governments. In removing it, we have strengthened our government's right to regulate in the public interest, to protect public health and the environment."

It was a smart public relations move: more than a quarter of submissions for Trudeau's public consultation on renegotiating NAFTA called for Chapter 11 to be removed. But it was in fact Trump's trade negotiators who had insisted on its removal from the USMCA deal—for their own America-first reasons—while Canada had pushed for a remodeled version based on CETA. "The reality is that on NAFTA negotiations around ISDS," note Maude Barlow and Sujata Dey of the Council of Canadians, "Canada was the least progressive partner and the Trump White House was, ironically, more progressive."[16] They wondered out loud why, if Freeland had suddenly embraced the removal of these pro-corporate private tribunals, the government persisted in asking for it in other agreements. "If ISDS-free is good enough for the largest trading partner, surely it is good enough for Europe or for our Asian partners," they wrote.

Some knowledgeable observers favourable to Trudeau's trade agenda had long recognized the progressive branding exercise as a cynical ploy—and embraced it. "Since many so-called progressive voters are assumed to be anti-free trade and anti-globalization, what better way to differentiate Liberal trade policies from those of the Harper government than to declare that the Trudeau trade agenda is progressive?" wrote Hugh Stephens, a former Assistant Deputy Minister for Policy and Communications at the Department of Foreign Affairs and International Trade, in a specialty trade publication. "If you are a unionized worker, an environmentalist, a social or human rights activist, a feminist, or even just a self-identified member of the middle class or an aspirant to join it, how could you possibly object to a progressive trade agenda? From a domestic political perspective, it's brilliant."[17]

By 2018, however, the Trudeau government quietly instructed its officials to drop the word "progressive," according to access-to-information documents. While it had served well, it had become too "politically-loaded" an adjective, on the heels of criticisms from the Conservatives at home and the rise of right-wing leaders abroad. The policies would not change, but the government would describe them instead as an "inclusive approach to trade."[18] The directive didn't seem to stick. As of mid-2019, the new Minister Jim Carr on the file was still using "progressive trade," and one Global Affairs official remarked in a document that Freeland remained "attached dearly" to the term. After peddling a fable for so long, she had come to fully believe in it herself.

From Public Trust to Private Clutch

It was the fall of 2016, and at the luxury Shangri-La Hotel in Toronto, Justin Trudeau was promising the world's financial titans that Canada was open for business. The MC and host of the summit was Larry Fink of BlackRock, a New York-based shadow bank so vast that it manages nearly ten percent of the planet's assets. The other envoys of global capital in the room—closed off to media and surrounded by high-level security—were nothing to scoff at either: Norway's Norges Bank, the largest sovereign wealth fund; Olayan Group from Saudi Arabia, with assets of $100 billion; Singapore's Temasek Holdings, worth double that; and the Hong Kong Monetary Authority, worth almost quadruple that. None accepted interview requests, as Paul Wells reported, but a government press release boasted that they represented an astonishing $21 trillion in wealth.[19] Trudeau had arrived for the occasion flanked by no less than nine of his cabinet ministers.

Political stability was a major asset in increasingly short supply, Trudeau told the media during a brief press conference later, summing up what he had pitched to investors. The populist right was on the rise in Europe, the U.K. had voted for Brexit, and the Republican party had just nominated a certain presidential candidate—but in Canada, where "diversity is a strength," investors could find a safe harbour. "Our offer is really based on long-term stability," he said, "much more than four years." He wanted the world's wealthiest money managers to consider the potential of a new Canadian bank, which would facilitate investment in "transformative" infrastructure—with private pools of money funding, building, and operating the projects.

"I think it's unprecedented," exclaimed John Manley from the Business Council of Canada. "A once-in-a-generation opportunity," enthused Dominic Barton, global director of McKinsey & Co. and the new chair of Trudeau's Advisory Council on

Economic Growth. "If the prime minister really takes it in his hands and runs with it, he will change the future of this country," gushed Kenneth Courtis, a former Goldman Sachs Vice-President who also sat on Trudeau's 14-person pro bono council.

Their quotes made for good filler in the news write-ups of the summit, but Manley and Barton couldn't actually have been surprised: they and their corporate colleagues had designed and urged the idea on Trudeau, and written and workshopped the talking points of his ministers.

According to access-to-information documents, BlackRock executives had spent months in advance of the summit working with senior civil servants and political aides to prepare ministers to make a pitch to "help Canada realize its full potential."[20] The executives from the shadow bank had formed small working groups with government officials to "test" presentations to make sure they would resonate with astonishingly wealthy investors at the Shangri-La—many of whom were BlackRock clients. The company's officials had even prepared the PowerPoint that Innovation Minister Amarjeet Sohi would present in Toronto. The Trudeau government wasn't merely consulting the voices of finance; it had fused the apparatus of the state to the world's most powerful financiers.

There was little doubt that the infrastructure gap in Canada was real. Roads and bridges were crumbling, subways and buses overcrowded and underfunded. The country needed a roll-out of renewable energy to avert catastrophic climate change, and a build-up of defenses to protect us from the floods and fires we had already locked in. But the "innovative solutions" offered by the BlackRock executives were anything but.

Manley and Barton were giddy because Trudeau was about to turn public infrastructure, a long-neglected responsibility of governments, into a new frontier for private profit-making. Larry

Fink, who had been introduced to Trudeau by Barton over break-fast at the World Economic Forum in Davos earlier in 2016, had long been calling on governments to move in this direction.[21] Barton, who had begun chairing Trudeau's economic council that spring, was keen on the same idea. So was Mark Wiseman, president of the Canadian Pension Plan and another appointee to economic council (epitomizing how financiers were moving through an open archway between government and the corporate world, he would soon jump to BlackRock himself). These high-powered men—who were to become three financial Magi to Trudeau—had formed a think tank with the innocuous name of Focusing Capital on the Long Term in 2013. A report they produced in 2015 pointed out that, in a slow-growth world, infrastructure investments "should present a rich opportunity…with predictable income streams and time spans measured in decades."[22] So when Trudeau's economic council released its first set of recommendations to the government, it was no surprise that it endorsed the idea of a bank to unlock private investment in toll highways, bridges, high-speed rail, and power transmission projects.

This didn't look like the infrastructure bank that had been promised in the Liberals' 2015 election platform: that was supposed to be a vehicle for Ottawa to use its ability to borrow cheaply to help municipalities build much-needed public infrastructure. Underwriting capital for public-private partnerships was a turn in the exact opposite direction.[23] And those secret preparatory meetings with BlackRock executives for the Toronto summit had even broached an idea that Canadians overwhelmingly opposed: full privatization. "The potential privatization of major Canadian airports will likely be of significant interest to the investor audience," government documents noted.[24] While the Liberals responded to criticisms from the Conservatives by noting that only $35 billion in government money would go to the bank, BlackRock had in fact preferred it this way: they wanted the bulk—$140 billion—to come from private financing.

At the Canadian Council for Public-Private Partnerships conference in Toronto in November 2018, there was a buzz about the opportunities. In the SNC-Lavalin Grand Ballroom in the Sheraton Hotel, John Manley touted high value assets in a turbulent period. In a side room, speed-networking activities saw government officials gabbing for five minute sessions with reps from credit agencies, banks, construction companies, public pensions, and engineering giants like SNC-Lavalin. Breakfast entertainment was a speech from venture capitalist and futurist Leonard Brody, who sung the praises of hologram technology, which could project simulations of musicians, staging concerts in several cities simultaneously. "And with holograms, you wouldn't need to worry about unions!" he joked. The bankers and lawyers sitting at my table tittered.

When then-Opposition Leader Justin Trudeau had showed up at this annual conference in 2014, he trotted out the most common argument for public-private partnerships. "I think what citizens see P3s as is, first and foremost, a way of sharing risk," he suggested. "We're talking of big investments over a long period of time. And knowing that the private sector has a stake in its success is going to be an important guarantor that the public monies going in are going to be well spent. But more than that, it's about accessing not just more capital outside of the public funds but accessing the innovation and the responsibility that the private sector brings to any project."[25]

By responsible and innovation, did Trudeau have in mind the result of past Canadian experiments in privatization? Unsafely constructed schools. Packed, dangerous prisons. Water treatment systems flooded with sewage. Super hospitals built with faulty wiring in emergency rooms. Senior care homes overrun with inedible food and filth.

The private sector covering the risk of projects: this is the enabling lie for P3s that cannot for its life find supporting evidence. Time and again, the costs of these public-private partnerships have instead been borne by the public. In Ontario, which the Liberals had turned into the most established P3 market in the world, the cost-overruns of such projects in just the last ten years had burdened citizens with an extra $8 billion and racked up $30 billion in public liabilities—the equivalent of $6,000 per household.[26] Michael Sabia, president and chief executive of the Caisse, Quebec's province's pension fund, and another member of Trudeau's economic council, gave an idea why. "For long-term investors, infrastructure offers something that's not easy to find today: stable predictable returns in the seven to nine percent range with a low risk of capital loss—exactly what we need to meet our clients' long term needs," he told the Toronto Board of Trade. But corporate and pension-fund backers could expect to make such high profits in only one way possible—higher bills, user fees, hidden government subsidies, diminishment in the quality of service, or cuts in jobs and pay. Carving off public infrastructure for profits was something Sabia knew about: having worked under Mulroney and CN, he was basically Canada's privatization king. No wonder Trudeau's economic council advisors were offering their advice free of charge: the financiers were going to make a killing, while ordinary people carried the cost.

Sabia's own efforts on Trudeau's economic council soon seemed to be rewarded. He had given a presentation on the design of the infrastructure bank to Innovation Minister Navdeep Bains and senior public servants from several departments.[27] Less than a year later, Sabia and the Caisse would get awarded the first federal infrastructure bank funds—a $1.28 billion subsidy—for an electrified light rail project.[28] The fully-automated REM project, which would connect Montreal to its airport and suburbs and be one of the largest public transit projects in Canada, quickly became a poster child of Trudeau's infrastructure bank. It was supposedly resilient, innovative, and green—and poorly planned and expensive. It would be built by a private consortium—which included SNC-Lavalin—risking the privatization of public transit, and would privatize important transit infrastructure in Montreal, limiting the potential to expand other rail lines. The developer's route would be favourable to its own real estate holdings and suburban development, in which it was a major investor. And though public money was flowing to get it off the ground, the private consortium project would get guaranteed profits until between eight and ten percent annual return is achieved—and if they didn't get that sum, then taxpayers would pick up the tab.[29]

These costs are not an oversight of privatization but their objective—the inevitable result of opening up the public sphere to private profit-making. For more than 30 years in Canada, such measures have been a tool of an elite agenda promoted by successive Liberal and Tory governments: the transfer of wealth from the poorer to the wealthy, from the public trust to the private clutch. Indeed, Liberal Premier of Ontario Dalton McGuinty—whose closest advisor was Gerald Butts—boasted in his memoir that the Liberals were able to advance the P3 model further than the Conservatives: "We did more work in concert with the private sector than the Conservatives could ever have dreamed, largely because Liberals were trusted by the public to implement this policy in a balanced way."[30] And yet 75 percent of Canadians surveyed years later opposed such privatization schemes and in many cases across the country have petitioned successfully for these services to be returned to public control.[31] So it was no surprise that Trudeau's government didn't dare call privatization by its name. Instead, his Ministers have been using glitzy, ambiguous terms like "asset recycling" and the "flywheel of reinvestment" to describe their proposed schemes. And the public opposition to privatization might explain why the Liberals' proclivity for consultations never extended to this matter.

Because privatization serves the elite, it always spawns contempt for democracy. In the early 2000s, a slideshow used by a Canadian legal firm promoted public-private projects in British Columbia. One slide describing the obstacles to privatization is titled "Inherent diseases." The obstacles? "Stakeholders," "transparency," and "public justification."[32] For corporations chasing endless profits, the basic values of democracy are not essential to a healthy, thriving society. They are a scourge to be avoided.

All this secrecy, euphemism, and dismissive rhetoric was meant to obscure a single, glaring fact: there was no good reason to privatize public assets. The Bank of Canada is already an infrastructure bank, and its purpose is to make low-interest loans to government. And government borrowing rates are at historic lows. The Liberals could have simply taken out loans and build infrastructure at a fraction of the cost—at rates below 2.5 percent over 30 years. So why would they want to borrow at high-interest rates from private investors?

Clear-thinking economists call it privatization. Liberal spin-doctors call it fanciful names. I call it the legalized fleecing of Canadians, a giant corporate giveaway.

9

Sunni Ways

As soon as you look at the jet ski on display, you can tell it wasn't made for a leisurely spin during a weekend at a lake. For one thing, it's super-sized, the length almost of a boat. For another, it's painted an unfriendly, stealthy black. But most startling is what's mounted on its rear: a heavy, high-powered machine gun. The man describing the jet ski's features trails his hand along its shiny sides. "You can hitch a few more light machine guns here and it can carry as many as eight soldiers," he says proudly.

I feel like I'm watching everyone's favourite part of a spy blockbuster, when the lab-coated technician runs through the newest gadgets and gizmos with which he'll outfit his Double O agent. Except the man giving the preview isn't with Bond—he's with Bombardier. And we're in a giant converted air hangar on the outskirts of Ottawa, where I'm attending CANSEC, Canada's biggest weapons trade show. For the last 30 minutes, I've been tailing an official delegation from Saudi Arabia, as Canadian companies try to sell them products with a licensed capacity to kill.

"What did they think of your ocean viper?" I ask the Bombardier salesman after the Saudis have moved on to the next stall. "They were interested, they could use them, and they have the money," he says, chuckling.

The Saudi delegation's next stop is with General Dynamics Missions Systems, a Canadian subsidiary of the U.S. weapons-manufacturer General Dynamics. After a company official—a deferential, grateful smile drawn across his face—shakes hands good-bye with the Saudis, I ask him to show me the monitoring console he was demonstrating for them. Embedded into fighter jets, it taps into a global network of satellites, distinguishing "hostile" and "friendly" targets during air strikes. "It makes your kills much more effective," he says. But when I tell him I'm a journalist, his smile vanishes. "I'm not supposed to talk to you," he whispers.

The caution is almost certainly because, while several Canadian companies are eagerly hawking arms to Saudi Arabia, General Dynamics has attracted most of the notoriety. In 2014, the Conservative government announced that the London, Ontario plant of General Dynamics Land Systems-Canada—another of the U.S. company's subsidiaries—had won a major contract to build an undisclosed number of weaponized military vehicles for Saudi Arabia. The deal was worth a stunning $15 billion, the biggest weapons deal—indeed, biggest export deal of any kind—in Canadian history.

You need only rudimentary knowledge of Saudi Arabia to realize that selling it military vehicles or souped-up jet skis may not be the wisest idea. The country remains in the authoritarian clutch of a few thousand men. This very extended royal family, when not in-breeding or in-fighting or lavishly spending their inordinate oil wealth, are practitioners as well as global propagators of a fundamentalist version of Sunni Islam known as Wahhabism. It regards Shia Muslims—not to mention Christians, Jews, and other religions—as heretics. Women, considered by law to be minors, are subjected to a form of institutional infantilization: they are shackled for their entire lives to a male guardian, usually a relative, who can deny them access to a passport, job, marriage, or apartment. In 2018, after decades of feminist activism under hostile conditions, restrictions were finally loosened to allow women to drive a car, get healthcare, or open a business.[1] But the Saudi rulers hadn't had a feminist awakening on the Road to Mecca. They simply needed more drivers and businesswomen to boost a flagging economy.

The minor reforms haven't been extended to democratic rights. Amnesty International regularly reports how planned demonstrations are "ruthlessly suppressed." A crackdown on dissidents escalated under Bin Salman, who oversaw a secret assassination team that roamed the world, disappearing journalists and human rights activists long before the world focused its attention on the killing of Saudi journalist Jamal Khashoggi in the Turkish Embassy in the fall of 2018.[2] The sentence of ten years in prison and 1,000 lashes given to liberal critic Raif Badawi, whose wife has since taken refuge in Montreal, is one of the only cases to get media coverage in Canada.

Much of what Saudi Arabia does is given tacit or formal approval by the United States. Their tight relationship is usually characterized as a trade of military protection for cheap oil. But in fact it goes deeper: alongside other western countries, the U.S. has generously armed the Saudis, helping build it into a militarized, fundamentalist state that treats as a mortal enemy any secular, progressive governments in the region. This contributes crucially to the main reason why the Saudi despots haven't yet been toppled by their own people: the threat of violence, readily exercised.[3] So in selling military combat vehicles to such a regime, what did the Canadian government expect they'd be used for—road trips to the beach? In Saudi Arabia, even asking such a question could land you in jail: the rulers have declared they will punish any acts of satire with sentences of up to five years.

While in opposition, the Liberals rightly poured scorn on the Conservatives. Roland Paris, Trudeau's senior foreign affairs advisor, told media that Conservatives have "allowed an arms sale to trump human rights." Justin Trudeau announced that Canada "must stop arms sales to regimes that flout democracy such as Saudi Arabia." At the time, the Conservatives had made ISIS their number one enemy abroad. Trudeau's main advisor Gerald Butts shared on Twitter an infographic that showed the policies Saudi Arabia has in common with ISIS: beheadings for homosexuality, stoning to death for adultery, chopping off hands for stealing. "Principled foreign policy indeed," Butts tweeted triumphantly.[4]

The remark would not age well. When the Liberals came to power, far from abandoning the arms deal, they cleared the remaining obstacles out of its way. Already a few days before the 2015 election, by which point his victory seemed assured, Trudeau indicated he had shifted position. During an appearance on the popular Quebec talk show *Tout Le Monde En Parle*, Trudeau pledged to maintain the arms deal and brushed off worries about human rights violations. But he made a promise to listeners: "We will behave in a way that is transparent and open going forward, to ensure that Canadians have confidence that their government is abiding by the rules, principles, and values that people expect of their government."

What has followed is an astonishing campaign of deceit and concerted violations of Canadian regulations meant to provide oversight over the exports of weapons. While never abandoning a posture of concern for human rights, the Liberals have subordinated and sacrificed any "rules, principles and values" to a short-term electoral calculus, to pandering to a U.S.-based weapons industry and corporate lobby, and to colluding in a Saudi-led war in Yemen that has killed and starved to death tens of thousands of innocent civilians and children. If there was one thing that distinguished the Liberal approach from that of the Conservatives, it wasn't heightened scrutiny of Saudi human rights violations. It was heightened sensitivity to any consequences for their public image.

Not your Grandfather's Jeeps

In December 2015, the Global Affairs Ministry received a message from the government of Saudi Arabia, proposing to send their Foreign Minister Adel al-Jubeir to visit Canada. According to documents obtained through access-to-information request, officials at Global Affairs Canada went into a panic.

If al-Jubeir was the first foreign minister of any country to make an official visit to Canada after the Liberals came to power, officials wondered, what would be the "the signal this sends"? They worried about the "risks," especially the "high likelihood" of criticism from media and protests from human rights groups. Finally, however, Canadian officials concluded that the benefits outweighed any drawbacks and recommended moving forward with the visit. It was a "positive step toward further strengthening our ties." [5] Any risks to their image could be "mitigated through an appropriate communications strategy."

This included arranging for the Canadian ambassador to speak to Saudi authorities, giving them advance notice that the Liberal government would speak out about the case of Raif Badawi. Giving a bully a heads-up before you denounce them is a dubious sort of bravery. But this have-your-cake-and-eat-it-too approach established a Liberal pattern for the following years: wanting to come across like human rights champions, yet going out of their way to assure the Saudis that little would undermine the key aspects of a vital relationship. This Liberal communication strategy would eventually pay off and win them global plaudits for seeming to stand tough against the Saudis, especially during a diplomatic spat through 2018.

But before then, the Liberals would make several gaffes, none more ridiculous than the Liberals' initial attempts to minimize the nature of the military combat vehicle deal. "They aren't weapons; they're Jeeps," Trudeau remarked during his appearance on

Quebec television. Business Council of Canada President John Manley chipped in soon after to say they were "basically fancy trucks."[6] All of which might sound plausible to anyone who hasn't looked up the combat vehicles on Youtube, or had a chance, as I did at the Ottawa weapons trade show, to inspect one closeup.

The light-armoured vehicle resembles a tank dropped over an eight-wheeled chariot. The outer shell has the feel of concrete sandpaper and is pock-marked with metal protrusions, like the rough hide of a hideous mechanized beast. It can move over fields and deserts at a speed of 100 km/hour, rarely needing to refuel, its long antennae swaying wildly. A front hull protects against land mines and improvised explosive devices, and can even withstand hits from canons. Besides the three-person crew who operates the vehicle, it can carry six or seven soldiers who spill out quickly from a rear ramp. Fully upgraded, with extra armour, it weighs over 28 tonnes—which is light, I guess, in comparison to a Boeing 747.

When I hitchhiked in my twenties, I liked getting rides in Jeeps or trucks. But a LAV is not something I'd like to meet on a roadside. It's equipped with machine guns, grenade launchers, and a 300-pound chain gun. Any light tanks, helicopters, or even slow-moving aircraft that come with a range of three kilometres are liable to be destroyed. In case that's insufficient firepower, a canon can be affixed to the vehicle's turret, firing 105-mm shells and armour-penetrating missiles. The Belgian supplier of this component boasts that it will "deliver high lethality at very light weight."[7] The assortment of LAVs that General Dynamics is supplying to Saudi Arabia includes more than 100 of this "heavy assault" variety. It must be a fearsome sight to behold on the battlefield. That is, if someone has a chance to see it—the thermal sights allow the gunner, in day or night, to spot, track, and shoot a person up to 1.2 kilometres away.

Media outlet *PressProgress* pointed out that if the government considers this a Jeep or fancy truck, the Canadian military could probably overhaul the names of all the military equipment in their arsenal. "Flamethrowers are basically high-powered barbecue lighters," it suggested.[8] Fighter jets could be armoured hang-gliders, warships ironclad jumbo rowboats. And bombs? Behind-the-counter fireworks.

What's Done Is (Not Quite) Done

In early 2016, the Liberal campaign of misinformation went into overdrive. That was when Saudi Arabia executed 47 people for the crime of terrorism (which includes engaging in dissent, demanding reforms, or exposing corruption). Suddenly, the Liberals' maintenance of the combat vehicle deal came under greater criticism.

Trudeau insisted the deal with the Saudis had been struck not by the government, but by General Dynamics. This was making a fine distinction, but the Liberals seemed to believe it could put enough distance between them and the deal. "First of all, the government is not approving this contract," Foreign Affairs Minister Stephane Dion told a Senate committee. "The government is simply refusing to cancel a contract approved by the former government, a contract between a private company and Saudi Arabia." There was one flaw to this line of argument: it was completely untrue. The deal in fact had been brokered and signed by the Canadian Commercial Corporation (CCC), a crown corporation overseen by the federal government that helps companies sign deals abroad.[9] It was also a well-known fact in the industry that the Saudis had a strict preference for "government-to-government" deals. At the weapons trade show in Ottawa, the CCC had one of the largest booths, complete with towering red columns, in the very centre of the convention floor. Young, well-dressed officials, smiling keenly at passersby, offered workshops for companies hoping to get support from the crown corporation. This could include promotion, marketing, financing, aid from diplomatic channels, and even weapons trainings, as it had arranged for the Saudis. The delegation from Saudi Arabia were themselves escorted around by CCC officials. When I drifted closer, trying to interview the Saudis, the officials scowled, then hurried the Saudis along.

In January 2016, Dion shifted tack, insisting that his hands were tied, that the deal had already been finalized. "What's done is done," he said, an expression that incidentally entered the English lexicon via Shakespeare, when Lady Macbeth uttered it to soothe her regicidal husband's conscience, as Canadian poet Michael Lista pointed out on Twitter. As you might recall from high school literature class, the murderer's attempts to feign innocence didn't turn out well.

It took only a few months to learn that what was supposedly a done deal wasn't exactly that. Challenged in federal court by Daniel Turp, a law professor and former Bloc Québécois MP, the Liberals were forced to publicly disclose a revelatory document. The memo from Global Affairs officials to Dion, stamped "Secret," spelled out a rationale for why the deal should go forward. It asked Dion to approve export permits for 70 percent of the military vehicles being shipped to Saudi Arabia. The memo offered the Minister three options in response: "I concur," "I don't concur," or "I wish to discuss." Granted an opportunity to block a hugely controversial deal, Dion did not take it. Nor did he defer this sensitive matter for a more fulsome discussion at Global Affairs. He left a checkmark next to "I concur," signalling his assent for the deal to move ahead.[10] The memo was dated April

2016—three months after Dion had insisted it was a done deal. It was a shambling charade worthy of Lord Macbeth himself.

In the uproar that followed, Dion shifted tactics again: he pledged to scrap the deal if the government found out the LAVs were being used to commit human rights violations. He told the media that he "could block the exports at any time if there were serious evidence of misuse of the military equipment." Except, this time, he was misrepresenting Canada's export control rules. They are in fact much stricter than Dion implied: there does not need to be "serious evidence of misuse" in order to halt weapons shipments, but merely evidence that the recipient regime has a "persistent record of serious violations of the human rights of their citizens," and "reasonable risk that the goods might be used against the civilian population." A quick perusal of Wikipedia would give anyone a firm impression that the Saudi regime is basically the embodiment of "serious violation of human rights."

And there wasn't merely a "reasonable risk" that the Saudis would deploy the LAVs against civilian populations. The fact was they already had. In 2011, the Saudis had deployed them against their own civilians in the eastern part of the country. That same year, inspired by uprisings in Egypt and Tunisia, youth activists in Bahrain had begun a non-violent revolt against their dictatorship. When several peaceful protestors were killed, the movement occupied the capital's main square. The country's rulers appealed to their allies, the Saudi government, to help them put down the protests. In photos of the convoy of Saudi forces that soon rolled ominously toward Bahrain along the interstate highway, you can make out several armoured, wheeled vehicles with roof-mounted heavy machine guns—the unmistakable features of Canadian-made LAVs.[11] But even this would pale alongside Canada's military contribution to the Saudi war on Yemen.

Arsonists Playing at Firefighting

Each time she got word that Saudi bombs were falling on Yemen, Shireen Al-Adeimi would rush to her cellphone. Living an ocean away in the United States, she'd scroll through WhatsApp chats to check that her friends and family back home were safe—an anxious habit by which to endure war in a hyper-connected world.

Yemen's own Arab Spring uprising had been an exhilarating development to witness from afar, the Yemeni-Canadian professor at Michigan State University told me over the phone in late 2018. But like elsewhere across the region, hope was soon dashed by a counter-revolution. Not long after a movement led by rebels from Yemen's north overthrew the Saudi-backed dictator, the Saudis launched a war on the country in 2015.

Over the following four years, the Saudis and their allies like the United Arab Emirates (UAE) launched a campaign of indiscriminate bombing of schools, hospitals, and mosques. The war killed more than 50,000 Yemeni civilians.[12] On top of that, a blockade of the port—in a country dependent on imports for 90 percent of its food—led to widespread hunger. There was an unprecedented outbreak of cholera. Photos of emaciated babies and children, looking like bags of skin and bone, were a glimpse of how, in just two years, at least another 85,000 children died of hunger.[13] In the fall of 2018, when I spoke to Al-Adeimi, the United Nations was warning that Yemen was on the verge of the "world's worst famine in 100 years."[14]

Al-Adeimi's family had come to Canada after leaving Yemen in the late 1990s and settled in London, Ontario—the same city where the General Dynamics factory makes its vehicles for Saudi Arabia. When she realized the Saudi war, as well as the Canadian and U.S. military involvement, were barely being covered by the media, she started a Twitter account, and became an outspoken critic.

Al-Adeimi's grandmother, who died in 2016, spent the last year of her life in a Yemeni city surrounded by Saudi bombing. "She was evacuated out of the city in a wheelbarrow," Al-Adeimi said, her voice cracking. "I can never forget that image."

The United States provided jets, bombs, midair refuelling to Saudi and UAE bombers, intelligence, targeting assistance, on-the-ground military personnel, and more—constrained only by growing opposition in the U.S. Congress, led by Senator Bernie Sanders. But while U.S. involvement in backing the war on Yemen was eventually debated on the floors of Congress, in Canada there was silence on the country's involvement in Yemen. "Media coverage left people in Canada to think this was just a civil war, and that we should figure it out for ourselves, ignoring the crucial military backing the Canadian government was providing Saudi Arabia," says Al-Adeimi.

This was despite the fact that the 2016 memo signed by Dion, approving the export of export vehicles, included a startling admission. It showed that the Ministry of Global Affairs recommended approval of the export permits in part to help Saudi Arabia wage war in Yemen. Saudi Arabia, the memo stated, is a "key military ally who backs efforts of the international community to fight the Islamic State of Iraq and Syria and the instability in Yemen. The acquisition of these next-generation vehicles will help in those efforts." But the instability Canada claimed to be helping fight, it was in fact stoking.

The Liberal government had pledged to closely monitor the use of its weapons in Saudi Arabia. But they must not have tried very hard, because the entire apparatus of the Canadian state was soon outperformed by a lone independent scholar. Anthony Fenton, an author and PhD student at York University studying Canadian foreign policy and military exports to the Middle East, had come up with an ingenious research strategy. He closely tracked posts on social media by Saudi military officials who were showing off their weapons or vehicles—what Fenton called "bling videos" and "Saudi selfies." Over the course of years of monitoring, he unearthed a trove of evidence about Canadian complicity in the war on Yemen.

In one photo posted on Instagram, a Saudi soldier sat cross-legged on a carpet next to a miniature mosque constructed out of ammunition boxes. A few metres from his makeshift shrine is parked a giant, dusty, weaponized Canadian combat vehicle. In a separate video, a long convoy of the same military vehicles cruised over sand dunes in Hajjah province, Yemen, as the heavy beats of electronic Arabic music pulsated from open tank hatches. In certain videos found online and verified by military experts, the Canadian combat vehicles—likely from previous shipments—were turning up in Yemen with large 'C' painted onto their sides, which marked them specifically for Yemeni operations. Armoured military vehicles made by three other Canadian companies—Terradyne, Streit Group, and IAG Guardian—turned up in Yemen as well. The evidence Fenton uncovered showed the Canadian contributions went well beyond just the armoured vehicles. In another Instagram photo, a soldier stood in front of a portrait of King Salman of Saudi Arabia while proudly cradling a Canadian-made sniper rifle. The caption issued a warning to Yemenis: "Beware of the Saudi Army."

The social media images were the visual tip of a story that had been kept hidden from Canadians: the involvement of Canadian companies in arming the destructive war on Yemen, with the approval of the Trudeau government. Canadian companies provided prestige sniper rifles, surveillance aircraft, and surveillance technology, and they trained drone pilots and U.S. pilots who refuelled Saudi fighter jets in mid-flight. They were involved in a major and unprecedented project with Saudi Crown Prince

Mohammad Bin Salman: to produce a plane in the country, for the first time in the kingdom's history. Another Canadian company, in a successful pitch to the UAE, suggested that Saudi Arabia had no need to send expensive F-16 fighters to eliminate Yemeni rebels armed with small arms—they could simply buy a "counterinsurgency" aircraft, the Archangel, an agricultural plane that was modified to carry up to 6,000 pounds of bombs and missiles.[15] Between the beginning of the war in 2015 and the end of 2018, a total of at least $2.4 billion in military goods—mostly weaponized combat vehicles, but much else as well—had been shipped to Saudi Arabia.[16] Labeled non-military, many of the aircraft sales eluded accounting in Canada's export figures. And there was no way to know just how many of the weapons had ended up in Yemen.

There was such a boom in business, in fact, that Canada under Trudeau became the second-biggest weapons exporter to the Middle East, after the United States.[17] Canadian companies opened or expanded several centres throughout the region to promote sales, and to maintain, repair, or update vehicles, aircraft, and war components sold to the Saudis and their allies like the UAE. "It's rare that a week has gone by without a Canadian-made combat vehicle or weapon showing up in Yemen, providing overwhelming and incriminating evidence of their widespread use," Fenton says. "Yet the silence in Canada about the profitable complicity of our government and companies in the Yemen war is striking."

This didn't stop a Global Affairs spokesperson from boasting in 2018 that Canada has provided $44 million "this year alone" in humanitarian assistance to Yemen. "Canada remains deeply concerned by the ongoing conflict in Yemen and its humanitarian impact on civilians, particularly women and children, who continue to bear the brunt of the fighting," the spokesperson said. Al-Adeimi saw it otherwise. "Justin Trudeau can't be an arsonist and then sometimes play at firefighting," she said. "Saudi Arabia doesn't have their own weapons industry; they only have their oil money. This war wouldn't be possible without Canada and others arming them. Western countries are literally holding their hand while they wage war. It's as simple as this: you have to stop helping kill Yemenis."

White-Washing Saudi Crimes

At the end of April 2019, the cousin of Abdullah Al Asreeh said a prayer for the 24-year old man, at a ceremony attended by relatives and friends in a mosque in Toronto. Without a warning, by phone-call or other means, they had learned on the news that Al Asreeh had been beheaded by the Saudi government, alongside three dozen men mostly from the country's persecuted Shia minority.

His crime? Peacefully protesting the Saudi regime's brutal treatment of his community.

Al Asreeh, just 20 years old at the time of his arrest, was a human rights activist and worked on his father's farm near the town of Awamiyah in Saudi Arabia's eastern province. "He was a normal person," his cousin told CBC News. "He wanted to build his life, but the government didn't give him a chance."[18]

Foreign Affairs Minister Chrystia Freeland expressed being "very concerned" about the mass executions, but she did not mention that Canada was complicit in Al Asreeh's fate. His town of Awamiyah—the heart of Saudi Arabia's brief Arab Spring protests—had long been a target of Saudi security forces, which regularly used Canadian armed vehicles. They had invaded the town in 2011, arresting and torturing several activists, forcing others into hiding, and executing a popular cleric and vocal advocate of non-violence.[19] In 2017, again using Canadian combat vehicles, they launched an operation that killed more than two dozen civilians, razed a historic neighbourhood, and displaced tens of thousands of people. Did the Liberal government seize the chance to collect evidence and make it the basis for a re-evaluation of their exports? To the contrary, they soon undertook a breathtaking exercise in white-washing.

In its campaign of harassment of Awamiyah, the Saudi government announced in late 2016 that it would demolish—or "renovate," in their words—the town's oldest neighbourhood, Al-Masora, a 400-year-old walled village lined with narrow streets, farmers' markets, clay buildings, and sea-stone houses. The situation was closely monitored by the United Nations experts, who petitioned the Saudi government to halt the demolition, which in their words threatened "the historical and cultural heritage of the town with irreparable harm, and may result in the forced eviction of numerous people from their businesses and residences."[20]

When many families refused to leave their homes, engaging in sit-ins, the Saudi government cut off their electricity and water supply. Soon after, Saudi security forces laid siege to the town, with some residents taking up arms in self-defence. According to testimonials collected by Human Rights Watch (HRW), the Saudi forces shot into populated areas, occupied a public school, closed clinics and pharmacies, and barred access to ambulances. The siege, which sealed off the town, continued for months. One resident told HRW that "the town was constantly bombarded by shelling, and security forces were going around shooting in residential neighbourhoods at random. We were too scared to leave our homes and most of the shops were shut down or burned. Anything that moved became a target."[21] Some 20,000 to 25,000 of the town's 30,000 population were forced to flee. By August, Saudi security forces had rid the town of "terrorists and criminal elements," they claimed, and completed the demolition of the old neighbourhood.[22] "The scale of devastation was shocking," wrote a BBC journalist, one of the rare reporters allowed by the Saudi authorities to visit. "It looked like a war zone—as if we were in Mosul or Aleppo."[23]

Researcher Anthony Fenton was monitoring social media and was the first to discover that pro-Saudi military accounts had posted videos showing Canadian Terradyne Gurkha vehicles rolling through the streets, firing ammunition, amidst crumbling and destroyed buildings.[24] When the news hit the front pages, Minister Freeland announced an investigation, emphasizing officials would "very energetically and very carefully review" the events with "a real sense of urgency," while temporarily suspending permits for the export of Terradyne vehicles.[25]

Six months later, in February 2018, Freeland announced that there "was no conclusive evidence that Canadian-made vehicles were used in human rights violations." The export of the armoured vehicles recommenced.[26] The investigation itself, released in partially-redacted form months later, claimed "there is no credible information that [the] Saudi Ministry of Interior forces committed serious human rights violations in the conduct of that operation, with Gurkhas or otherwise." The use of force, it concluded, was "proportionate and appropriate."[27]

Had Canadian investigators interviewed residents of Awamiyah? No. Had they spoken to the human rights organizations that had documented far from proportionate actions? No. Had they consulted the United Nations experts who had issued warnings about the consequences of Saudi actions? No, again. Their sources were "close allies and like-minded partners"—in other words, unnamed Saudi government officials. What kind of picture had these Saudi officials helped the investigators draw? The town was a "haven for criminality," rather than a courageous epicentre of civil resistance. Its situation was "deteriorating," not because the state had set itself to bulldozing a neighbourhood against the will of its residents, but "due to militancy in the Shia community." Saudi forces were "deployed in response to increased security threats" and "made a concerted effort to minimize civilian casualties." No mention of years of violent harassment of peaceful activism. And that video evidence of the Canadian armoured vehicles rolling through the town's street? It was dismissed as not providing "any insight as to the context or nature of the activity." The only organization named to back up the investigation's findings was the Saudi National Society for Human Rights, which "did not express concerns about the conduct of the operation." Why? Perhaps because this group was funded by a trust of former Saudi King Fahd's estate, is populated by government figures, and was in fact created by the Saudi dictatorship to ward off calls for more meaningful reform (none of which is mentioned in the Canadian government's report).[28]

The investigation concluded by expressing concern for Terradyne, which would lose business if they couldn't sell the custom-made vehicles to the Saudis. "It is reasonable to expect that the Kingdom of Saudi Arabia would continue to use Gurkhas to mitigate risk to security forces during the conduct of legitimate security operations," it concluded. But there was yet more astonishing commentary. "While one can question the wisdom of the Saudi plan to evacuate and raze the old section of Al-Awamiya and the manner in which the operation was conducted, one cannot dismiss the security-related motivations at play in the exercise." Question the wisdom? In its haste to protect and preserve a major arms deal, the Canadian government had stooped to toying with a justification for the political cleansing of a city. When a group of NGOs called for a truly independent investigation, it was no surprise that it went unacknowledged by the government.[29]

A Family Business

Under a tent on a moonlit night in an Arabian desert, a caftan-clad Pierre Elliott Trudeau swirled around a dancefloor with Sheikh Ahmed Yamani, the famous, goateed Oil Minister of the Kingdom of Saudi Arabia.

The festivities, reported by *The Globe and Mail* on its frontpage in 1980, were part of an opulent caravan along the Great Incense Route that the prime minister's entourage were treated to during his official state visit to Saudi Arabia. Justin, eight years old, remained at home, but his brother Sacha, six, climbed over sand dunes and slept beneath cliffs carved into ancient tombs. True to reputation, Pierre Elliott toyed with scandal when he danced with Liliane Jenkins, the wife of Canadian Ambassador William Jenkins, in front of the party of 100 Saudi royals. "Dancing with women is a no-no in this strict society, and dancing with one who isn't your wife is close to adultery. Saudi smiles froze until Mr. Jenkins jumped up and got into the act," *The Globe and Mail* reported.[30] "It was a night to remember—desert feasts, gutted sheep, Arab men doing grinds with scarves tied around their hips and a camel ride for Sacha," the reporter effusively wrote. It was also a night that would pay off handsomely for Canada's weapons industry.

We don't have a record of what words Trudeau exchanged, but in the coming months, on the basis of a relationship strengthened by the revelry of an Arabian night, the Saudis began looking into buying Canadian military equipment. It was the armoured vehicles made in London, Ontario, that caught their eye. Up until then, arms manufacturers based in Canada had not been able to sell to the Saudis, though not for lack of desire. While they had persistently tried to establish Saudi Arabia as a market for their exports from the 1950s onward, stricter Canadian export permit policies thwarted any sales. Countries engaged in widespread abuses like Saudi Arabia—which just a few months before Trudeau's visit had publicly executed, without trial or judicial proceeding, 63 Salafist militants who had seized a Grand Mosque in Mecca—were barred from buying Canadian-made weapons.[31]

But under Pierre Elliott Trudeau, this would soon change. At first, Trudeau seemed to endorse the restrictions, and even curbed the promotional activities of Canadian officials abroad. But under lobbying from the arms industry, in 1975, he radically watered down the restrictions: commercial considerations took on greater weight; the Department of Foreign Affairs and Defence no longer had a veto over exports; and within government, the onus to make their case now lay with those opposed to sales, rather than those who were supportive. Weapons exports to human rights abusers around the world exploded.[32]

All that was left to do to initiate sales of armoured vehicles to Saudi Arabia was the approval of the Trudeau government. Officials at the Department of Foreign Affairs, according to a 1980 document that Fenton uncovered in the federal archives, underlined that this required a "policy decision departing from the traditional Canadian approach on military sales to Middle East."[33] But with the blessing of Pierre Trudeau himself, the green-light was given by his Cabinet and the initial export permit for LAVs was issued in 1981. This paved the way for the first mega-sale of armoured vehicles. At first they were shipped through the United States, but after the government of Brian Mulroney made export laws even more permissive in the mid-1980s, they were sold directly to Saudi Arabia. Through the 1990s, under Chrétien, LAV exports jumped again. Today, some $50 billion worth of LAVs—numbering in the thousands—have been shipped to Saudi Arabia, many finding their way into Yemen.

Sound and Fury, Signifying Nothing

It was a cringe-inducing image: Russian President Vladimir Putin, grinning like the Grinch, high-fiving Saudi Crown Prince Mohammad Bin Salman at the G20 summit in Argentina in late 2018. With controversy over the killing of journalist Jamal Khashoggi and the Yemen war dogging the Saudi ruler, their greeting sent an obvious message: watch us flaunt our violent impunity with giddy abandon.

Putin's crude antics—much like Donald Trump's outlandish dismissal of the evidence connecting the Crown Prince to Khashoggi's murder—has given other western leaders a chance to pretend their hands were clean of the Saudis' brutal abuses. Emmanuel Macron tut-tutted in the Prince's ear on the summit's sidelines, though France hasn't stopped selling the Saudis naval vessels, tanks, and artillery. Theresa May insisted she snubbed him in private conversation, while saying nothing about the British bombs and missiles that continued to rain down on Yemen's children.[34] But no one put on a more dramatic show than Justin Trudeau.

In contrast to Putin's chummy bro-down, Trudeau engaged in some virtuous finger-wagging. Following a meeting with Bin Salman, he announced that he had underlined that Canada will "always stand up strongly and clearly for human rights."[35] Trudeau's brand of diplomacy had long been geared to send its own obvious message: watch us flaunt our brave stance toward Saudi Arabia. It continued a script that the Liberal government had followed since the time it came to office. Its most dramatic moment came when Canada's Foreign Affairs Minister tweeted in August 2018 that she was "extremely concerned" about the Saudi detention of female activists. When the tweet went viral and netted widespread media attention, the Saudi rulers reacted sharply, trying to send a signal to the world that they wouldn't accept criticism.[36] They expelled Canada's ambassador, started making plans to remove thousands of Saudi students and medical patients from Canada, and suspended new trade.[37] But there was a certain flow of trade between the two countries that didn't let up: oil and arms. Meanwhile, the world's media rushed to Canada's corner, and Freeland basked in her status as a champion of women's rights, declaring that "Canada will always stand up for human rights in Canada and around the world, and women's rights are human rights."[38]

But fine talk is meaningless if you're enabling the very abuses you're criticizing. Trump and Putin may make their indifference to Yemeni lives crassly obvious, but at least they're not brazen hypocrites. While it was clear that the Liberals never expected quite such a harsh Saudi reaction, they were completely willing to play it up to its fullest effect. The drama of a stormy diplomatic spat granted the Liberal government greater leeway to pursue the parts of the relationship with the Saudis that mattered to them most. In December 2018, as the global outcry over the murder of Jamal Khashoggi reached its diplomatic peak, Trudeau insisted several times that he was "looking into how to cancel the contracts." Freeland announced she would halt the issuance of any new permits for arms exports to Saudi Arabia, pending a "review." But since the spat broke out, and while concerned Canadians waited in vain for the review's results, Canada did not stop exporting. Indeed, between August 2018 and July 2019, Canada has exported more than a billion dollars worth of armoured vehicles, which had their permits already approved.[39] All that posturing, to invoke a last passage from Macbeth, "full of sound and fury, signifying nothing."

In January 2019, a young Saudi woman flew to Thailand and barricaded herself in a hotel room in a desperate attempt to flee her abusive family in Saudi Arabia. As she broadcast her fight for asylum on social media, her situation captivated the world's attention, and a number of countries expressed interest in granting her refugee status—but Canada moved the fastest.[40] "That is something that we are pleased to do because Canada is a country that understands how important it is to stand up for human rights, to stand up for women's rights around the world," Justin Trudeau announced. Soon after, the 18-year-old Saudi woman landed at Toronto's airport and emerged at arrivals, accompanied by Minister of Foreign Affairs Chrystia Freeland. "This is Rahaf al-Qunun, a very brave new Canadian," Freeland said to a throng of waiting reporters, her arm around al-Qunun's shoulders.

It was the latest in a series of stunts by the Liberal government, milking the symbolic power of an otherwise humane gesture to deflect attention from their continuing complicity in Saudi crimes. *The Guardian* reported that the "decision is likely to exacerbate Canada's already poor relations with Saudi Arabia," getting taken in yet again, like most of the world's media, by the Liberals' clever communications strategy.

10

#WelcomeToCanada

In her lap, Lucy Granados cradles her limp left hand. As she describes her journey to Canada as a refugee, her time in Montreal separated from her three children, and her recent forced return to Guatemala, she strokes the hand gently, as if it belonged to another person. Most days it feels like it does: ever since she was aggressively arrested by Canadian border security agents inside her apartment in Montreal, she hasn't been able to move her fingers.

A decade ago, Granados fled Guatemala to escape harassment by gangs targeting people for extortion. The gang violence had taken a horrendous toll on her family: a cousin, deliberately run over; another cousin, found dead in his fruit orchard; an uncle, discovered dismembered by the river. In 2007, after her husband was killed in an accident, and after the closure of the *maquila* where she had worked sewing six days a week, she felt she had no choice but to go north.

Leaving behind three young children with her mother, she travelled on the "death train" through Mexico to reach the U.S. border, evading drug-dealers and ranchers who have taken to shooting migrants for sport. By some estimates, one out of every three women who pass through this trail are sexually assaulted.[1] For three days and three nights, she walked through the border-lands, a desert littered with human bones.

Lucy was one of the lucky ones—for a time. She reached Canada and settled in Montreal. Though her refugee claim was denied a year later, she stayed in the country, fearing a return to Guatemala. "I only thought of my children," she says. "I had to protect them, pay for their education and their needs, and support a sick brother and mother." She worked as a housekeeper, a job that few Canadians care to do, and developed a wide circle of friends, involving herself in community work supporting other undocumented women.

In September 2017, she filed an application for permanent residency on humanitarian grounds. But in the early hours of March 20, 2018, two border security agents surprised her at her front door. In her gown and slippers, Granados tried to exit out the back door, but there were two more agents waiting there. Government documents indicate that, by the border security agency's own account, a terrified Granados cooperated and returned inside. But when she took her phone out and called a friend, the agents grabbed her, slammed her against her kitchen table, twisted her left arm behind her back, and threw her onto the floor.[2]

Medical tests later confirmed that Granados suffered nerve damage caused by an injury to two vertebrae, consistent with her account of a blow to her neck at the time of her arrest. Her hand had still not regained full capacity after six months, although she has slowly recovered feeling and partial mobility since then.

During interrogation by agents at Canadian border security headquarters in Montreal, she lost consciousness, her heart stopped beating, and she was rushed to the hospital, but the border agency neglected to alert lawyer or friends. When her friends finally found out, they were not allowed into the hospital room, where Granados had her feet shackled together, an agent watching over her. During a review hearing of her case, the border security agency told the judge that Granados had fainted, as if to try to delay her deportation—not telling the judge they had in fact performed emergency CPR to revive her.

Migrant justice organization Solidarity Across Borders launched a campaign over the next weeks, with letters to MPs, rallies, and peaceful sits-in. The day of her deportation—carried out against the advice of medical experts and with only the clothes on her back—Granados was smuggled out of the Migrant Detention Centre in Laval to a waiting van, while dozens of friends and activists peacefully blockaded the entrance. "It felt like I was being kidnapped," she remembers. It was only when an MP intervened that her luggage was finally returned. Her friends are now seeking to take her case to the United Nations, urging the international body to sanction Canada for her treatment.

Granados's story is not unique. It is a common story of an undocumented racialized woman in the age of Trump—and Trudeau. Her experience was worlds apart from the image of Canada cultivated by Trudeau's Liberals, but deeply in line with their actions and behind-the-scenes policies.

A Dangerous Third Country

It was the tweet heard around the world. In late January 2017, on the day Donald Trump's travel ban on Muslim immigrants was brought into effect, Justin Trudeau issued a pointed rejoinder. "To those fleeing persecution, terror & war, Canadians will welcome you, regardless of your faith," Trudeau's message on Twitter read. "Diversity is our strength. #WelcometoCanada." An antidote to the hatred coming from the White House, within days it had been retweeted hundreds of thousands of times and received effusive praise in media coverage around the world.

But as Trump's administration unleashed an anti-immigrant agenda that would eventually involve not just travel bans but increased surveillance, deportations, and separating children from their parents at the U.S.-Mexico border, there were more than a few wrinkles in Trudeau's tweet.

Asked to clarify if the prime minister's tweet meant that Canada would be accepting more refugees, Trudeau's immigration minister assured a reporter they were already "doing [their] part." There would be no increase the country's refugee intake. In reality, Canada was at that moment hardly a leader in openness to those fleeing violence and persecution. The number of refugees it accepted in 2016 totalled 38,000—ranking Canada in 20th place among industrialized countries, judged on a per capita basis.[3] Germany, by contrast, accepted 300,000 in 2016 and nearly 900,000 the year before.

And of the refugees that Canada did accept, nearly half were privately sponsored by citizens, not the government itself. Unlike some other countries, Canada doesn't have a formal system for integrating refugee claimants. Dozens of aid agencies, funded by government grants and private donations, take the lead in housing refugees and helping them find schools and jobs. While responsibility is often outsourced to ordinary Canadians, Trudeau had not been shy to claim the benefits to his image.

In late 2016, the month before that tweet, the government had quietly capped applications for private sponsorship of refugees from war-torn Syria and Iraq—after families and community groups brought in nearly 14,000 the previous year. The number now accepted? A mere 1,000. In other words, many desperate and endangered people from Syria would not be able to come to Canada, despite the existence of groups in civil society ready to welcome and host them.[4]

There were other wrinkles. An asylum seeker from the United States cannot just show up at an official Canadian border post. If someone first arrives and makes an application for refugee status in the United States—deemed a safe place for refugees by a "Safe Third Country" agreement signed between the previous Liberal government and the George Bush administration in 2004—they are then barred from seeking refuge in Canada.[5]

Asylum seekers crossing the border at places other than official border posts, however, are not automatically deported and may make asylum claims, because Canada is a signatory of the United Nations' 1951 Refugee Convention. Which is why, as Trump's anti-immigrant agenda stirred enormous fear in the U.S., we began to see desperate people increasingly turning to such irregular crossings—so they could at least get a hearing.[6] (This is also why, though such crossings are irregular, they are not "illegal," as media outlets and right-wing politicians constantly suggest.)

If Trudeau's government was sincere about his tweet, he could have taken a very specific follow-up step: he could have opted out of the "Safe Third Country" agreement, making the reasonable point that the U.S. is clearly not a safe third country for refugees and immigrants. Groups like Amnesty International and the Canadian Council of Churches, backed by over 200 law professors, soon launched a legal challenge to contest the designation that Canada had granted the U.S.[7]

New Arrivals and Coup Arrivals

While the Liberal government cultivated an image of Canada's refugee system as the political equivalent of airport hugs and teddy bears, refugee rights advocates warned about what would come to pass: desperate people would start believing in the promise embedded in Trudeau's branding exercise.

In the summer of 2017, hundreds of Haitian refugees from the United States began to cross the border—terrified of being sent back to Haiti by Donald Trump, who had cancelled a temporary stay on their deportation. The Liberal government may have been happy to reap the political benefits of Trudeau's PR posture, but in this case they were a step ahead of Trump: they had already been deporting hundreds of Haitians back to the country, ever since they lifted a freeze on deportations to the island nation in 2016—a freeze the Harper government had put into effect after the earthquake that hit the country.[8]

The people trudging across the border, mainly between Quebec and New York, eventually prompted the Canadian military to set up a temporary tent encampment in Quebec. Far-right groups and mainstream political parties seized the opportunity to stoke racism. By the end of 2018, nearly 40,000 people would walk into Canada from the United States to file refugee claims.[9]

But the Liberals wouldn't consider scrapping the agreement and regularizing crossings and appeals for status. Trudeau turned to admonishing Haitians, dispatching a Minister to the United States to warn Haitians against seeking asylum in Canada. "For someone to successfully seek asylum it's not about economic migration," Trudeau warned. "It's about vulnerability, exposure to torture or death, or being stateless people."[10]

"Economic refugees," of course, are not entitled to asylum. And this is where the base ranting of right-wing tabloids and anti-immigrant racists, who have stoked hate and fear of "selfish queue-jumpers," dovetails with the high-minded reasoning of elite pundits and Liberal policy-makers preaching pragmatic limits and strict refugee criteria. Both adhere to a brand that is much more enduring than this latest prime minister's: the image of an innocent Canada, whose benevolence is indisputable, whose humanitarian impulse is never in doubt. What they disagree about is whether Canada should share its virtues with refugees.

Unmentioned in even a single mainstream discussion was that Canada didn't stand at a remove from the misery that Haitians were fleeing: we had a direct hand in it. Ignoring this history— and absolving Canada of responsibility for Haiti's situation—has created the greatest barrier of all to refugees receiving the welcome they deserve. Haiti's long-suffering people, who have endured a line of dictatorships, had a brief respite in the last quarter century: a popular democratic wave that swept priest Jean-Bertrand Aristide to power. He raised the minimum wage from mere pennies, disbanded an army that terrorized the population, and started providing education and medical care to the poor majority.

Defying the agenda of the Haitian elite and multinational companies who used the country for cheap labour made Aristide enemies—the U.S., France, and Canada. In 2003, the Liberal government of the time hosted U.S. and French officials to plot Aristide's ouster.[11] They cut aid to his government. And when U.S. marines invaded the country, Canadian soldiers guarded the airport while they flew out Aristide and dumped him in Africa. A United Nations military force, commanded for a period by Canadians, occupied the country, providing cover for the regime installed after this *coup d'état*.[12] Thousands of Haitians were killed.

The Canadian government's role was hardly based on humanitarianism. Having refused a full role in the U.S. war on Iraq, they needed to get back in the good graces of U.S. President George Bush. In a moment of candour out of sync with our humanitarian brand, ex Liberal Foreign Affairs Minister Bill Graham explained: "[The] Foreign Affairs view was there is a limit to how much we can constantly say no to the political masters in Washington… eventually we came on side on Haiti, so we got another arrow in our quiver."[13]

The cost to Haitians of this cynical calculus was enormous. Since the coup, Haiti has lurched from disaster to disaster, compounded by governments more accountable to the U.S. than their own people. The devastating earthquake of 2010 was shaped by inequality and deliberate underdevelopment that Haiti was plunged back into after Aristide's ousting. The impact of similar storms on neighbouring Cuba—whose measures to lift people out of the most impoverished infrastructure have not been blocked by western governments—was a fraction of what it was in Haiti.

Western governments have tried to wash their hands of their victims. In the wake of the earthquake, Obama's administration built a fortress around Haiti: Coast Guard ships cruised the waters to prevent any from fleeing; Air Force bombers dropped messages in the country, warning that "if you leave, you will be arrested and returned"; and a U.S. private prison company started setting up a detention centre in Guantanamo Bay, all while Haitians had not yet dug themselves out of the rubble.[14]

And the reconstruction effort that millions of people around the world compassionately contributed to? It left Haiti with plenty of industrial parks for sweatshop employers and luxury hotels for tourists and NGO officers, but virtually no new housing for the million Haitians who had been made homeless. To make matters even worse, the occupying UN force introduced the world's largest cholera epidemic into the country—it has killed 30,000, infected 2 million people, and rages on.[15]

Canada has "slapped some make-up" on the situation to justify deporting people back to the country, says Haitian human rights lawyer Patrice Florvilus, who fled to Montreal from Haiti in 2013 after facing death threats. "Canada claims things have returned to normal," he told me in 2017. "They have not. There is criminalization of homosexuality and dissent, assassinations, a corrupt justice system. So much suffering has flowed from the coup onward, and the state now has no capacity to protect its citizens. Canada should assume responsibility for the chaos and injustice it helped create."

Haiti is today sliding back toward dictatorship: disastrously bad elections, sanctioned by the U.S. and Canada, have produced a parliament packed with thugs and drug dealers, the old army is being revived, and leading figures in the current government have links to the dictatorships of old. All of this could hardly be a better example of the slogan repeated by migrant justice movements around the world: "We are here because you were there."

Western governments' wars, their ransacking of resources, the manipulation and impoverishment of poor countries, has led to an inevitable flow of displaced and persecuted to our shores.

"If Canada wants to become a real beacon for refugees, here is an opportunity to prove it," said Florvilus, who believes Canada should grant special refugee status to the arriving Haitians. He's right. After all of our crimes toward that country, asylum should serve as the barest of reparations. The refugees arriving are hardly a "flood," or "unsustainable"—they are a drop in the bucket alongside the immigrants that arrive every year. As climate change wreaks devastation around the world, these numbers are sure to grow. But by the end of 2017, Canada had granted refugee status to only ten percent of the Haitian asylum seekers. Those numbers would hold. In the final account, welcoming refugees isn't a matter of generosity; it's a matter of justice.

Exploitation and Exclusion

In Saint-Bernard-de-Lacolle, Quebec, at one of the spots used for irregular crossings, a new government sign now greets asylum seekers. "Don't be the victim of misinformation," it reads. "Claiming asylum is not a free ticket into Canada."

Installed at the end of 2017, it was one of the many signs that the Trudeau government had started to change its tune on refugees. Canada isn't "some magical place that doesn't have worries about immigration, worries about security, worries about division and intolerant minds," Trudeau said at a press conference late that year.[16]

Rather than rescinding the Safe Third Country Agreement, they chose to make it worse. In early 2017, the government quietly reviewed the the designation it had granted the U.S., but astonishingly concluded it "continues to meet the requirements for designation as a safe third country."[17] Then they began making repeated secret entreaties to the U.S. Department of Homeland Security to rewrite the agreement. They wanted it to apply to the entire border, which would give the government legal authority to turn back asylum seekers rather than hearing their claims.[18] "We'd like to be able to get them to agree that we can, if somebody comes across, we just send them back," a government official anonymously told *Reuters*.[19]

Already, asylum seekers making attempts to cross into Manitoba in the winter had gotten frostbite and had to have fingers amputated. If the Canadian government were to bar irregular crossings—in violation of its UN convention obligations—it would be sure to drive asylum seekers into more dangerous attempts to cross the border without being apprehended.

In 2017, the government announced that over the next three years even fewer resettled refugees would be government-sponsored.[20] They invested some extra money to speed up the hearings that judge a refugee claimant's status in Canada, but these remained majorly backlogged. A life of limbo followed for refugees, because without status and only temporary social insurance numbers, asylum seekers find it hard to convince employers to hire them or get landlords to rent them apartments. They can't access loans or student aid, nor update their credentials to meet Canadian standards.

The Trudeau government also initiated a global dissuasion campaign. An MP was dispatched to California to talk to Salvadoran and Mexican communities. They sent government officials to embed with U.S. visa office in Lagos, Nigeria, to prevent people from reaching Canada after arriving first in the U.S. via ports in Nigeria. "They're interdicting people at airports, pulling people from flights, not just in Nigeria but even as they land in the United States, and that work is jointly being done by Canada," Hussen told reporters in 2018.[21]

Far from being a genuine haven for refugees, Trudeau has continued policies—dating back to the Conservative government of Stephen Harper or well before—that make life for refugees fleeing to this country exceedingly difficult and dangerous. Ten thousand people every year—including hundreds of children—are detained in facilities that go by disturbing names like Montreal's "Immigration Prevention Centre," surrounded by razor-wire fences, on the outskirts of major cities. Others are thrown into provincial prisons, including maximum-security, which makes Canada the only western country that jails refugees and migrants in the same place as convicts.[22] Hunger strikes to protest conditions have been a regular occurrence, but instead of acceding to demands, the Liberal government has deported key strike organizers.[23] These policies have been condemned by the United Nations—not the kind of international attention that Trudeau is used to.[24]

And far out of the sight of ordinary Canadians, a bureaucratic machine operated by security officials has ripped apart families and deported, often to lethal situations, a staggering number of refugees or migrants. Lucy Granados is just one of over an astonishing 100,000 people in the last decade who have been deported. These policies are presided over by Trudeau with none of Trump's venom, but the result is still exclusion, suffering, and heartbreak. This is not the violence of overt hate. It is the violence of empty gestures.

And in a process started by Harper, the Trudeau government, while limiting its intake of refugees, has thrown its doors open to migrant workers—so long as they remain precarious, low-wage, and without permanent residency or access to the labour protections and social services that Canadians take for granted. The number of migrants to Canada has exploded. Hundreds of thousands are now brought in to work on farms, care for our elderly, and staff fast-food joints—good enough to work, but not good enough to stay. These migrant policies are the flip-side of a system that treats people—especially people of colour from the Global South—as disposable.

This is the key to understanding Canada's current refugee and immigration policies, and to unraveling all the myths of their benevolence. The incredible fortressing of Canada, much like Europe, has nothing to do with the burden these populations supposedly pose to the resources of this country. Canada has always relied on enlarging its larger labour force with a huge influx of immigrants. But in an age of increasing inequality, the precarity imposed on refugees and migrants is no accident. It is by design. It is a callous and calculated management of vulnerable populations—exploiting some, excluding others.

The Pseudo-Centre Shifts Rights

The Conservative Party in Canada has stoked anti-Muslim and anti-refugee sentiments with proposals for a "barbaric cultural practices hotline" or screenings for "anti-Canadian values." This sowed the seeds for a gunman's rampage on a mosque. It also meant that even when the right-wing lost particular policy goals—as Trump did with aspects of his Muslim ban—they still won another way: they dragged the political climate further to the right, making racism more acceptable and discriminatory policies more possible.

In 2018, the Liberal government shifted rightward on its immigration policies, aiming to steal some oxygen from the right-wing. The Trudeau government established a new ministry called "Border Security and Organized Crime," and put former Toronto Police Chief Bill Blair in charge. It was a barely-veiled attempt to foster a connection in people's minds—non-existent, in truth—between organized crime and irregular migration. Blair began speaking of deterring "asylum shopping." Government officials anonymously admitted to a *Reuters* journalist that they had begun prioritizing the deportation of people who walked across the border, with the border security agency telling media that it "classifies border-crossers with criminals as a top deportation priority."[25]

Far away from the media spotlight, the Canadian border security agency is working overtime, even calling people in on Saturdays to get their deportation dates. Some Haitian refugees were ordered to come to CBSA offices to "choose" a deportation date while their cases were still before a Federal Court. Many come without a lawyer or any accompaniment and are all the more easily pressured into "agreeing" to deportation before exercising all their legal rights. They also created plans to build new migrant prisons.[26]

It remains to be seen if Trudeau's Liberals will pivot again, and once again attempt to appear as the open and humane alternative to right-wing xenophobia. Whatever their choices at the level of PR strategies, the legacy of their deeds will remain the institutionalization of cruelty toward migrants in service to corporate profits.

11

The Green New Deal of the North

"Alexandria Ocasio-Cortez's 'Green New Deal' is actually an old socialist plan from Canada," blared the headline on Fox News.[1] The right-wing U.S. broadcaster isn't exactly known for integrity and accuracy in reporting, but in this exceptional case, they weren't far from the truth.

In June 2018, a 28-year-old bartender and democratic socialist, Alexandria Ocasio-Cortez, unseated a high-ranking establishment Democrat in a Congressional primary race in the Bronx. After the stunning upset, Merriam-Webster reported that searches for the word "socialism" jumped by 1,500 percent.[2] Ocasio-Cortez—or AOC, as she quickly became known—provided an electrifying spark to left-wing politics in the United States with her moral clarity, flair for social media, and dazzling ability to communicate public policies (turning an episode of *60 Minutes*, for instance, into a workshop on why the ultra-rich should pay a 70 percent marginal tax rate). On her very first day on the job in Washington D.C. in the fall of 2018, young climate justice activists from the Sunrise Movement occupied the office of Democratic Speaker of the House Nancy Pelosi, calling on Democrats to get behind a plan for a Green New Deal. Ocasio-Cortez joined them at the sit-in, endorsing their demand. Overnight, the proposal was vaulted into the national spotlight.

Ocasio-Cortez soon introduced a resolution into the House that outlined a Green New Deal, which before long was endorsed by a large and growing number of U.S. Representatives and many leading Democratic presidential hopefuls. It proposed to treat climate change as the emergency it was, making massive, unprecedented investments to shift toward 100 percent renewable energy. This would involve a WWII-level transformation of the economy—but rather than gearing up to fight war, it would fight poverty and injustice. Connecting the dots between the overlapping crises of racism, inequality, and ecological collapse, the Green New Deal would use climate action to unleash millions of good, high-wage unionized jobs, build out affordable housing, public transit, and sustainable agriculture, and repair the "historic oppression of frontline and vulnerable communities."[3] And it would do all this with incredible velocity, because the UN's latest landmark report on climate change had told us we have just over a decade to cut our carbon emissions by half. In other words, the Green New Deal was a U.S.-style Leap Manifesto, only even more ambitious—and a Fox News reporter had put two and two together and realized as much.

The arrival to the mainstream of this transformative political agenda had been prepared by the work of a global climate justice movement for more than a decade—and indeed, the particular name and idea of the Green New Deal had been bandied about in different forms for some time. But unknown to Fox News, there was in fact a trail of influence from the Leap Manifesto to the newest and most popular incarnation of this agenda. Members of the youth-led Sunrise Movement, whose organizing was the galvanizing force behind the Green New Deal, had closely studied Naomi Klein's *This Changes Everything* and *No Is Not Enough*. In the latter book, Klein had argued that it wasn't sufficient for the progressive movement to merely resist Donald's Trump's agenda—they would have to offer a compelling and inspiring alternative, a blueprint that could reclaim the populist ground from the right-wing and lay out a path for a more just, post-carbon society. As a model, she described in detail the coalition-building process that had created the Leap Manifesto in Canada.

That process had brought together a diverse group of Indigenous land defenders, Quebec student leaders, feminists, food justice and migrant rights groups, environmentalists and even unions representing Albertan tar sands workers (I was one of its organizers). This silo-busting coalition recognized that taking on the narrow corporate interests holding us back from tackling the climate crisis required building a broad movement that would have everything to gain from a transition off fossil fuels.

A few weeks after the Green New Deal began dominating U.S. headlines, Klein met with members of Sunrise. When she expressed her gratitude for their activism, Klein was startled by their response: they were just doing, they told her, what she had laid out in her book. The political potency of the Leap Manifesto had been grasped by one of the most exciting new social movements in the United States, and by the most captivating progressive politician in a generation. The reception after its launch in Canada in 2015, however, had been markedly different.

An Ambitious Target for the NDP

In mid-September 2015, half-way through the federal election, a dartboard image went up on the wall of the Ottawa war room of the New Democrats. By that time, the early lead the party had enjoyed in the polls had evaporated, as the Liberals assumed the mantle of the most seemingly progressive alternative to the Conservative government. But the image eyed by the staffers in the war room was not, as one might have expected, of Justin Trudeau. Nor was it of Prime Minister Stephen Harper. It was the Leap Manifesto.

Meant as a joke, it was still a revealing gesture. The coalition behind the manifesto had been moved to act by the lack of urgent discussion of the climate crisis—and the disconnect between the narrow policy options on offer from the political parties and the ambitious vision that millions of Canadians were hungry for. But clearly, Tom Mulcair didn't regard the initiative as any sort of weather vane. If he had, he might have welcomed the spirit of the proposals, or encouraged the more than 100 signatory organizations to find a home among the New Democrats. The party might even have tried to shift course over the election, just as the Liberals had nimbly done, to channel some of this progressive energy. Their full New Democratic platform, after all, had not even been released, and wouldn't until ten days before the October 19th election.

Instead, Mulcair carefully distanced himself from the manifesto, while his consultants and closest staffers acted out their anger in the war room. To the leadership of the New Democratic Party in 2015, a bold left-wing agenda rooted in social movements was a threat to the brand they had tried to cultivate for the party as a safe and responsible choice for government. If this explained the dartboard image pinned to a wall, it also explained their eventual electoral collapse. At a moment when Canadians wanted to break with the neoliberal political consensus, the New Democrats mistakenly believed that sticking fast to this consensus was the key to their success.

The last time a Trudeau had been prime minister of the country, the New Democrats had a leader, David Lewis, who blasted Canada's "corporate welfare bums" for not paying their fair share of taxes. His campaigning in the 1972 election earned him the wrath of the corporate elite—who, reckoning with declining profits and the end of the post-war boom, were spurred into forming the Business Council of Canada to put an end to "the popular game of beating the hell out of business," as it was put by their first chair, the CEO of Imperial Oil.[4] Several decades later, Thomas Mulcair's efforts earned him only plaudits from that same elite, while the establishment media lauded his prosecutorial style of questioning Stephen Harper in the House of Commons—quietly pleased that this was the extent of his boat-rocking.

In the intervening years, the New Democrats had slowly accommodated themselves to the ascendent neoliberalism of the age. In a context of shrinking government revenues, an erosion of their industrial base of workers, and the new threats of capital flight, standing up for the causes they had once championed—public ownership, progressive redistribution, and strong workers rights—would have required a major reinvention, and deepening links with unions and social movements. The other option was to begin presenting themselves as superior technical administrators of the new neoliberal economy. Over the last four decades, they almost invariably chose the latter.

Their new policy toolkit included many of the policies of the right: privatization, cutting the welfare state, obsessing over balanced budgets. When they reached power, they often betrayed their allies through cutbacks or by suppressing the right to strike of public sector workers. "Today's NDP," as Manitoba New Democratic Premier Gary Doer styled it, had made a clean break with old-time social democracy. But by sliding toward the right, the New Democrats abandoned huge swaths of Canadians to be picked off by Liberals. Some tried to warn about this. "Canadians are social democrats, but most don't support the NDP," pollster Marc Zwelling observed in 2001. "The federal NDP is not in trouble because voters have turned conservative or because social democratic values are out of style. The polls put the blame for the party's demise squarely where it belongs: on the NDP. Its candidates have failed to harvest their potential vote."[5]

A Tri-Partisan Consensus

The party's slide toward the neoliberal consensus quickened, ironically, under the leader who is today remembered as its greatest progressive standard-bearer. Despite his start as a community activist who believed in the power of visionary grassroots movements, Jack Layton oversaw a transformation of the party—often described as a "modernization" process—that took it in a different direction. Over the course of four elections, from 2004 to 2011, the party became a much more professionalized machine that made success in elections its almost exclusive focus. Ad campaigns, staged photo-ops, polling, and focus groups took primacy, with consultants from the Obama administration brought in to help along this transformation. More than ever before, the party emphasized the personality of the leader, as opposed to the program and vision it offered. "Jack wasn't the pitchman...he was the product," wrote the NDP's former National Communications Director Brad Lavigne.[6] Layton's warm, impish, mustachioed face, blown up on giant posters, was impossible to avoid at party events and conventions.

The party underwent an accompanying centralization. Conventions became more stage-managed, glitzy affairs, a pageant intended to parade the leader before the membership rather than a venue for critical debate. The New Democrats' link to organized workers, already more tenuous than in other social democratic parties, was further loosened by abandoning the bloc votes guaranteed to labour unions. And these were the years in which a professional class of consultants took greater control over party decision-making. Rather than open themselves up to the energy and ideas of youth-driven social movements, the party grew more fearful of the grassroots.

"Just as 'only Nixon could go to China,'" political scientists Dennis Pillon and Murray Cooke write, "only someone with

Layton's credibility on the left of the party could shift the NDP so solidly toward the centre of the political spectrum without a murmur of discontent."[7] Layton backtracked on a widely-popular inheritance tax on the wealthy. The party abandoned "large multi-billion-dollar new programs," Lavigne wrote, in favour of "smaller, more immediate things." The title of the 2011 election platform was as inoffensively cautious as possible: "Practical First Steps." Lavigne's account of the development of the platform that year reveals how far they had come from being anchored in a distinct progressive social vision for Canada:

> "What's our response to a Conservative corporate tax cut?" I'd put to our talented policy team... "A corporate tax increase?" answered one. "No," I'd responded. "Our response to a corporate tax cut is a small business tax cut. What's our response to the Conservatives' purchase of multi-billion-dollar F35 fighter jets for the air force?" I asked them. "Cancelling the contract and opening it up to tender?" someone suggested. "Wrong. Our response is to invest in replacing our aging naval fleet. Their military priority is planes; ours is ships," I said.[8]

In spite of this transformation, Layton proved an effective opposition leader, pushing both Liberal and Conservative minority governments to make meaningful concessions. Next to the haughty, aloof Michael Ignatieff, who had penned urbane justifications for the Iraq War and torture, he stood out as a progressive choice. In the 2011 election, hobbling from event to event with a cane after hip surgery, he found his political stride. Asked on a Quebec television show why he was enjoying a rise in popularity in the province, he quipped, "la moustache?" Quebecers in fact had no stomach for Liberals still tainted by the sponsorship scandal and newly-tarnished by their support for extending the military occupation of Afghanistan. Soft nationalists voted in droves for the New Democrats in order to defeat Stephen Harper. The result was the Orange Crush, an outcome that elevated the New Democrats to opposition party status for the first time in their history. They had sacrificed left-wing politics, but they had come within reach of power.

While I was critical of the direction that Layton had taken the party, when news broke that he had been diagnosed with terminal cancer, I realized how much his authentic connection to people and his passion for social justice had moved me. The day he died, I felt like someone had kicked the wind out of me. As much of the country mourned, I spent a tearful afternoon in Montreal slumped in a coffee shop with my girlfriend. In the evening, we wandered to the Mont-Royal mountain for a memorial, where we lit candles and sang.

After Layton passed away, the rightward slide consolidated under him seemed to take on a momentum of its own. As the New Democrats eyed the possibility of government, it was no longer unthinkable to reach completely outside the party's traditions for its next leader. Mulcair—a former provincial cabinet minister in Quebec's Liberal government, which is considerably more right-wing than the federal Liberal Party—was chosen to replace Layton. He had won many people's support by helping the New Democrats break through in Quebec, even if they didn't recognize themselves in his politics. He proceeded to consolidate decision-making to a very small circle of advisors around him. He swore off ever hiking individual taxes on the wealthy and spoke only of "cautious increases" to taxes on corporations. He blocked candidates from running for the party who mildly criticized the Israeli military occupation and colonization of Palestinian territories. And he led a move to expunge the party's constitution of any hints of its radical past. Comedian and New Democrat Charles Demers remarked that "the party has officially removed 'socialism' from its preamble and unofficially added 'go along to get along' to its ethos." If the New Democrats were to win in 2015, it would be as a more compelling version of liberals than the Liberals.

When a video emerged of Mulcair delivering a speech in the Quebec legislature in 2001, in which he offered fulsome praise for former Conservative U.K. Prime Minister Margaret Thatcher— the godmother of neoliberalism—he didn't recant, issue a mild apology, or offer a sage reflection chalking it up to youthful indiscretion.[9] He shrugged and stood by the comments. The hollowing out of the NDP's left-wing legacy was complete: neoliberalism in Canada had become tri-partisan.

Leaping in a New Direction

As progressives reckoned with the New Democrats' crushing 2015 electoral defeat, many began to look more closely at the Leap Manifesto. Could it become a roadmap for a party searching for its political soul? It was the beginning of a drama that would, over the next year, generate incredible turbulence—but also enormous potential—for the party and for Canada's progressive movement. The behind-the-scenes story is worth telling in detail, because it may still offer guideposts to a path forward.

In the run-up to the party's convention in Edmonton in April 2016, where the future of Thomas Mulcair's leadership would be decided, a resolution calling on New Democrats to back the Leap Manifesto was passed in a Toronto riding association. It was drafted by a small caucus of older, well-meaning socialists who had worked diligently within the party for decades, but who had also acquired a reputation for alienating support for good ideas with their battle-hardened inflexibility. Their resolution called for the New Democratic Party to "promote the vision of the Leap Manifesto in all its future electoral endeavours." This wording would quite intentionally tie the hands of the party, preempting any democratic, participatory debate about how the manifesto could simply serve as an inspiration, or be reshaped to suit the party's needs.[10] Before long, however, nearly 20 riding associations across the country endorsed the resolution—showing the appetite for a new direction.

The resolution, however, would have had little chance of catalyzing a moment of truth for the party. Over the past two decades, the New Democratic conventions, just like those of the Liberals and Conservatives, had become highly choreographed spectacles. Party officials controlled the ranking of resolutions, and only a dozen of the hundreds submitted by members make it to the convention floor for discussion.[11] There was no way Mulcair's office would let this resolution make it that far. With that in mind, a few stalwart progressive members of the party— including recent MPs Libby Davies, Megan Leslie, and Craig Scott, party activist Janet Solberg, and Avi Lewis, a key drafter of the manifesto—formed a small group to navigate the situation. They began to rally support behind a different resolution passed by Davies in her Vancouver East riding. This version endorsed the spirit of the manifesto and suggested it was in line with the social justice traditions of the party. It called for the manifesto's study and adoption, but subject to modification to suit regional circumstances and only after a grassroots and democratic policy-making process. This took into account that the views of New Democrats in Alberta, where party leader and premier Rachel Notley had staked her fortunes on promoting pipelines, would be different than those in Quebec or British Columbia. "The NDP recognizes and supports the Leap Manifesto as a high-level statement of principles that is in line with the aspirations, history, and values of the party," the resolution read."[12] Some activists accused it of being watered down. But besides upholding the possibility of democratic debate, it was designed to appear innocuous enough to reach the convention floor, giving the grassroots of the party the opening they were clamouring for.

The resolution had the virtue of offering Mulcair a way out of his predicament. As he clung to leadership of the party after a disastrous election, it was clear he was in search of a way to demonstrate his progressive credentials and channel some of the new political spirit sweeping the continent. He began name-dropping "his friend Bernie Sanders," as hard as it must have been to stomach for an unrepentant fan of Margaret Thatcher. Inequality and climate change became regular talking points.[13] It wasn't like Mulcair was going to personally remove the dartboard image of the Leap Manifesto from the wall and place it on his desk next to the family photo. But he seemed to believe the new resolution gave him what he needed as a concession to the discontent in the party. He now openly welcomed its debate. Word started to spread that his office would give it a top spot in the ranking of resolutions, ensuring it could reach the floor at the convention. Even the top advisors in Rachel Notley's government, in whose backyard the convention would take place, were made aware of the progress of the resolution at every stage. They weren't thrilled, but gave signs that they would not organize their party's members against it. An unlikely fix seemed to be in. Mulcair would let a debate over the Leap Manifesto resolution proceed in order to save his leadership, hoping that it would generate as little turmoil as possible, whether or not it passed. Then the whole affair could be forgotten just as quickly as Mulcair had become a convert to democratic socialism. The proponents of the manifesto believed, on the other hand, that the resolution could not be bureaucratically managed into oblivion, and would take on a life of its own.

They were proven right. As buzz continued to build around the Leap Manifesto, Mulcair sat down for a major interview with Peter Mansbridge, just a few days before the convention's start. Sitting knee to knee, Mansbridge asked Mulcair whether he would respect the members' decision if they voted to support the manifesto's position that the tar sands in Alberta should be left in the ground. The question had one problem: this was not in fact in the manifesto. Apparently Mansbridge or his producers hadn't read the document (all of 1,400 words). It said nothing about "keeping oil in the ground"—that demand, in fact, had been negotiated out to satisfy the wishes of the union Unifor, an early coalition member that represented tar sands workers. What was in the manifesto, as per the global consensus of scientists, was that Canada not build any new fossil fuel infrastructure, an act which would lock in oil extraction for 50 years more. But Mulcair, who himself seemed unfamiliar with the document's contents, had cornered himself: he could hardly distance himself from a manifesto he was now clinging to like a lifeline, nor defy the democratic will of the party. Red in the face, he confirmed he would back his members regardless of what position they took.

This was the headline CBC blasted across its platforms that night: "Tom Mulcair will 'do everything' to keep oil in the ground if party tells him to."[14] The next day, the Alberta New Democrats tore up their non-aggression pact and launched an attack on the Leap Manifesto. Deputy Premier Sarah Hoffman told the provincial legislature: "Those remarks are unacceptable, and I will certainly be there [at the federal NDP convention] to convey that message to membership and to make sure that they know how important it is that we get our product to market."[15] Alberta's Environment Minister Shannon Philipps ratcheted up the rhetoric, calling the manifesto a "betrayal" of the province. Having by now acquainted himself more closely with the manifesto, Mulcair tried to back-peddle and point out that nowhere did it mention "leaving all the oil in the ground."[16] But it was too late. As the convention opened, the attempt to keep a lid on any turmoil had unravelled. A carefully scripted pageant was about to turn into a raucous battle of ideas.

The Power of Slogans and Dreams

The hallways in Edmonton's conference centre hummed with activity and debate. Corbyn and Bernie buttons could be seen everywhere. "NDP+Leap Manifesto" ones were popular too. Older members drew parallels to the founding conference of the Cooperative Commonwealth Federation, when the Regina manifesto had been launched. The convention had turned into a referendum not just over Mulcair's leadership, but about what kind of party the NDP should become.

Two of Canada's finest orators—Rachel Notley and former provincial party leader Stephen Lewis—went head-to-head over the merits of the manifesto in major keynote speeches. Notley appealed for a hard-nosed defence of blue collar workers. "We need to be able to get the best possible world price for the oil we produce here," she told the convention, "and the way to do that is through pipelines to tidewater." Lewis, at 78 an elderly statesman of the party, reminded the audience of a moral imperative they owed their grandchildren. "The damage we've done to the planet, and our refusal to confront that damage, constitutes nothing less than a monumental crime against humanity," he said. Yet, ambitious climate action was also the truly pragmatic way to look after workers' interests, if the shift to renewable energy was harnessed as "the greatest job creation program on the planet, a Marshall Plan for employment."

Delegates should not to be seduced by "slogans and dreams," Notley counselled. "We're acting, really acting, on the basis of a concrete plan that is actually being implemented. That is what you get to do when you move up from manifestos, to the detailed, principled, practical plans you can really implement by winning an election." Lewis didn't let the jab slide, underlining the manifesto was about, as the first order of business, super-charging the party's revival. "I'm attracted to the idea that it could become a centrepiece of constituency debate over the next couple of years, the kind of proposition that re-energizes and reanimates— through a lens of determinedly left-wing analysis."[17]

The next day, the debate continued on the convention floor. Alberta Federation of Labour President Gil McGowan gave a heated call-to-arms to oppose the resolution, eliciting a roar of approval from the Alberta delegate section, which had been packed for the day by the provincial party. Avi Lewis, Libby Davies, and Megan Leslie—with Unifor president Jerry Dias standing beside her in support—argued in favour of the Leap resolution.[18] The convention soon turned to voting. To cheering across the hall, the Leap resolution passed with a majority. Not long after, the votes were tallied for Mulcair. Analysts and party insiders had said he would need to secure at least 60 or 70 percent in the vote of confidence to stay on as leader. When the result was announced, silence gripped the room. He had barely managed to win half the delegates.

Rather than helping Mulcair come across as Canada's Bernie, the Leap Manifesto had proven to be his downfall. Alberta delegates had mobilized to vote against him because of his seeming embrace of the document. Many others from across the country, inspired by the Leap to believe the New Democrats could become an unapologetically bold left-wing party, realized that Mulcair was not the politician to lead them there.

When the Leap Manifesto had first launched in September 2015, the response from Canada's elite media and political class had been a mixture of breezy dismissal, mockery, and condescension. But the convention's results would send reverberations of anxiety through the halls and boardrooms of the corporate elite.

The Unfamiliar Sight of Elite Panic

Less than a week later, the Business Council of Canada gathered to celebrate their 40th anniversary on a top floor of the luxury Shangri-La hotel in Toronto. There were many familiar, friendly faces. Finance Minister Bill Morneau stopped by to discuss his first budget and hung around to answer questions. Dominic Barton, the director of McKinsey & Co. and chair of the Trudeau's Advisory Council on Economic Growth, gave one of his sweeping, big-picture talks about the global economy. Former Conservative Foreign Affairs Minister John Baird popped in, and so did current Liberal Foreign Affairs Minister Stephane Dion.

At dinner on the first evening, retired long-time president Tom d'Aquino rose to toast a who's who of Canada's most powerful people. He saluted the former CEO of SNC-Lavalin Guy Saint-Pierre, the former CEO of the Royal Bank of Canada Gord Nixon, and the current CEO of Power Corporation Paul Desmarais, Jr.. He pointed out that they were graced by the unusual presence of the Business Council's most generous funder, Ron Mannix, a reclusive Albertan billionaire with vast holdings in real estate, ranching, coal, and oil and gas (according to lore, the Mannix family cut their PR manager's pay each time their name appeared in print).[19]

D'Aquino proudly reminded everyone that the founder of the World Economic Forum, economist Klaus Schwab, had called them "the most effective CEO-based organization in the world." He listed off some of their accomplishments: scrapping the National Energy Program; successfully pushing for a free trade agreement with the U.S., despite the initial "opposition of all federal political parties;" getting the government to implement a "deeply unpopular" goods and services tax; "pressing for more muscle" in foreign policy and defence; and "helping to re-write Canada's competition laws." Since the 1980s, working with both

Liberals and the Conservatives, they had overseen a neoliberal revolution that had remade the country in the image of corporate interests. They had their critics, sure, with some "claiming that the Council had become something close to a parallel government—far too influential for their liking." But to their fans, he said, this was "business breaking out of its fetters," demonstrating "enlightened leadership at its best." He lifted his glass of wine. "I ask you to rise, raise your glasses, and drink to the Business Council of Canada," d'Aquino said. "Vive le conseil!"[20]

Not all the assembled well-wishers, however, were in a jovial mood. The gathering closed with a keynote address by Former Prime Minister Brian Mulroney, who seemed to feel he was the only one paying attention to what had just transpired at the New Democratic convention in Edmonton. It was a disturbing spectre from the past, he warned his audience. When he had abolished Pierre Elliott Trudeau's National Energy Program—with its mucking about of government in the regulation and management of fossil fuels—he thought he had "consigned it permanently to the dustbin of history." He shook his head. "I thought we would never again see political attitudes in Canada that would give rise to such egregious and nation-wounding policies, but I was wrong." Rather than mention by name the majority of New Democrats who had endorsed the Leap Manifesto, he referred to them by a choice pejorative. "Recently a group of Luddites attempted to seize control of a major political party in Canada by articulating a new philosophy of economic nihilism that would devastate the economy of Western Canada and seriously damage the long term economic prospects of our country as a whole." For Mulroney, imagining a prosperous Canada beyond the extraction of fossil fuels, beyond domination by corporate power, was impossible—it was the termination of the world as he knew it. "Despite all that you may have heard or read, the age of fossil fuels

is not about to end any time soon," he insisted. But the rise of a
new politics posed a challenge unlike anything he had seen. "This
must be resisted and defeated," he urged.[21]

Over the following days, expressions of similar outrage spilled
forth from the Canadian political and media establishment. BC
Premier Christy Clark claimed that if the Leap Manifesto were
implemented, "hundreds of towns would be wiped off the map,
tomorrow, and turned into ghost towns." Saskatchewan Premier
Brad Wall told a group of oil executives that the manifesto was
"an existential threat" to his province. *The Globe and Mail* published an editorial describing it as "madness" (all this to describe
a document whose subtitle was "a call for a Canada based on
caring for the earth and one another"). And CBC commentator
Rex Murphy, never one to be outdone in political hyperbole,
described it as the "most radical, anti-industrial, anti-trade, anti-
oil, anti-banks policy," a "wild-eyed, ultra-greenist, anti-capitalist
dogma-sheet." (The CBC has never disclosed that Murphy gave
more than two dozen public speeches paid by the oil industry
while employed at the public broadcaster).[22]

In an epic case of concern-trolling, the country's corporate
newspapers were filled with editorial cartoons of New Democratic politicians—primarily Mulcair, but others too—jumping
from high-rise windows, hang-gliding off cliffs, and lunging into
traffic-ingested streets. *Maclean's* magazine put aside all subtlety
and published a photo of Naomi Klein and Avi Lewis on its cover
with the title "How to Kill the NDP." Yet the unhinged outrage
about the Leap Manifesto, and the frantic insistence that it was
a prescription for electoral suicide, hinted at an underlying fear:
that a bold progressive alternative challenging elite interests might
be very popular indeed.

The Beautiful Backlash

For weeks, the corporate media continued to spout stern and dire predictions. Canadians would flee in horror from the Leap Manifesto. They were a "modest shift people," not "big shift people." And the New Democratic Party, merely by associating with the document, would surely court "irrelevance." Frank Graves, however, decided to conduct a poll. He was the only pollster who would. The first striking feature of his poll was that, unlike the corporate media, it accurately summarized the manifesto's proposals. The second striking feature was the result: rather than recoiling from the Leap Manifesto, people were embracing it. Nearly half of Canadians surveyed had heard about it, and of those, already half supported it.[23] That included a majority of New Democrats' and Greens' supporters, half of Liberal voters, and even twenty percent of Conservatives—and this was without any political party, or even a single politician, making the case for it, not to mention an environment of media hostility. Far from consigning the NDP to the fringes, it appeared that such a program could serve as the basis of a popular, winning movement.

Call it the beautiful backlash: the phenomenon of establishment smears boosting the strength of an insurgent campaign. In the U.S. and U.K., Senator Bernie Sanders's run for the Democratic nomination and Jeremy Corbyn's rise to the leadership of the Labour party benefited from this phenomenon. In each case, as the attacks from the political and media establishment against these left-wing politicians and their platforms increased, so too did their popularity—and on and on in a cycle of intensifying hostility and broadening appeal. The elite who unleashed the attacks inadvertently drew more attention to their targets' positions, underlined their anti-establishment bonafides, and fired up their supporters—revealing just how out of touch they were with ordinary people. Corbyn expressed his appreciation for the establishment backlash in a speech he gave to the U.K. Labour convention in 2017, soon after an election in which he dramatically reversed the expected fortunes of his party and brought it within reach of government. He pointed out that the right-wing newspaper *The Daily Mail* had devoted 14 pages to attacking him with apocalyptic warnings, the day before the election. "And the following day," he noted with a smile, "our vote went up nearly 10%." Corbyn offered a piece of cheeky advice to *The Daily Mail*'s editor: "Next time, could you please make it 28 pages?"[24]

While the New Democrats had no such leader or political program, there had been brief glimpses of the potential for beautiful backlashes even before the Leap Manifesto. In the lead-up to the 2013 provincial election, BC New Democratic leader Adrian Dix reversed his support for the Kinder Morgan pipeline and rightly came out against it. While the media establishment described his stance as "disturbing," "amateurish," and a "millstone," the provincial party set an all-time high for campaign donations the day after his announcement. When he lost the election, provincial party consultants agreed he'd made a mistake (flip-flopping might have been a mistake, but his new position itself was not).[25] During the 2015 federal election, journalist and New Democratic candidate Linda McQuaig argued on national television that "some" of the Alberta tar sands "may have to be left in the ground." Though climate science in fact calls for leaving all new deposits undeveloped, the comment ignited a week of intense denunciations in the media. She was criticized for this supposed "gaffe," and pushed by the party to go silent. But the day after her comment, her campaign was flooded with volunteer offers and donations.[26] Rather than harness these moments to their advantage, the New Democrats sought to stifle them—terrified of censure from the media and the political establishment. Their leadership hadn't grasped that the howls of the pundit and political class were not a mark of their failure but a sign of their promise.

More than anything, the wave of beautiful backlashes across the world—and the ripples in Canada—was the surest indication that the stranglehold of neoliberalism over political discourse was ending. Ideas that had been vanquished from mainstream debate were back, terrifying Brian Mulroney and his corporate allies. The demands spelled out by the Leap Manifesto coalition confronted every single one of the pillars of neoliberal capitalism: ending austerity and corporate-led trade that undermined local economies; raising the taxes on the wealthy and decreasing spending on the military; regulating big business and challenging the corporate capture of politics; using public planning to rapidly shift to 100 percent renewable energy; welcoming refugees more openly; and restoring land to Indigenous peoples. And yet these kinds of bold, transformational policies were now exceedingly popular—and could potentially serve as the building blocks of a progressive electoral majority.

There was someone else on the right-wing, besides Brian Mulroney, who understood the implications. *National Post* columnist Andrew Coyne was a rare voice in the establishment media who traded fear-mongering for lucid reflection. In the aftermath of the New Democratic convention, he lamented in a Twitter essay that Canadian conservatism had no answer to the Leap Manifesto. He recognized the movement behind the manifesto for what it was: an attempt to shift the terms of what was considered politically possible. "It's a model of how to marshall intellectual/activist opinion to maximum political effect," he wrote. This was what the right-wing in Canada had been so successful at doing between the 1980s and 2000s, something Coyne knew intimately. For years, he had quietly played a central role within the right-wing infrastructure, not merely as an editor and columnist, but as an advisor to the Manning Centre, a board member of a legal firm leading the attack on public healthcare, and a trustee at mining tycoon Peter Munk's Aurea Foundation, which funded conservative think tanks and advocacy organizations.[27] This network, in symbiotic relationship with the Conservative Party and its precursors, had acted as a stalking horse for more radical right-wing ideas, gradually but perceptibly transforming the public discourse (whereas the New Democrats seemed to believe that ideas to their left could only be threats that needed to be marginalized). Coyne noted that the right-wing no longer had, like the coalition behind the Leap Manifesto, an "organized, coherent intellectual movement of that kind." He conceded how formidable the New Democrats and the broader progressive movement could become. "The Leap manifesto sprang from fertile soil: a left that is confident both in its ideas and of their potential for adoption."[28]

New Democrats Try the Trudeau Formula

In the spring of 2016, riding associations of the New Democratic Party reported an influx of new members and returning former members, excited and energized about the outcome of the convention. The organizers of the Leap Manifesto received scores of requests from riding associations across the country to help them host the kind of forums the convention resolution had called for.

The party establishment, however, clearly wanted nothing to do with it. In the key riding of Ottawa Centre, activists started to organize a major public event at City Hall, but the local riding president blocked the initiative. He said he had communicated with the party leader's office, which had "pointed out that their understanding of the convention resolution is that ridings were asked to discuss the manifesto internally, not to engage the public or the media through mechanisms such as town halls." The party's central office did eventually produce a manual for hosting Leap Manifesto discussions, but many riding associations say they didn't even receive it.[29] And the party had set an impossible deadline: the discussions had to be conducted and finished in the summer, when activity is at its lowest ebb. These steps were so self-defeating that it was hard not to mistake them for an act of sabotage.

Some of the most bitter criticism of the manifesto had come from a particular corner: long-time New Democrat consultants, who had for more than a decade enjoyed a privileged, influential perch in the party, running its federal and provincial campaigns and staffing its governments.[30] Their hostility could be partially explained by what some call the iron law of organizations: those who control organizations are often more concerned with protecting their power within them than in growing the power of the organization itself. The consultant clique knew that in a more democratic and left-wing party they would not hold the kind of sway they had grown accustomed to. The other explanation was that their political imagination had been shrunk by neoliberalism and years of trying to out-Liberal the Liberals. They could only see left-wing ideas as a liability. The Leap offered the idea of a monumental job-creation program and just transition that would simultaneously reduce carbon emissions—a recipe with potential not only for electoral success, but to stave off climate catastrophe. Yet, to some, it appeared easier to imagine the end of the world than the transformation of a social democratic party.

The only way that the Leap Manifesto's success at the convention could have been built on is if Tom Mulcair were replaced by a leader with a movement behind them. This person would have to compellingly articulate forthrightly left-wing policies, help democratize the party, use the electoral pulpit to encourage grassroots organizing, and forge a bridge between often skeptical social movements and party activists who were hungry for such ties but felt electoral activity was often dismissed. My preference was Avi Lewis, the eloquent, principled broadcaster and journalist already popular with much of the membership. But when no comparable candidate ran, it was easy for the party's establishment to snuff out any discussion of Leap Manifesto—and to retroactively suggest, conveniently, that it didn't have much support to begin with. While promising grassroots networks like Courage soon emerged to push for bolder policies and greater democracy in the party, the lesson from the transformation of the U.K. Labour party was clear: changes at the very top were required to ensure that a groundswell from the bottom would have a significant impact.

The new leader, Jagmeet Singh, would initially adopt a very different approach from that promised by the Leap Manifesto. Forget about inviting a backlash from the elite. One of his first media successes, in January 2018, wasn't due to an ambitious policy announcement, a new organizing campaign, or a provocative interview response. Singh brought a clique of reporters to a restaurant in Toronto, where he proposed marriage to his girlfriend. The stunt gave him a bump in feel-good coverage, but it also reminded us of a certain other Canadian politician. That wouldn't have been the first time, either. Dapper suits, boasts about boxing or wrestling skills, hopey slogans, making a show of public media access to candid private moments: all these were as present in the playbook of Prime Minister Justin Trudeau as they had become in Singh's. One columnist called it the NDP's embrace of "Trudeau-style, leader-centric glam." Rather than distinguishing himself from the Liberal leader's brand of showy, symbolic politics, Singh gave the impression of trying to out-do him at his own game.

While the NDP dabbled in the Trudeau formula, social democratic parties elsewhere focused on something else: not flashy personalities, but far-reaching policies. The Democratic primary campaign of Bernie Sanders in 2016 had taken on the billionaire class and unleashed the activist initiative of hundreds of thousands of people through a model of "big organizing." It transformed the U.S. political landscape. In its wake, the race to pick a Democratic challenger to Donald Trump in 2020 saw a field of candidates endorsing policies that would have been unthinkable just a few years earlier: universal medicare, free college tuition, a wealth tax, a shift to renewable energy, and more welcoming immigration policies. In the U.K., Jeremy Corbyn was helping rebuild the Labour party into a more democratic force, open to thousands of diverse and long-neglected non-voters and animated by an ambitious social agenda. What the Leap Manifesto potentially added to the mix was a holistic vision to urgently address the climate emergency at the scale and speed of what was necessary, with radically integrated solutions to all the accompanying crises of our age. Even if the New Democrats didn't seem ready to embrace it, others soon would.

A Green New Deal of the North

By 2019, as the model of the Leap Manifesto found elaboration and amplification in the Green New Deal, a proposal once dismissed as fringe suddenly became obviously commonsensical. Its way of thinking surfed on the youth climate strikes inspired by the Swedish 16-year-old Greta Thunberg, which saw hundreds of thousands of students walking out of their schools, as well as on the headline-grabbing mass direct actions of Extinction Rebellion. The infectious energy made its way back to Canada, offering an unlikely second chance to pick up where the Leap Manifesto had let off.

A call from a coalition of Canadian organizations for people to assemble to begin defining a Canadian Green New Deal was met with an unprecedented response. Within a week, volunteers had set plans for more than 150 town halls. This time around, the organizing had a backdrop of climate change-induced terror: destructive flooding throughout Quebec and Ontario, and wildfires blanketing Alberta and BC with a disturbing and debilitating haze—which meteorologists declared "smoke season," a new fifth seasonal cycle. From Whistler to Waterloo, Halifax to Hamilton, massive crowds turned out to community centres, church basements, and union halls for impassioned discussions. In Edmonton, in the heart of oil country, an overflowing room of more than 250 people sang a rendition of the classic labour song, "Which side are you on?" rewritten to denounce the fossil fuel industry and Liberal and Conservative governments that subsidize them. There was even a small town hall in the Arctic village of Iqaluit, Nunavut, where temperatures that summer, usually just above freezing, hit an astonishing 23.5 degrees celsius.[31] Many of the town halls took place in June, the hottest month ever measured on Earth—a record then broken in July.[32]

Barely a few months into organizing, this new movement would already make its impact felt on the electoral landscape. The evident appetite for an epic transition off fossil fuels to a more prosperous and humane society was confirmed again in a poll, which showed that 60 percent of Canadians supported a Green New Deal, including 50 percent of Albertans—with that number jumping to 66 percent when the plan was paid for by increased taxation on corporations and the wealthy. (And, unlike the poll commissioned about the Leap Manifesto in 2016, this one was covered by some of the mainstream media).[33] Mostly on the strength of their name, the Green Party suddenly became a much more attractive option to Canadians, even though the New Democrats, at least on paper, still have better environmental policies. When Green Party candidate Paul Manly—a left-wing activist blocked from running for the New Democrats by Mulcair in 2015 over his support for Palestinian rights—convincingly won a federal by-election in BC in May, the New Democrats finally seemed to take notice. This was electoral logic that even they could grasp. Soon the two federal parties were vying for Canada's growing Green New Deal constituency with competing platforms. Though the New Democrat's "New Deal for Climate Action and Good Jobs" fell far short of the scale, speed, and equity provisions of the U.S. version, what it proposed amounted to the party's boldest policy platform in a generation: a climate bank to fund low-carbon investments, the building of 500,000 units of affordable housing, and free electrified public transit. Attempting to dampen some of this momentum, the Liberals declared a "climate emergency" in Parliament in June—only to approve the Trans Mountain pipeline the very next day, demonstrating in a compact way the difference between leadership and the mere performance of it.

It should be clear to Liberal Party strategists that a Green New Deal is like kryptonite to their politics: by offering a roadmap to accomplish everything that Justin Trudeau has claimed to champion, it exposes him as the establishment defender of the status quo that he is. It demonstrates the fantasy of an "all of the above" energy strategy, when science is telling us to say "no" to new fossil fuel frontiers. It shows us that genuine reconciliation must involve not just symbolic gestures, but the redistribution of power and land. It underlines how, if we want to take climate action at the speed and scale necessary, we must abandon incremental, market-based policies and re-embrace public planning and regulation. And if we're to pay for this kind of transition, we'll have to reverse the draining of the public purse by putting our hands on billions of dollars of under-taxed private wealth.

This would be an epic progressive agenda worthy of the name, serving the interests of a majority of people in Canada struggling with economic hardship, racism and insecurity. It would also be the most effective answer to a surging right, who are misdirecting insecurities and fears towards scapegoats like migrants, Muslims, and so-called foreign funded radicals—anyone but the one percent.

This much else is clear: the corporate architects of Canada's neoliberal revolution keenly understand the threat this agenda poses to their narrow self-interests. They understand its transformative potential—so far, better than the progressive movement itself. Winning continuously for as long as they have, after all, has given them a sense of what such an agenda looks like, and how quickly it can become a reality.

We too have to acquire a taste and habit for winning, and fast. In politics, we ever so rarely get an opportunity for a re-do, a second chance to win. But in an age of climate emergency that has put our efforts on a tight, existentially-charged deadline, we only get one. Our duty, to all the living beings on these lands, is to seize it.

Acknowledgements

My name is on this book, but it truly was a collective endeavor: as many people contributed as make up the social movements that constantly educate me and inspire me to write. But there are several individuals and groups whose contribution and support deserve special thanks.

I was so lucky to have Nikolas Barry-Shaw work as a brilliant researcher on this project at the beginning, when we hashed out many of its ideas together during long lunches at our local Polish restaurant (any mistakes in the book are mine, but I attribute some blame to the decadent servings of sour cream). Long after Nik's formal stint was over, he kept up a steady flow of the suggested readings accompanied by his incisive analysis.

Thanks to Dimitri Roussopoulos, Clara-Swan Kennedy, Nathan McDonnell and Dan Reid at Black Rose Books, for their openness, flexibility and commitment to this project. Shannon Daub, Bill Carroll and Thi Vu and the Corporate Mapping Project generously supported some of the research. Ricardo Acuna and the team at Parkland and Samir Gandesha and Huyen at SFU Institute for Humanities gave me a precious chance to work out some of these ideas in lectures. Isabeau Doucet, Will and Evie loaned their home for a month-long writing retreat with an inspiring view.

Anthony Fenton took me on a deep crash course in Canadian weapons exports abroad. Russ Diabo has been my guide to colonialism at home for a very long time. Thanks to those who spoke to me anonymously, and to some others who were just loose-lipped. The Prime Minister's office declined my requests to interview Justin Trudeau or Gerald Butts.

Many others provided inspiration, encouragement or support: Jackie Joiner, Holly Dressel, Molly Kane, Firoze Manji,

Preeti Dhaliwal, Naomi Klein, Courtney Kirkby, Amy Miller, Amanda Lewis, Trena White, Amanda Crocker, Dave Molenhuis, Ezra Winton, Svetla Turnin, Zi-Ann Lum, Rushdia Mehreen, Daniel Horen Greenford, Shiri Pasternak, Tamara Sandor, Kevin Skerrett, Anna Rabin, Gordon Laxer, Corvin Russell, Judy Rebick, Rajiv Sicora, Stefan Christoff, Aurore Fauret, Chloe Raxlen, Yves Engler, Rachel Zellars, Darrah Teitel, Sebastian Ronderos-Morgan, Sharmeen Khan, Geordie Dent, Nate Wallace, the Jeanne Mance family, Lina Nasr, Zoe Grams, and Mabel and Niko Jr..

Jonathan Dyck designed an incredible cover (and Arwen made the perfect contact). Friends at the Shakti bouldering gym helped me pick up some good new writing-related habits. Thanks to Jim, Anna, Merrily and the community at Weisbord Acres, where I wrote some of this book, though mostly got lured away from it by the lake. Javed Iqbam provided fresh fruit and procrastination breaks. Derek Rasmussen lifted my spirits. Peter McFarlane helped out in a pinch with great editing. Avi Lewis made surgical strikes and offered his incomparable cheerleading. And Amy Miller and Lucas Freeman caught some last errors.

Dru Oja Jay, my best friend, informal life coach, and book production wizard—I couldn't have done this without you. Donya Ziaee arrived near the end, but made all the difference. The next one will be yours. I owe so much to my family. Thanks to my sister Sophie Lukacs for the musical missives from across the ocean—can't wait for your first album to be the sound-track to any future writing. This book is dedicated to my parents, Gergely Lukacs and Judith Szapor, who gave me their love, kept me fed with Hungarian food, and passed on a passion for the written word.

Endnotes

Introduction

1. Angus Reid Institute, "As Government Presents Election-Year budget, Canadians Are Uneasy about Economic Fortunes," March 18, 2019, http://angusreid.org/wp-content/uploads/2019/03/2019.03.12-economics.pdf; Ekos Politics, "At the Crossroads of Hope and Fear: The New Axis of Societal Tension," February 5, 2019, http://www.ekospolitics.com/index.php/2018/02/at-the-crossroads-of-hope-and-fear.

2. Lars Osberg, *The Age of Increasing Inequality: The Astonishing Rise of Canada's 1%* (Toronto: James Lorimer & Company Ltd., 2018), 51.

3. The United Way, "Rebalancing the Opportunity Equation," May 2019, https://www.unitedwaygt.org/file/2019_OE_fullreport_FINAL.pdf.

4. Jordan Press, "Nearly 50 Percent of Indigenous Children in Canada Live in Poverty, Study Says," *The Globe and Mail*, July 9, 2019, https://www.theglobeandmail.com/canada/article-half-of-indigenous-children-live-in-poverty-highest-rate-of-child.

5. Frank Graves, "Canada 150: The End of Progress?" Presentation to the *Queen's Policy Review*, April 27, 2017, http://www.ekospolitics.com/index.php/2017/04/canada-150-the-end-of-progress.

6. There are 550 food banks and more than 3,000 agencies feeding people. At last count, there were 3,802 Tim Horton's chain stores in Canada in 2016. Use of food banks has grown by 30 percent since 2008.
Statista, "Number of Tim Hortons Restaurants in Canada and the United States from 2007 to 2018," last modified July 24, 2019, https://www.statista.com/statistics/291536/number-of-restaurants-north-america-tim-hortons; "Fewer Living Paycheque to Paycheque But More Overwhelmed By Debt: Survey," *CTV News*, September 5, 2018, https://www.ctvnews.ca/business/fewer-living-paycheque-to-paycheque-but-more-overwhelmed-by-debt-survey-1.4081177; "Almost 1 Million Canadians Give Up Food, Heat to Afford Prescriptions: Study," *CBC News*, February 13, 2018, https://www.cbc.ca/news/canada/british-columbia/canadians-give-up-food-heat-to-afford-prescriptions-study-says-1.4533476; Leslie Young, "Hundreds of Canadians Die Every Year Because They Can't Afford Medication: Nurses' Union," *Global News*, May 1, 2018, https://globalnews.ca/news/4178908/deaths-pharmacare-prescription-drug-costs.

7. Carly Weeks, "One Person Died Every Two Hours of Opioid-Related Overdose in Canada Last Year, Report Says," *The Globe and Mail*, June 13, 2019, https://www.theglobeandmail.com/canada/article-one-person-died-every-two-hours-of-an-opioid-related-overdose-in; Andrea Woo, "Overdose Crises Lowering Life Expectancy: Statistics Canada," *The Globe and Mail*, May 30, 2019, https://www.theglobeandmail.com/canada/british-columbia/article-overdose-crises-lowering-life-expectancy-statistics-canada.

8. Alex Boutilier, "Researchers to Probe Canada's Evolving Far-Right Movements," *Toronto Star*, March 6, 2019, https://www.thestar.com/politics/federal/2019/03/06/researchers-to-probe-canadas-evolving-far-right-movements.html; Shannon Carranco and Jon Milton, "Canada's New Far Right: A Trove of Private Chat Room Messages Reveals an Extremist Subculture," *The Globe and Mail*, April 27, 2019, https://www.

theglobeandmail.com/canada/article-canadas-new-far-right-a-trove-of-private-chat-room-messages-reveals; "Canada Hate Crimes Up 47% as Muslims, Jews and Black People Targeted," *The Guardian*, November 29, 2018, https://www.theguardian.com/world/2018/nov/29/canada-hate-crimes-rise-muslims-jews-black-people.

9.   David Macdonald, "Unaccommodating: Rental Housing Wage in Canada," *The Canadian Centre for Policy Alternatives*, July 18, 2019, https://www.policyalternatives.ca/unaccommodating.

10. "Opinion: More Than Ever Canada's Emission Reduction Targets Are Doomed," *Calgary Herald*, April 30, 2019, https://calgaryherald.com/opinion/columnists/opinion-more-than-ever-canadas-emission-reduction-targets-are-doomed.

11. Susan Cake et al., "Boom, Bust, and Consolidation: Corporate Restructuring in the Alberta Oil Sands," *Parkland Institute*, November 8, 2018, https://www.parklandinstitute.ca/boom_bust_and_consolidation; Sophia Harris, "Canada's Major Banks Hiking Fees while Pulling in Big Profits," *CBC News*, June 13, 2016, https://www.cbc.ca/news/business/banking-fees-profits-1.3629701; Doug Alexander, "Bonus Pools at Canadian Banks Climb 6.5% in a 'Polarizing' Year," *Toronto Star*, December 5, 2018, https://www.thestar.com/business/2018/12/05/bonus-pools-at-canadian-banks-climb-65-in-a-polarizing-year.html; Zach Dubinsky, "Wealthy Canadians Hiding up to $240B Abroad, CRA Says," *CBC News*, June 28, 2018, https://www.cbc.ca/news/business/wealthy-canadians-hiding-up-to-240b-abroad-cra-says-1.4726983; The Canadian Centre for Policy Alternatives, "CEO Pay Still Near Historic Levels at 197 Times More Than the Average Worker," January 2, 2019, https://www.policyalternatives.ca/newsroom/news-releases/ceo-pay-still-near-historic-levels-197-times-more-average-worker.

12. Canadians for Tax Fairness, "Canadian Corporate Cash in Top 12 Tax Havens Increases by 10% to All-time High in 2018," April 24, 2019, https://www.taxfairness.ca/en/press_release/2019-04/canadian-corporate-cash-top-12-tax-havens-increases-10-all-time-high-2018.

13. Alexander Sazonov, "Millionaires Flee Their Homelands as Tensions Rise and Taxes Bite," *Bloomberg*, April 30, 2019, https://www.bloomberg.com/news/articles/2019-04-30/millionaires-flee-their-homelands-as-tensions-rise-taxes-bite.

14. April Fong, "David Thomson Is Canada's Wealthiest on Forbes' Rich List, Again," *BNN Bloomberg*, March 5, 2019, https://www.bnnbloomberg.ca/david-thomson-is-canada-s-wealthiest-on-forbes-rich-list-again-1.1223918.

15. "David Thomson & family," *Forbes* profile, accessed March 23, 2019, https://www.forbes.com/profile/david-thomson; Diane Francis, *Who Owns Canada Now: Old Money, New Money and the Future of Canadian Business* (Toronto: HarperCollins, 2008), 266-270.

16. According to Susan Delacourt, "A search on the openparliament.ca website shows that "income inequality" was mentioned at least 100 times a year in parliamentary discussions from 2012 to 2014 but then, just 30 times last year and only about a dozen times so far in 2018."
     Susan Delacourt, "Losing Ground in the War against Inequality," *Toronto Star*, October 25, 2018, https://www.pressreader.com/canada/toronto-star/20181025/281535111977716.

17. Frank Graves, "From the End of History to the End of Progress," August 2014, http://www.ekospolitics.com/wp-content/uploads/from_the_end_of_history_to_the_end_of_progress_august_19_2014.pdf

18. Giuseppe di Lampedusa, *The Leopard* (New York: Pantheon Books, 1960).
19. Ashifa Kassam and Laurence Mathieu-Léger, "Justin Trudeau: 'Globalisation Isn't Working for Ordinary People'," *The Guardian*, December 15, 2016, https://www.theguardian.com/world/2016/dec/15/justin-trudeau-interview-globalisation-climate-change-trump.

Chapter 1

1. John Ivison, "Justin Trudeau Pinning His Hopes on a Class War Is a Losing Strategy," National Post, May 19, 2015, https://nationalpost.com/news/canada/john-ivison-justin-trudeau-pinning-his-hopes-on-a-class-war-is-a-losing-strategy; Konrad Yakabuski, "Taxing the Rich Will Not Pay Off for Trudeau," *The Globe and Mail*, May 18, 2015, https://www.theglobeandmail.com/opinion/taxing-the-rich-will-not-pay-off-for-trudeau/article24460706/.
2. Chrystia Freeland, "Plutocrats vs. Populists," *New York Times*, November 1, 2013, https://www.nytimes.com/2013/11/03/opinion/sunday/plutocrats-vs-populists.html; Chrystia Freeland, "Revolt Against the Global Super-Rich Is Underway," *New Perspectives Quarterly* 31, no. 2 (April 2014): 67-69, https://doi.org/10.1111/npqu.11455.
3. John Shmuel, "Bill Morneau Names Dominic Barton, Head of McKinsey & Co., to Government's Economic Advisory Council," *Financial Post*, February 23, 2016, https://business.financialpost.com/news/economy/bill-morneau-names-dominic-barton-head-of-mckinsey-co-to-governments-economic-advisory-council.
4. Edelman Insights, "2015 Edelman Trust Barometer: Canadian Results," February 2, 2015, https://www.slideshare.net/EdelmanInsights/2015-edelman-trust-barometer-canadian-findings.
5. Dominic Barton, "Capitalism for the Long Term," *Harvard Business Review* (March 2011), https://hbr.org/2011/03/capitalism-for-the-long-term; Sandro Contenta, "Dominic Barton, Capitalism's Go-To Guy," *Toronto Star*, December, 17, 2016, https://www.thestar.com/news/insight/2016/12/17/dominic-barton-capitalisms-go-to-guy.html.
6. Chrystia Freeland, "Revolt Against the Global Super-Rich," 67-69.
7. Justin Trudeau, "Why It's Vital We Support the Middle Class," *The Globe and Mail*, April 15, 2013, https://www.theglobeandmail.com/news/politics/justin-trudeau-why-its-vital-we-support-the-middle-class/article11209063.
8. Luke Savage, "Justin Trudeau Is Waging a Phony War Against Inequality," *The Guardian*, May 4, 2018, https://www.theguardian.com/commentisfree/2018/may/03/justin-trudeau-phony-war-against-inequality.
9. Justin Trudeau, "How Fairness and Growth for the Middle Class Benefits Everyone," Presentation to *The Canadian Club of Toronto*, May 11, 2015, https://www.vvcnetwork.ca/canclub/20150511.

10. On missile defence, d'Aquino told American audiences that "like many Canadians, I am greatly disappointed by the decision of my government to reject a course of action so manifestly in our national interest and so consistent with our long-standing commitment to the defence of North America. It is my hope that this decision will be reversed by a future Parliament...that will recognize the logic and wisdom of full Canadian participation and that will vigorously make the case for involvement to the electorate."

11. "'Mr Dithers' and His Distracting 'Fiscal Cafeteria,' *The Economist,* February 17, 2005, https://www.economist.com/the-americas/2005/02/17/mr-dithers-and-his-distracting-fiscal-cafeteria. The unsigned editorial was written by a Canadian journalist, Clyde Sanger.

12. "Every large business with registered lobbyists would have had people talking to Stephen Harper and his caucus for several years," one bank official said. Janet McFarland, "Business Seeks New Ties to Ottawa," *The Globe and Mail,* January 24, 2006, https://www.theglobeandmail.com/report-on-business/business-seeks-new-ties-to-ottawa/article1094197.

13. John Lorinc, "Can Earnscliffe Win Over Stephen Harper?" *The Globe and Mail,* June 20, 2006, https://www.theglobeandmail.com/amp/report-on-business/can-earnscliffe-win-over-stephen-harper/article1104653.

14. Erica Alini, "Jim Flaherty's Invitation Lists," *Maclean's,* August 21, 2013, https://www.macleans.ca/economy/business/flahertys-wakefield-confab.

15. Sean Kilpatrick, "Boardroom Confidential: What CEOs Are Asking of Jim Flaherty," *The Globe and Mail,* August 15, 2012, https://www.theglobeandmail.com/news/politics/boardroom-confidential-what-ceos-are-asking-of-jim-flaherty/article4483479.

16. Les Whittington and Susan Delacourt, "PM's Office Attacks Top Banker in Deficit Spat," Toronto Star, February, 11, 2010, https://www.thestar.com/business/2010/02/11/pms_office_attacks_top_banker_in_deficit_spat.html.

17. Bill Curry and Tara Perkins, "TD Chief Caught in Deficit Crossfire," *The Globe and Mail,* February 11, 2010, https://www.theglobeandmail.com/news/politics/budget/td-chief-caught-in-deficit-crossfire/article4188642.

18. James Cowan, "Justin Trudeau Might Be Better For Business Than Stephen Harper," *Canadian Business,* April 11, 2013, https://www.canadianbusiness.com/economy/justin-trudeau-friend-or-foe.

19. The NDP, on the other hand, were "still thrashing around in the deep end of climate change where very little is actually known," and putting forward the "insane demand for a boycott of Saudi Arabia," and other "hobbling foibles." Conrad Black, "The NDP Still Isn't Ready, But It Turns Out Trudeau May Be," *National Post,* October 2, 2015, https://nationalpost.com/opinion/conrad-black-the-ndp-still-isnt-ready-but-it-turns-out-trudeau-may-be; Conrad Black, "Stephen Harper Did Many Great Things for This Country, But He Hung on to Power a Little Too Long," *National Post,* October 17, 2015, https://nationalpost.com/opinion/conrad-black-stephen-harper-did-many-great-things-for-this-country-but-he-hung-on-to-power-a-little-too-long.

Chapter 2

1. Dalton McGuinty, *Dalton McGuinty: Making a Difference* (Toronto: Dundurn Press, 2015), 100.

2. Jonathan Gatehouse, "'When I Run': Justin Trudeau Considers Politics," *Maclean's*, December 23, 2002, https://www.macleans.ca/politics/ottawa/when-i-run-justin-trudeau-considers-politics-from-the-archives.

3. Adam Radwanski, "The BFF in the PMO," *The Globe and Mail*, September 2, 2016, https://www.theglobeandmail.com/news/gerald-butts-the-guardian-of-the-trudeau-narrative/article31692482.

4. Scott Reid, "Justin and Gerald," *The Walrus*, April 23, 2014, https://thewalrus.ca/justin-and-gerald.

5. Martin Patriquin, "Meet the Man Who Helped Make His friend Canada's Next PM," *Maclean's*, September 25, 2015, https://www.macleans.ca/politics/ottawa/how-gerald-butts-plans-to-make-justin-trudeau-the-next-prime-minister.

6. "Gerald was key to this," one Liberal senator said of the expulsion from caucus. "It was the right decision politically, but it was still a tough sentence for all of us."
    Reid, "Justin and Gerald"; Don Butler, "Trudeau Plants Seeds of 'Revolution' by Expelling Liberal Senators from Caucus," *Ottawa Citizen*, May 20, 2014, https://ottawacitizen.com/news/trudeau-plants-seeds-of-revolution-by-expelling-liberal-senators-from-caucus.
    Chrystia Freeland, "Plutocrats vs. Populists," New York Times, November 1, 2013, https://www.nytimes.com/2013/11/03/opinion/sunday/plutocrats-vs- populists.html

7. Susan Delacourt, *Justin Trudeau: Can He Bring the Liberal Party Back to Life?* (Toronto: Star Dispatches, 2009).

8. Matt Price, *Engagement Organizing: The Old Art and New Science of Winning Campaigns* (Vancouver: UBC Press, 2017), 137.

9. Price, *Engagement Organizing*, 141.

10. Jim Bronskill, "Bill C-51 Could Be Used to Target Activists: Amnesty International," *Huffington Post*, September 3, 2015, https://www.huffingtonpost.ca/2015/03/09/anti-terrorism-bill-could_n_6831898.html.

11. Jean Chrétien et al., "A Close Eye on Security Makes Canadians Safer," *The Globe and Mail*, February 19, 2015, https://www.theglobeandmail.com/opinion/a-close-eye-on-security-makes-canadians-safer/article23069152.

12. Chyrstia Freeland, "The 1 Percent vs President Obama" *Reuters*, July 12, 2012, https://www.reuters.com/article/column-freeland/column-the-1-percent-vs-president-obama-chrystia-freeland-idINDEE86B0KC20120712.

13. They would also scrap various benefits and measures that Stephen Harper had used to give a $2-billion yearly tax giveaway to Canada's richest. Trudeau accusing Harper of "giving child benefit cheques to millionaires." Radio ads kept up the messaging about ending Harper's tax giveaways to the richest.

14. "Several provinces are now at the 50 per cent rate," Mulcair said in a 2013 interview. "Beyond that, you're not talking taxation; you're talking confiscation. And that is never going to be part of my policies, going after more individual taxes. Period. Full stop."
    James McLeod, "Mulcair Says People Want Him to Kick Harper Out," *The Telegram*, August 8, 2013, https://www.pressreader.com/canada/the-telegram-st-johns/20130808/281535108624091.

15. Andrew Jackson, "Trudeau's Promised 'Middle Class' Tax Cut Excludes Most Canadians," *The Globe and Mail*, November 12, 2015, https://www.theglobeandmail.com/report-on-business/economy/economic-insight/trudeaus-promised-middle-class-tax-cut-excludes-most-canadians/article27215398.

16. Patriquin, "Meet the Man."

17. Maude Barlow and Bruce Campbell, *Straight Through the Heart: How the Liberals Abandoned the Just Society* (Toronto: HarperCollins, 1996), 6.

18. David Akin, "Trudeau's Deficit Flip-Flop, Grist for Harper's Mill," *Toronto Sun*, August 31, 2015, https://torontosun.com/2015/08/31/trudeaus-deficit-flip-flop-grist-for-harpers-mill.

19. Tristan Markle and Sarah Beuhler, "Balanced Budgets a Terrible Hill for the NDP to Die On," *rabble.ca*, October 27, 2015, http://rabble.ca/node/114985.
    "Within our means there are decisions that can be made around the kinds of investments that actually give us returns, whether it's in education or infrastructure like public transit, without having to fall into deficit," Trudeau had said back in January. David Ljunggren and Randall Palmer, "Canada Liberals can lift spending and avoid deficits: Trudeau," *Reuters*, January 27, 2015, https://ca.reuters.com/article/domestic-News/idCAKBN0L02LU20150127?pageNumber=2&virtualBrandChannel=0.
    As Markle and Beuhler pointed out, by the summer of 2015, it "made Keynesian sense to use infrastructure spending to get out of Harper's recession —even if that meant running deficits." In that first debate, Mulcair forced Harper to admit that the Canadian economy had shrunk consecutively for five months, just one month from a technical recession. As widely expected, later that week on September 1, Canada entered an official recession.
    For this section I also draw on my own article: "Trudeau's Bold Change Pledge Was a Ruse. But Canada Now Has a Fighting Chance," *The Guardian*, October 22, 2015, https://www.theguardian.com/environment/true-north/2015/oct/22/trudeaus-bold-change-pledge-was-a-ruse-but-canada-now-has-a-fighting-chance.

20. Allison Jones, "'(NDP's) First Budget Will Be a Balanced Budget': Mulcair," *Toronto Sun*, August 25, 2015, https://torontosun.com/2015/08/25/ndps-first-budget-will-be-a-balanced-budget-mulcair/wcm/d45473b6-27d6-4235-80a0-b5c607998c8f.

21. Bob Hepburn, "Justin Trudeau's Smartest Campaign Move," *Toronto Star*, October 18, 2015, https://www.thestar.com/opinion/commentary/2015/10/18/justin-trudeaus-smartest-campaign-move-hepburn.html.

22. Nick Logan, "'That's Probably the Election Right There': Trudeau Reveals Turning Point in Liberal Campaign," *Global News*, December 18, 2015, https://globalnews.ca/news/2410464/thats-probably-the-election-right-there-trudeau-reveals-turning-point-in-liberal-campaign.

23. Paul Martin, interviewed on *The House*, CBC Radio, August 29, 2015, https://www.cbc.ca/radio/thehouse/week-4-of-the-campaign-sees-parties-drawn-economic-battle-lines-1.3205839/paul-martin-blasts-ndp-for-move-to-far-right-1.3205843.

24. "Canada Election 2015: Justin Trudeau Accuses Tom Mulcair of 'austerity' Over Balanced Budget Pledge," *CBC News*, August 25, 2015, https://www.cbc.ca/news/politics/canada-election-2015-justin-trudeau-accuses-tom-mulcair-of-austerity-over-balanced-budget-pledge-1.3202773.

25. "Most voters — 58 per cent — are alright with modest deficit spending," Kyle Duggan wrote in *iPolitics*, "suggesting the campaign debate on deficits may help the

Liberals to poach NDP supporters and red Tories based on Justin Trudeau's promise to focus on economic growth rather than balancing the budget."
Kyle Duggan, "Most Canadians In Favour of Modest Deficits: Ekos Poll," *iPolitics*, September 11, 2015, ipolitics.ca/2015/09/11/most-canadians-in-favour-of-modest-deficits-ekos-poll; Greg Lyle, "Have the NDP Missed the Greatest Electoral Opportunity in Their History?" *The Hill Times*, September 25, 2015, https://www.hilltimes.com/2015/09/25/have-the-ndp-missed-the-greatest-electoral-opportunity-in-their-history/33515/43515.

26. New Democratic Party of Canada, "Campaign 2015 Review: Working Group Report," accessed June 16, 2018, http://xfer.ndp.ca/2016/-Debrief-Report/Campaign2015Review-Report-EN-Final.pdf.

Chapter 3

1. Michael Den Tandt, "Charity Boxing Match Strikes Blow for Charity," *National Post*, February 20, 2012, https://nationalpost.com/opinion/justin-trudeau-boxing-match.

2. Stephen Rodrick, "Justin Trudeau: The North Star," *Rolling Stone*, July 26, 2017, https://www.rollingstone.com/politics/politics-features/justin-trudeau-the-north-star-194313.

3. *God Save Justin Trudeau.* Directed by Guylaine Maroist. Quebec: Les Productions de la Ruelle, 2015.

4. John Powers, "Justin Trudeau Is the New Young Face of Canadian Politics," *Vogue*, December 9, 2015, https://www.vogue.com/article/justin-trudeau-prime-minister-canada; Jesse Ferreras, "Justin Trudeau Does 'Jazz Hands' At G20," *Huffington Post*, November 16, 2015, https://www.huffingtonpost.ca/2015/11/16/justin-trudeau-jazz-hands-g20_n_8579028.html; "Justin Trudeau's 7 Secrets to Being Extraordinarily Charming," *Inc.*, March 11, 2016, https://www.inc.com/leigh-buchanan/beach-sand-sculptures-santa-rosa-beach-florida-main-street.html; "Can Justin Trudeau's Socks Bring Peace to the World?" *The Guardian*, June 28, 2017, https://www.theguardian.com/world/shortcuts/2017/jun/28/can-justin-trudeau-socks-bring-world-peace; Jenna Guillaume, "Literally Just 27 Really Hot Photos of Justin Trudeau," *BuzzFeed*, March 2, 2017, https://www.buzzfeed.com/jennaguillaume/ohhhh-canada.

5. Lauren O'Neil, "Photo of Justin Trudeau Doing Yoga Makes the Internet Freak Out — Again," *CBC News*, March 30, 2016, https://www.cbc.ca/news/trending/justin-trudeau-yoga-photo-peacock-pose-2013-pierre-trudeau-1.3513238.

6. "Justin Trudeau Takes CHEO Kids to Private Star Wars Screening," *CBC News*, December 16, 2015, https://www.cbc.ca/news/politics/justin-trudeau-cheo-star-wars-force-awakens-1.3367268; "Justin Trudeau, 11, Reviews Return of the Jedi after Ottawa Premiere in 1983," *CBC News: From the Archives*, December 14, 2015, https://www.cbc.ca/news/canada/ottawa/return-of-the-jedi-justin-trudeau-1.3363979.

7. "I think Canadians are tired of politicians that are spun and scripted within an inch of their life, people who are too afraid of what a focus group might say about one comment or a political opponent might try to twist out of context," Trudeau also told Joan Bryden.

Joan Bryden, "Occasional Gaffe Part of Being Genuine Political Leader, Trudeau says in Interview," *The Globe and Mail*, December 11, 2013, https://www.theglobeandmail.com/news/politics/occasional-gaffe-part-of-being-genuine-unscripted-political-leader-trudeau-says-in-interview/article15866526.

8. Alexander J. Marland, *Brand Command: Canadian Politics and Democracy in the Age of Message Control* (Vancouver: UBC Press, 2017), xvi-xvii.

9. The National, "Behind-the-Scenes of Justin Trudeau's First Day as Prime Minister," *CBC News*, November 4, 2015, https://www.cbc.ca/news/thenational/behind-the-scenes-of-justin-trudeau-s-first-day-as-prime-minister-1.3304991.

10. Edward Greenspon and Anthony Wilson-Smith, *Double Vision: The Inside Story of the Liberals in Power* (Toronto: Doubleday Canada, 1996), 2.

11. The National, "Behind-the-Scenes."

12. Aaron Hutchins, "No, Trudeau Didn't Photobomb Those Prom Dids," *Maclean's*, May 23, 2017, www.macleans.ca/politics/no-trudeau-didnt-photobomb-those-prom-kids.

13. Standing in front of a chalkboard filled with complex math equations, as he announced funding at the Physics Institute in Waterloo, Ontario, the video seemed to show him calling the bluff of a condescending journalist who had suggested he try to explain quantum computing. *The Toronto Star* reported that "apparently eager to show he's more than a now globally recognized pretty face, Trudeau promptly showed he has computer-geek talents previously little known."
    Jim Coyle, "PM Shows Off Knowledge of Quantum Computing," *Toronto Star*, April 15, 2016, https://www.thestar.com/news/canada/2016/04/15/justin-trudeau-reveals-his-inner-computer-geek-at-waterloo.html.
    Meanwhile, a headline from *The Guardian* on April 16, 2016 read, "Justin Trudeau Stuns Audience with Quantum Computing Knowledge" (https://www.theguardian.com/world/video/2016/apr/16/justin-trudeau-stuns-audience-with-quantum-computing-knowledge-canada-video). But Trudeau had in fact told reporters at the press conference that he hoped someone would ask about quantum physics. One reporter jokingly obliged, referencing it before asking the question he really wanted an answer to. Trudeau ignored the real question and launched into a prepared riff—the perfect length of a short viral video.

14. An executive from McCann, the U.S. advertising agency that completed the contract, asked, "what ethnicities you would like us to cover? Asian? Native? Indian? Latino?" A photo of a woman in hiking boots with a laptop was meant to represent "innovation and skill." Another photo of a boy holding a cartoon bridge represented "infrastructure." The Finance Ministry had a long email discussion with the Prime Minister's Office over whether the boy should wear eyeglasses.

15. George Monbiot, "Celebrity Isn't Just Harmless Fun – It's the Smiling Face of the Corporate Machine," *The Guardian*, December 20, 2016, https://www.theguardian.com/commentisfree/2016/dec/20/celebrity-corporate-machine-fame-big-business-donald-trump-kim-kardashian.

16. Edelman Insights, "2016 Edelman Trust Barometer: Canadian Results," February 3, 2016, https://www.slideshare.net/EdelmanInsights/edelman-trust-barometer-canada-results.

17. "Trudeau Promises Ban on Oil Drilling in the Arctic, But What about Seismic Testing?" *APTN News*, December 21, 2016, https://aptnnews.ca/2016/12/21/trudeau-promises-ban-on-oil-drilling-in-the-arctic-but-what-about-seismic-testing.

18.   Bruce Cheadle, "Trudeau Says Image-Making Part of Governing, Not a Popularity Contest," *City News*, December 17, 2015, https://toronto.citynews.ca/2015/12/17/trudeau-says-image-making-part-of-governing-not-a-popularity-contest.

19.   "For #statedinner #SophieGrégoireTrudeau is wearing Lucian Matis dress, Ela handbag, Zvelle shoes, John de Jong earrings, Dean Davidson ring." (@CBCAlerts, March 10, 2016).

20.   Stephen Marche, "Canada in the Age of Donald Trump" *The Walrus*, August 25, 2017, https://thewalrus.ca/canada-in-the-age-of-donald-trump; Stephen Marche, "Trudeau Won Because the Youth Want Old Canada Back," *Huffington Post*, October 21, 2015, https://www.huffingtonpost.ca/stephen-marche/trudeau-youth-old-canada-back_b_8346112.html.

21.   Lee Berthiaume, "Trudeau and Macron Promise to Double Down on Climate-Change fight," *CBC News*, April 16, 2018, https://www.cbc.ca/news/politics/trudeau-jean-paris-environment-1.4621202.

22.   Katie Reilly, "'Fight Our Tribal Mindset' Read Justin Trudeau's Commencement Address to NYU Graduates," *Time*, May 16, 2018, http://time.com/5280153/justin-trudeau-nyu-commencement-2018-transcript.

23.   Matt Taibbi, "Obama Is the Best BS Artist Since Bill Clinton," *AlterNet*, February 14, 2007, https://www.alternet.org/2007/02/obama_is_the_best_bs_artist_since_bill_clinton.

24.   "Justin Trudeau Promises to Grow the Economy 'From the Heart Outwards' — Whatever That Means," *National Post*, August 12, 2015, http://nationalpost.com/news/politics/justin-trudeau-grow-the-economy-from-the-heart-outwards.

25.   Justin Trudeau, *Common Ground* (Toronto: HarperCollins, 2014), 204.

26.   The organization promises that the "combination of Trudeau's electric charisma and inspirational message leaves audiences educated, entertained and ready to make a difference." See: https://web.archive.org/web/20071009075527/https://www.speakers.ca.

27.   Glen McGregor, "Justin Trudeau Admits That He 'Won the Lottery' with $1.2 Million Inheritance and Successful Speaking Business," *Ottawa Citizen*, February 13, 2013, https://o.canada.com/news/justin-trudeau-admits-that-he-won-the-lottery-with-1-2-million-inheritance-and-successful-speaking-business.

28.   When Trudeau was set to mount his run for the Liberal leadership, there was a brief controversy. He was still pulling in a quarter of a million dollars from speaking fees, despite the fact that parliamentarians are generally expected to speak for free. His rationale for taking speaker fees from charities and non-profit organizations? Trudeau said his speeches were focused on youth issues, education, and the environment. "I talked non-political stuff," he said, revealing more than he realized.

Chapter 4

1.   Marco Chown Oved, Alex Boutilier, and Robert Cribb, "Liberal Fundraisers Held Family Millions in Offshore Trust, Leaked Documents Reveal," *Toronto Star*, November 5, 2017, https://www.thestar.com/news/paradise-papers/2017/11/05/trudeau-bronfman-kolber-offshore-trust-taxes.html.

2.   Sharon Batt, "The Big Money Club: Revealing the Players and Their Campaign to Stop Pharmacare," *Canadian Federation of Nurses Unions*, March 2019, https://nursesunions.ca/wp-content/uploads/2019/03/CFNU_bigmoneyclub_low.pdf.

3. National Public Relations, "Securing Regulatory Approval for Pacific NorthWest LNG," February 14, 2018, https://www.national.ca/en/expertise/portfolio/detail/pacific-northwest-lng-regulatory-approval/; National Public Relations, "Elevating Lockheed Martin in Canada," February 14, 2018, https://www.national.ca/en/expertise/portfolio/detail/lockheed-martin/; National Public Relations, "Speechwriting for Prime Minister Justin Trudeau," February 14, 2018, https://www.national.ca/en/expertise/portfolio/detail/public-policy-forum-justin-trudeaus-speech.

4. Liberal Party of Canada, "Constitution of the Liberal Party of Canada," as adopted at the Biennial Convention on May 28, 2016, https://www.liberal.ca/wp-content/uploads/2016/07/constitution-en.pdf; Tim Naumetz, "Justin Trudeau, Party Brass Set to Gain More Power Over Campaigns, Policy Under New Proposed Liberal Constitution," *The Hill Times*, April 15, 2016, https://www.hilltimes.com/2016/04/15/justin-trudeau-party-brass-set-to-gain-more-power-over-campaigns-policy-under-new-proposed-liberal-constitution/58608.

5. Stephen Clarkson, *The Big Red Machine: How the Liberal Party Dominates Canadian Politics* (Vancouver: UBC Press, 2005), 24-27.

6. Clarkson, *The Big Red Machine*, 8.

7. Julie Van Dusen, "Justin Trudeau Joyfully Mobbed by Federal Civil Servants," *CBC News*, November 06, 2015, https://www.cbc.ca/news/politics/trudeau-dion-duncan-civil-servants-cheered-pearson-1.3308271.

8. Sue Montgomery, "Environmentalist Jim MacNeill Was An Early Warrior Against Climate Change," *The Globe and Mail*, March 22, 2016, https://www.theglobeandmail.com/news/national/environmentalist-jim-macneill-was-an-early-warrior-against-climate-change/article29345345.

9. Emily Chung, "More Than Half of Federal Government Scientists Still Feel Muzzled, Poll Finds," *CBC News*, February 21, 2018, https://www.cbc.ca/news/technology/muzzled-scientists-1.4545562.

10. Paul Wells, "Trudeau's Reforms, Three 'Ifs' and a Set of Ginsu Steak Knives," *Maclean's*, June 16, 2015, https://www.macleans.ca/politics/ottawa/trudeaus-reforms-three-ifs-and-a-set-of-ginsu-steak-knives.

11. The Liberal Party of Canada, "Justin Trudeau Delivers Change," June 18, 2015, https://www.liberal.ca/justin-trudeau-delivers-real-change.

12. John Ivison, "Scuttled Electoral Reform Betrays Those Who Saw Trudeau as Antidote to Political Cynicism," *National Post*, February 1, 2017, https://nationalpost.com/opinion/john-ivison-scuttled-electoral-reform-betrays-those-who-saw-trudeau-as-antidote-to-political-cynicism.

13. Debates of May 11th, 2016, House of Commons Hansard #53 of the 42nd Parliament, 1st Session, https://openparliament.ca/debates/2016/5/11/justin-trudeau-3.

14. Éric Grenier, "Change to Preferential Ballot Would Benefit Liberals," *CBC News*, November 26, 2015, https://www.cbc.ca/news/politics/grenier-preferential-ballot-1.3332566.

15. "PM Trudeau Backs Away from Electoral Reform Pledge," *CTV News*, October 19, 2016, https://www.ctvnews.ca/politics/pm-trudeau-backs-away-from-electoral-reform-pledge-1.3122167.

16. Peter Mazereeuw, "Feds to Release Data from Electoral Reform Town Halls: Monsef," *The Hill Times*, December 14, 2016, https://www.hilltimes.com/2016/12/14/electoral-reform-town-halls-didnt-poll-preferred-voting-system/90790.

17. Fairvote Canada, "Consultations Provide Strong Mandate for Proportional Representation," November 3, 2016, https://www.fairvote.ca/2016/11/03/strong-mandate.

18. Aaron Wherry, "'A Dating Website Designed by Fidel Castro': Opposition Blasts Liberal Electoral Reform Survey," *CBC News*, December 06, 2016, https://www.cbc.ca/news/politics/monsef-survey-electoral-reform-1.3882359.

19. Bertolt Brecht, "The Solution," https://www.poemhunter.com/poem/the-solution.

20. CBC News, "Trudeau explains his electoral reform U-turn," video, 8:16, February 10, 2017, https://www.youtube.com/watch?v=QVtTr-RO1Ts.

Chapter 5

1. "Are the Liberals Planning To Flip Flop on Their Promise To Close a Big Tax Loophole For The Rich?" *PressProgress*, February 23, 2016, https://pressprogress.ca/are_the_liberals_planning_to_flip_flop_on_their_promise_to_close_a_big_tax_loophole_for_the_rich.

2. What was inconvenient for this explanation was that the Liberals' own calculations, contained in their platform's fiscal and costing document, pointed out that the tax loophole was being almost entirely used by just 8,000 of Canada's wealthiest one-percenters.
The Liberal Party of Canada, "Growth for the Middle Class: The Liberal Fiscal Plan and Costing," September 2015, page 10, https://www.liberal.ca/wp-content/uploads/2015/09/The-Liberal-fiscal-plan-and-costing.pdf.

3. Sean Silcoff, "Liberals Drop Controversial Stock Options Tax Plan," *The Globe and Mail*, March 22, 2016, https://www.theglobeandmail.com/report-on-business/small-business/startups/liberals-drop-controversial-stock-options-tax-plan/article29337792; The Liberal Party of Canada, "Growth for the Middle Class"; "Bay Street Pressured Liberals to Break Promise to Close CEO Tax Loophole, Documents Show," *PressProgress*, January 6, 2017, https://pressprogress.ca/bay_street_pressured_liberals_to_break_promise_to_close_ceo_tax_loophole_documents_show.

4. Theophilos Argitis and Doug Alexander, "Tax Changes Won't Apply to Existing Stock Options, Morneau Says," *The Globe and Mail*, November 20, 2015, https://www.theglobeandmail.com/report-on-business/economy/tax-changes-wont-apply-to-existing-stock-options-morneau-says/article27409116.

5. *United We Fall*. Directed by Bryan Law. Canada: KITG Productions, 2010.

6. Peter C. Newman, "A Man of Influence: Thomas d'Aquino," *Canadian Business*, October 12, 2009, https://www.canadianbusiness.com/business-strategy/a-man-of-influence-thomas-daquino.

7. Business Council of Canada, "Reforming Canada's Corporate Tax System Would Help Companies Grow and Create Jobs, Report Says," September 16, 2015, https://thebusinesscouncil.ca/news/reforming-canadas-corporate-tax-system-help-companies-grow-create-jobs-report-says.

8. David Langille, "The Business Council on National Issues and the Canadian State," *Studies in Political Economy: A Socialist Review* 24, no. 1 (1987): 59, https://doi.org/10.1080/19187033.1987.11675557; Murray Dobbin, *The Myth of the Good Corporate Citizen: Canada and Democracy in the Age of Globalization* (Toronto: James Lorimer & Company Ltd., 1998).

9. Newman, "A Man of Influence," 68.

10. Murray Dobbin, "Our Grand Ayatollah," *The Tyee*, September 12, 2007, https://thetyee.ca/Views/2007/09/12/Ayatollah.

11. When thousands showed up to protest in Montebello, Quebec during a meeting between PM Stephen Harper and Presidents Bush and Calderón, Tom d'Aquino likened them to barbarians. "I do not say to myself, 'If I don't get an hour with the prime minister in the next six months, I'm going to go out and protest and reject the system outright,'" he told the media. "I don't do that because civilized human beings—those who believe in democracy—don't do that."

12. Adam Radwanski, "'I Have My Own Brand'," *The Globe and Mail*, August 16, 2009, https://www.theglobeandmail.com/news/politics/i-have-my-own-brand/article1201566.

13. Julian Beltrame, "Dumb as a Bag of Hammers", *Maclean's*, February 3, 2003, https://archive.macleans.ca/article/2003/2/3/dumb-as-a-bag-of-hammers.

14. Jane Taber, "Corporate Donors Reluctant to Come to Liberals' Table," *The Globe and Mail*, April 16, 2003, https://www.theglobeandmail.com/news/national/corporate-donors-reluctant-to-come-to-liberals-table/article25282704.

15. Jane Taber, "A Summer of Backyard Party Politics," *The Globe and Mail*, June 27, 2006, https://www.theglobeandmail.com/news/national/a-summer-of-backyard-party-politics/article711777.

16. The company also gave $8,000 to the Conservative Party and its ridings. Monique Scotti, "SNC-Lavalin Illegally Donated Over $117K to Federal Parties: Elections Canada," *Global News*, September 8, 2016, https://globalnews.ca/news/2927286/snc-lavalin-illegally-donated-over-117k-to-federal-parties-elections-canada.

17. Althia Raj, "Trudeau Government In No Hurry To Reinstate Per-Vote Subsidy," *Huffington Post*, May 17, 2016, https://www.huffingtonpost.ca/2016/05/17/per-vote-subsidy-canada-trudeau-harper_n_10014486.html.

18. Yamri Taddese, "Elections Ontario Data Shows Some Law Firms Still Donate to Political Parties," *Law Times*, February 10, 2014, http://www.lawtimesnews.com/author/yamri-taddese/elections-ontario-data-shows-some-law-firms-still-donate-to-political-parties-11054.

19. Robert Fife and Steven Chase, "Morneau Fundraiser One in List of Liberal Cash-For-Access Events," *The Globe and Mail*, October 20, 2016, https://www.theglobeandmail.com/news/politics/morneau-fundraiser-one-in-list-of-liberal-cash-for-access-events/article32450347; Justin Ling, "The Liberal Party Has Scheduled More Than 100 Cash-For-Access Events in 2016 Alone," *VICE*, October 28, 2016, https://www.vice.com/en_ca/article/9b8jba/the-trudeau-government-scheduled-more-than-100-cash-for-access-events-in-2016-alone; Robert Fife and Steven Chase, "Drug Firm Executive Helps Organize Cash-For-Access Fundraiser Featuring Bill Morneau," *The Globe and Mail*, October 25, 2016, https://www.theglobeandmail.com/news/politics/drug-firm-executive-helps-organize-cash-for-access-fundraiser-featuring-bill-morneau/article32509138; Campbell Clark, "Trudeau's New Era of Transparency Off to an Iffy Start," *The Globe and Mail*, April 21, 2016, https://www.theglobeandmail.com/news/politics/globe-politics-insider/trudeaus-new-era-of-transparency-off-to-an-iffy-start/article29704923; Robert Fife and Steven Chase, "Trudeau Defends Cash-For-Access Fundraising," *The Globe and Mail*, October 25, 2016, https://www.theglobeandmail.com/news/politics/trudeau-defends-cash-for-access-fundraising/article32523956.

20. Sherman and Apotex were eventually investigated by the Lobbying Commissioner for having hosted an earlier fundraising dinner for Justin Trudeau in 2015,

potentially breaching the prohibition on registered lobbyists improperly influencing someone in public office. But the Commissioner dropped it after Sherman passed away.

21. Campbell Clark, "Liberals Shrug Off Their Own Ethical Guidelines with Fundraiser," *The Globe and Mail*, October 23, 2016, https://www.theglobeandmail.com/news/politics/liberals-shrug-off-their-own-ethical-guidelines-with-fundraiser/article32486963.

22. Robert Fife and Steven Chase, "Drug Firm Executive."

23. "A Detailed Timeline of All the Excuses Used to Explain Liberal Party Cash-For-Access Fundraisers," *PressProgress*, December 25, 2016, https://pressprogress.ca/a_detailed_timeline_of_all_the_excuses_used_to_explain_liberal_party_cash_for_access_fundraisers.

24. New Democratic Party of Canada, "Majority of Canada's Richest Donate to the Liberals," September 11, 2018, https://www.ndp.ca/news/majority-canadas-richest-donate-liberals.

25. Anthony Fenton, "Hostile Takeover: Canada's Outsourced War for Iraq's Oil Riches," *This Magazine,* September 1, 2009, https://this.org/2009/09/01/canada-iraq-oil.

26. "Scott Brison Takes Job with Bank of Montreal, Weeks after Resigning from Cabinet," *CBC News*, February 14, 2019, https://www.cbc.ca/news/canada/nova-scotia/former-liberal-cabinet-minister-scott-brison-joins-bmo-1.5018143.

27. Chrystia Freeland, "Plutocrats vs. Populists." *New York Times*, November 3, 2013, https://www.nytimes.com/2013/11/03/opinion/sunday/plutocrats-vs-populists.html.

28. Bill Curry, "Bill Morneau's Office Made 'Angry' Calls Over Bank Bill, Insurance Group Says," *The Globe and Mail*, May 14, 2018, https://www.theglobeandmail.com/politics/article-insurance-group-received-angry-calls-from-finance-ministers-office.

29. Elizabeth Thompson, "Banking Industry Has Lobbied Officials, MPs Hundreds of Times," *CBC News*, June 12, 2017, https://www.cbc.ca/news/politics/banks-finance-lobbying-government-1.4155703.

30. Personal calculations of Duff Connacher.

31. Erica Johnson, "'We Are All Doing It': Employees at Canada's 5 Big Banks Speak Out About Pressure to Dupe Customers," *CBC News*, March 15, 2017, https://www.cbc.ca/news/business/banks-upselling-go-public-1.4023575.

32. Erica Johnson and Enza Uda, "Bank Regulator's Report on Aggressive Sales Tactics Weakened After Government — and Banks — Reviewed Drafts," *CBC News*, April 10, 2019, https://www.cbc.ca/news/politics/fcac-bank-report-on-sales-tactics-weakened-1.5091115.

33. Beatrice Britneff, "Lobbying Activity More Than Doubled After Liberals Elected," *iPolitics*, January 13, 2017, https://ipolitics.ca/2017/01/13/lobbying-activity-more-than-doubled-after-liberals-elected; Bill Curry and Tom Cardoso, "SNC-Lavalin Lobbied PMO 19 Times Since Start of 2017, Records Show," *The Globe and Mail*, February 19, 2019, https://www.theglobeandmail.com/politics/article-snc-lavalin-had-access-to-governments-top-decision-makers-lobbying.

34. Derek Abma, "Federal Lobbying Activity Heats Up, Reflects Liberals' Friendlier Stance with Consultant Lobbyists," *The Hill Times*, March 21, 2016, https://www.hilltimes.com/2016/03/21/federal-lobbying-activity-heats-up-reflects-liberals-friendlier-stance-with-consultant-lobbyists/54614.

35. Samantha Wright Allen and Beatrice Paez, "Meet the Top-Lobbied Political Gatekeepers in 2018," *The Hill Times*, January 30, 2019, https://www.hilltimes.com/2019/01/30/meet-top-lobbied-political-gatekeepers-2018/185776; Samantha Wright Allen, "Canada's Most-Lobbied Staffers Drive Policy Tied to Federal Purse," *The Hill Times*, October 18, 2017, https://www.hilltimes.com/2017/10/18/canadas-most-lobbied-staffers-drive-policy-tied-to-federal-purse/122495.

36. Daniel Tencer, "Canada's Most And Least Reputable Industries," *Huffington Post*, May 4, 2017, https://www.huffingtonpost.ca/2017/05/04/reptrak-canada-2017-report_n_16412480.html.

37. Jesse Cnockaert, "Earnscliffe Plans More Hires in 2019 for Fourth Floor Expansion," *The Lobby Monitor*, December 17, 2018, http://www.lobbymonitor.ca/2018/12/03/earnscliffe-plans-more-hires-in-2019-for-fourth-floor-expansion/16569.

38. Beatriz Paez, "Trudeau's Nominee for Lobby Watchdog Sought Other Post, Committee Hears," *The Hill Times*, December 6, 2017, http://www.lobbymonitor.ca/2017/12/06/ethics-committee-votes-in-favour-of-grits-nominee-for-next-watchdog/15946.

Chapter 6

1. Anne Kingston, "Inside the Progressive Think Tank That Really Runs Canada," *Maclean's*, October 12, 2017, https://www.macleans.ca/politics/ottawa/inside-the-progressive-think-tank-that-really-runs-canada; BJ Siekierski and James Munson, "Capp Bolsters Lobbying Efforts with Bluesky Strategies," *iPolitics*, November 16, 2016, https://ipolitics.ca/2016/11/16/capp-bolsters-lobbying-efforts-with-bluesky-strategies.

2. https://www.blueskystrategygroup.com/stuart-mccarthy

3. Dave Lazzarino, "Non-Peaceful Pipeline Protests Will Be Met By Police And Military, Federal Minister Tells Edmonton Business Leaders," *Edmonton Journal*, December 1, 2016, https://edmontonjournal.com/news/local-news/pipeline-protests-will-be-met-by-police-and-military-federal-minister-tells-edmonton-business-leaders.

4. Gordon Kent, "People 'Are Going To Die' Protesting Trans Mountain Pipeline: Former Bank of Canada Governor," *Edmonton Journal*, June 13, 2018, https://edmontonjournal.com/business/energy/people-are-going-to-die-protesting-trans-mountain-pipeline-former-bank-of-canada-governor.

5. Damien Gillis, "Justin Trudeau's Two-Faced Climate Game," *New York Times*, May 2, 2018, https://www.nytimes.com/2018/05/02/opinion/trudeau-climate-kinder-morgan-pipeline.html.

6. Melanie Green, "Meet the Self-Described 'Sinister Seniors' Taking a Stand against Trans Mountain — And Going to Jail for It." *Toronto Star*, August 23, 2018, https://www.thestar.com/vancouver/2018/08/20/meet-the-self-described-sinister-seniors-taking-a-stand-against-trans-mountain-and-going-to-jail-for-it.html.

7. "1 In 4 Pipeline Opponents Would Consider Civil Disobedience: Poll," *Vancouver Courier*, February 19, 2018, https://www.vancourier.com/news/1-in-4-pipeline-opponents-would-consider-civil-disobedience-poll-1.23178843.

8. Jesse Ferreras, "Watch the Kelowna-Area Wildfire Erupt Like a Volcano in This Stunning Timelapse," *Global News*, August 24, 2017, https://globalncws.ca/news/3695237/watch-the-kelowna-area-wildfire-erupt-like-a-volcano-in-this-stunning-timelapse.

9. Sharon J. Riley, "How Climate Change Is Making B.C.'s Wildfire Season Hotter, Longer, Drier," *Narwhal*, August 13, 2018, https://thenarwhal.ca/how-climate-change-is-making-b-c-s-wildfire-season-hotter-longer-dryer; Bethany Lindsay, "2018 Now Worst Fire Season on Record as B.C. Extends State of Emergency," *CBC News*, August 29, 2018, https://www.cbc.ca/news/canada/british-columbia/state-emergency-bc-wildfires-1.4803546.

10. Intergovernmental Panel on Climate Change, "Summary for Policymakers of IPCC Special Report on Global Warming of 1.5°C approved by governments," October 8, 2018, https://www.ipcc.ch/2018/10/08/summary-for-policymakers-of-ipcc-special-report-on-global-warming-of-1-5c-approved-by-governments.

11. Valerie Richardson, "Obama Takes Credit for U.S. Oil-and-Gas Boom: 'That Was Me, People,'" *AP News*, November 28, 2018, https://www.apnews.com/5dfbc1aa177 01ae219239caad0bfefb2.

12. Joanna Smith, "Trudeau Wants Canada to Play Key Role in Fighting Climate Change," *Toronto Star*, March 2, 2016, https://www.thestar.com/news/canada/2016/03/02/canada-will-play-leading-role-in-new-economy-trudeau-says.html.

13. Marc Lee, "Enbridge Pipe Dreams and Nightmares: The Economic Costs and Benefits of the Proposed Northern Gateway Pipeline," *Canadian Centre for Policy Alternatives*, March 2012, https://www.policyalternatives.ca/sites/default/files/uploads/publications/BC%20Office/2012/03/CCPA-BC_Enbridge_Pipe_Dreams_2012.pdf.

14. Martin Lukacs, "Revealed: Trudeau Government Welcomed Oil Lobby Help for US Pipeline Push," *The Guardian,* February 9, 2018, https://www.theguardian.com/environment/true-north/2018/feb/09/trudeau-government-welcomed-oil-lobby-help-for-us-pipeline-push-documents.

15. Jeremy Berke, "'No Country Would Find 173 Billion Barrels of Oil in the Ground and Just Leave Them': Justin Trudeau Gets a Standing Ovation at an Energy Conference in Texas," *Business Insider*, March 10, 2017, https://www.businessinsider.com/trudeau-gets-a-standing-ovation-at-energy-industry-conference-oil-gas-2017-3.

16. Gerald Butts, "Carbon Capture No Silver Bullet for Tar Sands," *Toronto Star*, February 27, 2009, https://www.theguardian.com/environment/2013/may/19/tar-sands-exploitation-climate-scientist.

17. Butts, "Carbon Capture."

18. Pembina Institute, "Declaration of U.S. and Canadian Environmental and Conservation Leaders on U.S.-Canada Cooperation on Climate, Energy, and Natural Areas Conservation," June 4, 2009, http://www.pembina.org/pub/1849.

19. Natural Resources Canada had warned that any planned expansion of the tar sands "would not be sustainable because the Athabasca River does not have sufficient flows." Andrew Nikiforuk, *Tar Sands: Dirty Oil and the Future of a Continent* (Vancouver: Greystone Books, 2010), 61-62.

20. World Wildlife Canada, "Annual Report, 2009," http://awsassets.wwf.ca/downloads/wwfcanada_annualreport_2009.pdf.

21. "Old Guard & Vanguard," *National Post*, June 2, 2007, https://www.pressreader.com/canada/national-post-latest-edition/20070602/282716222571869.

22. Manulife Asset Management Limited, "Units of Oil Sands Sector Fund: Annual Information Form for the Year Ended December 31, 2015," March 28, 2016, http://manulifemutualfunds.ca/en/pdf/regulatory/AIF_OSSF.pdf.

23. Goldring did not respond to written questions about why he left the board of directors.

World Wildlife Canada, "Annual Review," October 2010, http://d2akrl9rvxl3z3. cloudfront.net/downloads/wwfcanada_annualreport2010_1.pdf.

24. Emma McIntosh and David Bruser, "Oilsands Waste Is Collected in Sprawling Toxic Ponds. To Clean Them Up, Oil Companies Plan to Pour Water on Them," *Toronto Star*, November 23, 2018, https://www.thestar.com/news/investigations/2018/11/23/oilsands-waste-is-collected-in-sprawling-toxic-ponds-to-clean-them-up-oil-companies-plan-to-pour-water-on-them.html.

25. Peter O'Neil, "The Inside Story of Kinder Morgan's Approval," *Vancouver Sun*, January 6, 2017, https://vancouversun.com/news/local-news/the-inside-story-of-kinder-morgans-approval.

26. Gerald Butts did not respond to extensive efforts to get comment from him on this story.

Gerald Butts, "A Message from Gerald Butts," *WWF-Canada Blog*, October 16, 2012, blog.wwf.ca/blog/2012/10/16/a-message-from-gerald-butts.

27. World Wildlife Canada, "Loblaw Launches National Plastic Shopping Bag Reduction Program," April 20, 2009, http://www.wwf.ca/newsroom/?3500.

28. Rich Bell, "Justin Trudeau Bashes National Energy Program in Calgary," *Edmonton Sun*, October 3, 2012, https://edmontonsun.com/2012/10/03/bell-justin-trudeau-bashes-national-energy-program-in-calgary.

29. Stephen Clarkson, *Canada and the Reagan Challenge: Crisis in the Canadian-American Relationship* (Toronto: James Lorimer & Company Ltd., 1982), 55.

30. "Though some oil barons shout confiscation and nationalization to the congressional cronies there is no talk of the multinationals being forced out of the play. Their take would be handsome, not astronomical, when the field was ultimately developed. What irked them most, though they did not admit this, was the prospect of a considerable Canadian governmental presence around their boardroom tables to keep an eye on their operations." (Stephen Clarkson, *Canada and the Reagan Challenge*, 75).

31. Making it the aberration in the world: Former CIBC chief economist Jeff Rubin calculates that the tar sands represent 50 to 70 percent of all the private investment in oil reserves in the world.

32. Gordon Laxer, *After the Sands: Energy and Ecological Security for Canadians* (Madeira Park, BC: Douglas and McIntyre, 2015), 47.

33. Liberal Party of Canada, "Liberal Party of Canada Leader Justin Trudeau's Speech to the Calgary Petroleum Club," October 30, 2013, https://www.liberal.ca/liberal-party-canada-leader-justin-trudeaus-speech-calgary-petroleum-club.

34. I have relied closely on Donald Gutstein's brilliant account to understand the development of the Business Council's strategy in the lead-up to the Trudeau government. Donald Gutstein, *The Big Stall: How Big Oil and Think Tanks are Blocking Action on Climate Change in Canada* (Toronto: James Lorimer & Company Ltd., 2018), 64.

35. Kaija Belfry Munroe, *Business in a Changing Climate: Explaining Industry Support for Carbon Pricing* (Toronto: University of Toronto Press, 2016), 53.

36. The left-wing think tank Parkland Institute was in fact the first to use the term Canadian Energy Strategy, but it was appropriated by the oil lobby, which quickly transformed its meaning.

Laxer, *After the Sands*, 14.

37. Karen Kleiss, "Provinces Look to Find Common Ground on Energy Strategy," *Financial Post*, January 16, 2012, https://business.financialpost.com/commodities/energy/provinces-look-to-find-common-ground-on-energy-strategy.

38. The Business Council of Canada, "Clean Growth: Building a Canadian Environmental Superpower (A Policy Declaration of the Canadian Council of Chief Executives)," October 1, 2007, https://thebusinesscouncil.ca/publications/clean-growth-building-a-canadian-environmental-superpower-a-policy-declaration-of-the-canadian-council-of-chief-executives.

39. Belfry Munroe, *Business in a Changing Climate*, 4-6.

40. Trudeau, *Common Ground*.

41. Kevin Taft, *Oil's Deep State: How the Petroleum Industry Undermines Democracy and Stops Action on Global Warming — in Alberta, and in Ottawa* (Toronto: James Lorimer & Company Ltd., 2017), 30.

42. Taft, *Oil's Deep State*, 30.

43. Bill Curry and Dawn Walton, "Climate Change Report 'Irresponsible,' Prentice Says," *The Globe and Mail*, October 29, 2009, https://www.theglobeandmail.com/news/politics/climate-change-report-irresponsible-prentice-says/article4297333; Tyler Hamilton, "TD Chief Distances Bank from Greenhouse-Gas Report," *Toronto Star*, November 4, 2009, https://www.thestar.com/business/2009/11/04/td_chief_distances_bank_from_greenhousegas_report.html.

44. "Justin Trudeau Calls Dan Gagnier's Letter to Pipeline Officials 'Inappropriate'," *CBC News*, October 15, 2015, https://www.cbc.ca/news/politics/canada-election-2015-liberals-trudeau-gagnier-pipeline-letter-campaign-1.3272049; Ira Basen, "Dan Gagnier's Departure from Liberal campaign Highlights Murky World of Ottawa Lobbying," *CBC News*, October 16, 2015, https://www.cbc.ca/news/politics/canada-election-2015-gagnier-lobbying-1.3274251.

45. "Syncrude and Suncor were chafing under the agreements they had signed with the Lougheed team, and potential investors were uncertain about negotiating new agreements with the government," Kevin Taft writes. "The oil sands industry wanted a change that would open up their opportunities and reduce their risks." (Taft, *Oil's Deep State*, 156.)
Gillian Steward, "Betting on Bitumen: Alberta's Energy Policies from Lougheed to Klein," *Parkland Institute*, June 7, 2017, https://www.parklandinstitute.ca/betting_on_bitumen.

46. Glenbow Museum, Petroleum History Society Oil Sands Oral History Project, Interview with Anne McLennan, Former Minister of Natural Resources Canada, July 11, 2011, https://www.glenbow.org/collections/search/findingAids/archhtml/extras/oilsands/McLellan_Anne.pdf.

47. Taft, *Oil's Deep State*, 35.

48. Glenbow Museum, 8.

49. Glenbow Museum, 9.

50. "I remember Eric at one of our meetings, and there were many of one kind or another, I remember saying to Eric that 'Look if you want me to try and sell this to the Minister of Finance and to my colleagues around the Cabinet table at this difficult time, you really do have to go across this country and try and sell this as a national project, that this isn't just about the Province of Alberta. This is a national endeavour that will, in fact, inure to the benefit of all Canadians.' And Eric said that he would do that, and he and I have often laughed, because I think he visited every

Chamber of Commerce he could possibly get an invitation to talk about the benefits, the potential benefits for other parts of the country." (Glenbow Museum, 10.)

51. Syncrude lobbyist Hyndman says he was inspired to rewrite Canada and Alberta's tar sands royalty and tax structure by a paper published in 1975 by two Australian economists. They had served as colonial administrators in Papua New Guinea; one of them later as a board member of heavily polluting mining companies operating there. The paper was a blueprint, Hyndman says, for "how governments in third world countries should treat natural resource projects to maximize the value." In other words, he had sought to implement an even more cutthroat version of a colonial model that already existed in Canada: usurp the rights of Indigenous peoples, get huge government handouts, and make bucket loads of money despoiling the land and air.
Glenbow Museum, Petroleum History Society Oil Sands Oral History Project, interview with Al Hyndman, audio, 91 mins, June 29, 2011, https://www.glenbow.org/collections/search/findingAids/archhtm/extras/oilsands/Hyndman_Al-pt1.mp3.

52. Taft, *Oil's Deep State*, 181.

53. Amy Taylor, "Standing Committee on Finance Submission," *Pembina Institute*, February 2007, https://www.pembina.org/reports/Subm_SC_Finance_ACCA_Feb2007.pdf.

54. Tony Clarke, *Silent Coup: Confronting the Big Business Takeover of Canada* (Toronto: James Lorimer & Company Ltd., 1997), 97.

55. Regan Boychuck, "Misplaced Generosity: Extraordinary Profits in Alberta's Oil and Gas," *The Parkland Institute*, November 25, 2010, https://www.parklandinstitute.ca/misplaced_generosity.

56. Gutstein, *The Big Stall*, 73.

57. Gutstein, *The Big Stall*, 67.

58. Belfry Munroe, *Business in a Changing Climate*, 59.

59. Gutstein, *The Big Stall*, 66.

60. Shawn McCarthy, "Oil Sands Tax Break to End — In 2010," *The Globe and Mail*, March 20, 2007, https://www.theglobeandmail.com/news/national/oil-sands-tax-break-to-end----in-2010/article17993063.

61. "There's no question that the changes that were made at the time on the fiscal side, both within the province on the royalties side, on the federal side with the tax act, helped enormously and also provided a psychological boost," McLellan recalled. (Glenbow interview with Anne McLennan, 21.)

62. Peter O'Neil, "The Inside Story Of Kinder Morgan's Approval," *Vancouver* Sun, January 6, 2017, https://vancouversun.com/news/local-news/the-inside-story-of-kinder-morgans-approval.

63. Gutstein, *The Big Stall*, 188.

64. Claudia Cattaneo, "'A Key Test': Canadian Oil Executives Await Trudeau's Grand Bargain on Pipelines," *Financial Post*, November 28, 2016, https://business.financialpost.com/commodities/energy/canadian-oil-executives-await-trudeaus-grand-bargain-on-pipelines.

65. Mike De Souza, "Government Insiders Say Trans Mountain Pipeline Approval Was Rigged," *National Observer*, April 24, 2018, https://www.nationalobserver.com/2018/04/24/kinder-morgan-opponents-suspected-trudeau-government-rigged-its-review-pipeline-federal.

"Cost to expand Trans Mountain pipeline now $1.9 billion higher, Kinder Morgan says," *Canadian Press*, August 7, 2018, https://calgaryherald.com/commodities/energy/cost-to-twin-trans-mountain-pipeline-now-1-9b-higher-kinder-morgan-says/wcm/bdac74a1-712c-4c8e-80f0-c0563d0bfe08

66. Shawn McCarthy, "Ottawa to Dramatically Scale Back Carbon Tax on Competitiveness Concerns," *The Globe and Mail*, August 1, 2018, https://www.theglobeandmail.com/business/industry-news/energy-and-resources/article-ottawa-to-dramatically-scale-back-carbon-tax-on-competitiveness.

67. Keith Stewart, "Could Trump Derail Canada's Climate and Energy Plan?" *Policy Options*, February 9, 2017, https://policyoptions.irpp.org/magazines/february-2017/could-trump-derail-canadas-climate-and-energy-plan.

68. Mia Rabson, "Canada Delays Methane Regulations for 3 Years Following U.S. Retreat," *CTV News*, April 22, 2017, https://www.ctvnews.ca/business/canada-delays-methane-regulations-for-3-years-following-u-s-retreat-1.3380204.

69. Taryn Grant, "Why Coal Will Continue to Power Nova Scotia Beyond 2030," *The Signal*, December 2, 2017, https://signalhfx.ca/why-coal-will-continue-to-power-nova-scotia-beyond-2030.

70. Don Pittis, "Zero-Emission Rules Mean Fewer Electric Car Choices for Most Canadians: Don Pittis," *CBC News*, November 19, 2018, https://www.cbc.ca/news/business/zero-emission-canada-1.4906767.

71. Patrick DeRochie, "Oil and Gas Is Trying to Weasel Its Way Out of Playing by the Rules," *Environmental Defence*, November 13, 2018, https://environmentaldefence.ca/2018/11/13/oil-and-gas-is-trying-to-weasel-its-way-out-of-playing-by-the-rules.

72. Jesse Snyder, "Industry Groups Warn Federal Government Against Proposal for Energy Project Exemptions," *Calgary Herald*, November 6, 2018, https://calgaryherald.com/news/politics/industry-groups-warn-federal-government-against-proposal-for-energy-project-exemptions/wcm/470221e9-1e16-450a-a66f-57259d42c4f2.

73. VICE Canada Staff, "70 Bad One-Liners About the Great Conservative Resistance Photo," *VICE*, November 7, 2018, https://www.vice.com/en_ca/article/qvq4am/70-bad-one-liners-about-the-great-conservative-resistance-photo.

74. Marieke Walsh, "Ford Doubles Down on Falsehoods About Federal Carbon Tax," *iPolitics*, October 30, 2018, https://ipolitics.ca/2018/10/30/ford-doubles-down-on-falsehoods-about-federal-carbon-tax.

75. Colin Perkel, "Ontario to Appeal Court's Ruling Upholding Federal Carbon-Pricing Law," *CBC News*, June 28, 2019, https://www.cbc.ca/news/canada/toronto/ontario-court-appeal-carbon-tax-ruling-1.5192914.

76. Dave Sawyer, Seton Stiebert, and Michael Bernstein, "An Emission and Cost Assessment of 'A Real Plan to Protect Our Environment'," July 2019, https://www.cleanprosperity.ca/wp-content/uploads/2019/07/A-Real-Plan-to-Protect-Our-Environment-Document-Nm05.pdf.

77. Robin V. Sears, "Conservatives Feel Heat on Climate Change," *Toronto Star*, June 16, 2019, https://www.thestar.com/opinion/contributors/2019/06/16/conservatives-feel-heat-on-climate-change.html.

78. Carl Meyer, "Skeptical of Trudeau's Carbon Pricing? There's An Institute for That," *National Observer*, April 9, 2019, https://www.nationalobserver.com/2019/04/09/news/skeptical-trudeaus-carbon-pricing-theres-institute.

Chapter 7

1. "Indian Affairs Prefers to Keep Low Profile," *Edmonton Journal*, March 14, 2004.

2. Indigenous and Northern Affairs Canada, "Public Service Renewal: Working for Reconciliation," December 6, 2016, https://www.aadnc-aandc.gc.ca/eng/148069814 8684/1480698208423.

3. Dan David, "All My Relations," *This Magazine*, 1997.

4. The Royal Commission on Aboriginal Peoples had its origins in a little-known gesture of Tory realpolitik. When Cree NDP parliamentarian Elijah Harper had scuppered the Meech Lake Accord in the spring of 1990 by blocking a needed consensus in the Manitoba legislature, Prime Minister Brian Mulroney included the offer of a Royal Commission in a political package to buy Harper's support for his constitutional designs. Rebuffed then, he repurposed it at the end of the Oka Crisis.

5. Minister of Indian Affairs and Northern Development, "Gathering Strength: Canada's Aboriginal Action Plan," 1997, http://publications.gc.ca/collections/collection_2012/aadnc-aandc/R32-189-1997-eng.pdf.

6. Glen Coulthard, *Red Skin, White Masks: Rejecting the Colonial Politics of Recognition* (Minneapolis, University of Minnesota Press, 2014), 121.

7. See: https://www.kijiji.ca/v-terrain-a-vendre/laval-rive-nord/terrain-a-vendre-oka-pour-auto-construction.

8. APTN News, "Ellen Gabriel and Oka Mayor Have Words at a Protest This Morning," video, 1:46, July 13, 2017, https://www.youtube.com/watch?v=tXm15drUUUs.

9. Personal communication, Ellen Gabriel, May 15, 2018.

10. Arthur Manuel, *The Reconciliation Manifesto* (Toronto: James Lorimer & Company Ltd., 2017).

11. John Paul Tasker, "Ottawa Spent $110k in Legal Fees Fighting First Nations Girl Over $6k Dental Procedure," *CBC News*, September 29, 2017, https://www.cbc.ca/news/politics/health-canada-legal-fees-first-nations-girl-dental-coverage-1.4310224.

12. Carolyn Bennet, "'See You In Court': An Expensive, Time-Consuming Wrong-Headed Strategy," *Huffington Post*, November 14, 2013, https://www.huffingtonpost.ca/hon-carolyn-bennett/aboriginal-litigation-canada_b_4273893.html; Department of Justice, "The Attorney General of Canada's Directive on Civil Litigation Involving Indigenous Peoples," last modified January 11, 2019, https://www.justice.gc.ca/eng/rp-pr/other-autre/litigation-litiges.html;
    Jody Wilson-Raybould, Address to the Premier, BC Cabinet, and Chiefs of BC, November 29, 2018, https://www.justice.gc.ca/eng/news-nouv/speech11292018.html.

13. Jorge Barrera, "Ottawa Initially Fought St. Anne's Residential School Electric Chair Compensation Claims," *CBC News*, December 2, 2017, https://www.cbc.ca/news/indigenous/st-annes-residential-school-electric-chair-compensation-fight-1.4429594; "Ottawa Must Apologize for 'Sixties Scoop' and Compensate Survivors," *Toronto Star*, August 22, 2016, https://www.thestar.com/opinion/editorials/2016/08/22/ottawa-must-apologize-for-sixties-scoop-and-compensate-survivors-editorial.html; "Supreme Court Rules in Favour of Yukon First Nations in Peel Watershed Dispute," *CBC News*, December 1, 2017, https://www.cbc.ca/news/canada/north/peel-watershed-supreme-court-canada-decision-1.4426845; Jorge Barrera, "Ottawa Spent

$2.3M on Court Battles with St. Anne's Residential School Survivors," *CBC News*, September 20, 2018, https://www.cbc.ca/news/indigenous/federal-legal-battle-costs-stannes-residential-school-1.4831887;

John Paul Tasker, "Supreme Court Quashes Seismic Testing in Nunavut, But Gives Green Light to Enbridge Pipeline," *CBC News*, July 26, 2017, https://www.cbc.ca/news/politics/supreme-court-ruling-indigenous-rights-1.4221698;

Kelly Geraldine Malone, "Jane Philpott: Liberal Government Has Complied With Tribunal Ruling On First Nations Child Welfare," *Canadian Press*, April 2, 2018, https://www.huffingtonpost.ca/2018/04/02/jane-philpott-cindy-blackstock-first-nations-child-welfare_a_23400895;

Colin Perkel, "Woman Wins 32-year Fight for Indian Status; Argued Rules Were Discriminatory," *Canadian Press*, April 20, 2017, https://www.cbc.ca/news/indigenous/woman-wins-32-year-fight-for-indian-status-1.4078317;

Kathleen Harris, "Supreme Court Ruling Removes Barrier for Year-round Ski Resort on Sacred First Nation Land," *CBC News*, November 2, 2017, https://www.cbc.ca/news/politics/indigenous-rights-ski-resort-1.4381902.

14. Public Accounts of Canada, "Volume III, Section 3—Professional and Special Services," 2018, https://www.tpsgc-pwgsc.gc.ca/recgen/cpc-pac/2018/vol3/ds3/index-eng.html.

15. Arthur Manuel, *Unsettling Canada: A National Wake-up Call* (Toronto: Between the Lines, 2015), 47.

16. Geoff Dembicki, "'Native Land Claims Scare the Hell Out of Investors': Energy Expert," *The Tyee*, May 19, 2011, https://thetyee.ca/Blogs/TheHook/Environment/2011/05/19/native-land-claims-enbridge-expert.

17. Martin Lukacs, "Aboriginal Rights A Threat To Canada's Resource Agenda, Documents Reveal," *The Guardian*, March 4, 2014, https://www.theguardian.com/environment/true-north/2014/mar/04/aboriginal-rights-canada-resource-agenda.

18. Meeting of the Standing Committee on Indigenous and Northern Affairs, House of Commons of Canada, October 17, 2017, http://www.ourcommons.ca/DocumentViewer/en/42-1/INAN/meeting-75/evidence.

19. BC Treaty Commission press release, "Treaty Negotiations Embody Reconciliation and the UN Declaration," October 13, 2016, http://www.marketwired.com/press-release/treaty-negotiations-embody-reconciliation-and-the-un-declaration-2166480.htm.

20. Jennifer Stahn, "Trudeau: 'Only Communities Can Grant Permission'," *InfoNews.ca*, July 24, 2013, https://infotel.ca/newsitem/trudeau-only-communities-can-grant-permission/it3456; Liberal Party of Canada, "Justin Trudeau's Speech To The Calgary Petroleum Club," October 30, 2013, https://www.liberal.ca/liberal-party-canada-leader-justin-trudeaus-speech-calgary-petroleum-club; APTN News, "Trudeau Talks Pipelines," video, 0:55, November 30, 2016, https://www.youtube.com/watch?v=GMpBiYYGkaA.

21. Bruce Cheadle, "UN Declaration on Rights of Indigenous Peoples 'Should Not Be Scary': Bennett," *Canadian Press,* May 12, 2016, http://www.macleans.ca/news/canada/un-declaration-on-rights-of-indigenous-peoples-should-not-be-scary-bennett.

22. *Cut-Off,* Viceland documentary, February, 2017, https://cutoff.vice.com/page/documentary; Jorge Barrera, "Trudeau Government Eyeing Nwt's 'Collaborative Consent' Model As Part of UNDRIP Implementation," *APTN News*, May 9, 2016, https://aptnnews.ca/2016/05/09/trudeau-government-eyeing-nwts-collaborate-consent-model-as-part-of-undrip-implementation.

23. Larry Innes, Merrell-Ann Phare, and Michael Miltenberger, "Collaborative Consent: Considering a Framework for Building Nation-to-Nation Relationships in Environmental Assessment," presentation, 2016, https://d3n8a8pro7vhmx.cloudfront.net/envirolawsmatter/pages/290/attachments/original/1461534532/Phare_Miltenberger_Innes_Beyond_EA_Final.pptx.pdf.

24. Indeed, there was a deep connection between bodily and territorial violations: sexual and gender violence has always been integral to land dispossession. The attacks on Indigenous bodies and minds—once carried out through the residential schools, and today through the child welfare system, Christianity, patriarchal norms—has been about breaking Indigenous peoples, and breaking their connection to land. Anishnaabe writer and professor Leanne Betasamosake Simpson describes the procession of theft that extends beyond land alone, "expansive dispossession." "The removal and erasure of [Indigenous] bodies from land makes it easier for the state to acquire and maintain sovereignty over land because this not only removes physical resistance to dispossession, it also erases the political orders and relationships housed within Indigenous bodies that attach our bodies to the land." Leanne Betasamosake Simpson, *As We Have Always Done: Indigenous Freedom through Radical Resistance* (Minneapolis: University of Minnesota Press, 2017), 43, 87.

25. "Trudeau Says First Nations 'Don't Have a Veto' Over Energy Projects," *Postmedia News*, December 21, 2016, http://business.financialpost.com/news/trudeau-says-first-nations-dont-have-a-veto-over-energy-projects.

26. Peter O'Neil, "The Inside Story of Kinder Morgan's Approval," *Vancouver Sun*, January 6, 2017, https://vancouversun.com/news/local-news/the-inside-story-of-kinder-morgans-approval.

27. A poll commissioned by the BC environmental organization the Dogwood Collective offers a fascinating confirmation of the power of a fear-mongering phrase. When British Columbians were asked if Indigenous peoples should have a "veto" over pipelines, only 33 percent said yes. But when asked if they should have "final say over resource developments on their land," support jumped massively to 52 percent. And when asked if governments should "obtain their consent," support increased further to 57 percent. (Source: unpublished poll)

28. The Yellowhead Institute, "Legislation on Indigenous Issues," June 2018, https://yellowheadinstitute.org/resources/legislation-on-indigenous-issues-2/, https://yellowheadinstitute.org/wp-content/uploads/2018/06/yi-indigenous-legislation-infographic.pdf.

29. "We have heard that some Indigenous groups continue to equate these techniques to the extinguishment of rights, which does not reflect evolving nation-to-nation relationships," the government said. "Although these techniques move us towards greater flexibility in agreements, it is anticipated that the new policy that will be developed under the Framework may go further in seeking to achieve intergovernmental agreements that provide predictability and enable the continuation of rights (rather than extinguishing rights) through evolutionary provisions and periodic review processes." Parliament of Canada, "Government of Canada Response to the Standing Committee on Indigenous and Northern Affairs," February 2018, https://www.ourcommons.ca/DocumentViewer/en/42-1/INAN/report-12/response-8512-421-356.

30. Jody Wilson-Raybould, "The Recognition and Implementation of Rights Framework Talk," *Department of Justice Canada*, April 13, 2018, https://www.canada.ca/en/department-justice/news/2018/04/the-recognition-and-implementation-of-rights-framework-talk-1.html.

31. Chantelle Bellrichard, "Budget 2019: $1.4B In Loans To Be Forgiven Or Reimbursed To Indigenous Groups for Treaty Negotiations," *CBC News,* March 19, 2019, https://www.cbc.ca/news/indigenous/budget-2019-treaty-loans-forgiven-1.5063128.

32. "Justice Minister Jody Wilson-Raybould Says Adopting UNDRIP Into Canadian Law 'Unworkable'," *APTN News,* July 12, 2016, https://aptnnews.ca/2016/07/12/justice-minister-jody-wilson-raybould-says-adopting-undrip-into-canadian-law-unworkable.

33. The Yellowhead Institute, "Carceral Colonialism in Canada: Systemic Racism & Corrections Canada Risk Assessments," September 2018, https://yellowheadinstitute.org/wp-content/uploads/2018/09/carceral-colonialism-in-canada-final-version.pdf.

34. John Geddes, "Jody Wilson-Raybould's Vision to Save Canada," *Maclean's,* March 2, 2018, http://www.macleans.ca/politics/ottawa/jody-wilson-rayboulds-vision-to-save-canada.

35. Jody Wilson-Raybould, "Recognition, Reconciliation and Indigenous People's Disproportionate Interactions with the Criminal Justice System," *Department of Justice Canada,* September 13, 2018, https://www.justice.gc.ca/eng/news-nouv/speech.html; Jody Wilson-Raybould, "Opening Remarks at 'Raising the Bar: Indigenous Women's Impact on the Law-scape,'" *Department of Justice Canada,* October 30, 2018, https://www.canada.ca/en/department-justice/news/2019/01/opening-remarks-at-raising-the-bar-indigenous-womens-impact-on-the-law-scape.html; Department of Justice Canada, "Address by the Honourable Jody Wilson-Raybould, PC, QC, MP to the BC Leaders Gathering," November 29, 2018, https://www.justice.gc.ca/eng/news-nouv/speech11292018.html.

36. Jorge Barrera, "Trudeau Told Aesop's Fable About Sun and Wind During Meeting With AFN Chiefs," *CBC News, January 30, 2019,* https://www.cbc.ca/news/indigenous/trudeau-aesop-fable-afn-meeting-1.4997980.

37. "Indigenous Activist Kanahus Manuel Arrested After Trans Mountain Protest in B.C.," *Canadian Press,* July 15, 2018, https://www.nationalobserver.com/2018/07/15/news/indigenous-activist-kanahus-manuel-arrested-after-trans-mountain-protest-bc.

Chapter 8

1. Paul Magnette, *CETA: Quand l'Europe déraille* (Waterloo: Luc Pire, 2017), 68.

2. Magnette, *CETA,* 69.

3. Les Whittington, "Ottawa Faces $250-Million Suit Over Quebec Environmental Stance," *Toronto Star,* November 15, 2012, https://www.thestar.com/news/canada/2012/11/15/ottawa_faces_250million_suit_over_quebec_environmental_stance.html.

4. Robert Fife, "Trudeau's Davos Trip 'All About Selling Canada'," *The Globe and Mail,* January 22, 2016, https://www.theglobeandmail.com/news/politics/trudeau-insists-davos-trip-all-about-selling-canada-as-place-to-invest/article28361304.

5. Scott Sinclair and Stuart Trew, "What Trade Agreements Have Meant for Canada," in *Canada after Harper,* edited by Ed Finn (Toronto: James Lorimer & Company Ltd., 2015).

6. Magnette, *CETA,* 67.

7. Magnette, *CETA*, 76.
8. Magnette, *CETA*, 73.
9. Magnette, *CETA*, 74.
10. Magnette, *CETA*, 76.
11. Magnette, *CETA*, 90.
12. Magnette, *CETA*, 83-85.
13. Magnette, *CETA*, 127.
14. "Paul Magnette ne croit pas aux larmes "stratégiques" de Mme Freeland lors des négociations CETA," *RTBF*, February 9, 2017, https://www.rtbf.be/info/insolites/ detail_paul-magnette-ne-croit-pas-aux-larmes-strategiques-de-mme-freeland-lors-des-negociations-ceta?id=9526181.
15. In her previous life as a journalist, Freeland had been well-aware of the deep problems with trade. In writing about the U.S.-China trade relationship, she wrote: "What is striking, and frightening, is the extent to which, at least in the U.S.-China trade relationship, the knee-jerk, populist fears intellectuals tend to deride actually turned out to be true. Shipping middle-class jobs to China, or hollowing them out with machines, is a win for smart managers and their shareholders. We call the result higher productivity. But, looked at through the lens of middle-class jobs, it is a loss. That profound difference is why politics in the rich democracies are so polarized right now. Capitalism and democracy are at cross-purposes, and no one yet has a clear plan for reconciling them." But if in her previous life she was critical of trade deals, in government she would become a savvy spokesperson for them. Chrystia Freeland, "Technology, Trade and Fewer Jobs," *New York Times*, February 14, 2013, https://www.nytimes.com/2013/02/15/us/15iht-letter15.html.
16. Maude Barlow and Sujata Dey, "Liberals Should Consistently Fight Trade Deals That Let Corporations Sue Canada," *Huffington Post*, October 19, 2018, https://www.huffingtonpost.ca/maude-barlow/free-trade-investor-state-dispute-settlement_a_23566289; Greg Quinn, "Canadian Opposition to Nafta's Chapter 11 Gives Trudeau Leeway," *Bloomberg*, April 17, 2018, https://www.bloomberg.com/news/ articles/2018-04-17/canadian-opposition-to-nafta-s-chapter-11-gives-trudeau-leeway.
17. Hugh Stephens, "Canada's 'Progressive' Trade Agenda: Let's Be Careful How Far We Push It," *Canadian Global Affairs Institute*, January 2018, https://www.cgai.ca/ canadas_progressive_trade_agenda_lets_be_careful_how_far_we_push_it.
18. Marie-Danielle Smith, "Canadian Officials Instructed To Stop Using 'Progressive' To Describe Trade Deals, Documents Show," *National Post*, July 4, 2019, https://nation-alpost.com/news/politics/canadian-officials-instructed-to-stop-using-progressive-to-describe-trade-deals-documents-show.
19. Paul Wells, "Trudeau and Cabinet Woo International Money: Paul Wells," *Toronto Star*, November 15, 2016, https://www.thestar.com/news/canada/2016/11/15/ trudeau-and-cabinet-woo-international-money-paul-wells.html.
20. Bill Curry, "Private-Sector Role in Canada Infrastructure Bank Raises Conflict-of-Interest Questions," *The Globe and Mail*, May 5, 2017, https://www. theglobeandmail.com/news/politics/ottawas-dealings-to-secure-infrastructure-funds-raise-questions/article34904963.
21. Andy Blatchford, "What is BlackRock, and Why Does It Matter Now in Ottawa?" *Maclean's*, May 11, 2017, https://www.macleans.ca/politics/blackrock-liberal-canada-infrastructure.
22. The report recommended loosening "outdated accounting rules" and "government red tape" to provide better returns on infrastructure investments. FCLTGlobal, "2015 Long-Term Value Summit: Discussion Report," https://www.

fcltglobal.org/docs/default-source/default-document-library/fclt_march-10-ltv-summit-discussion-report.pdf; BlackRock Transparency Projcct, "New Evidence Shows Blackrock's Role in Canada Infrastructure Bank May Have Also Included Advising on Key Personnel," August 27, 2018, https://blackrocktransparencyproject.org/2018/08/27/how-canadas-infrastructure-bank-was-created-by-and-set-up-to-benefit-blackrock.

23. A report by the Canadian Centre for Policy Alternatives noted that the plan had "taken a 180 degrees turn"—shifting from "providing low-cost financing to 'leveraging' higher cost private sector financing for infrastructure."
Toby Sanger, "Creating a Canadian Infrastructure Bank in the Public Interest," *Canadian Centre for Policy Alternatives*, March 2017, https://www.policyalternatives.ca/newsroom/news-releases/private-financing-infrastructure-bank-could-double-cost-infrastructure.

24. Bill Curry, "Private-Sector Role."

25. The Canadian Council for Public-Private Partnerships, "Keynote Speakers from 22nd Annual CCPPP National Conference on Public-Private Partnerships," video, 2:12, November 14, 2014, https://www.youtube.com/watch?v=VvUi1k6uxas.

26. Toby Sanger, "Ontario Audit Throws Cold Water on Federal-provincial Love Affair With P3s," Canadian Centre for Policy Alternatives, February 2, 2015, https://www.policyalternatives.ca/publications/monitor/ontario-audit-throws-cold-water-federal-provincial-love-affair-p3s.

27. Bill Curry, "Private-Sector Role."

28. Jason Magder, "Trudeau Confirms $1.283 Billion in Federal Cash for REM Train," *Montreal Gazette*, June 15, 2017, https://montrealgazette.com/news/local-news/federal-money-moves-rem-closer-to-funding-6-million-price-tag.

29. Within the first year of the announcement, it was already set to cost $300 million more, and be built one year later than promised.

30. Dalton McGuinty, *Making a Difference*, 162.

31. Kevin Connor, "Public Support for Public-Private Partnerships Plummets: Poll," *Toronto Sun*, November 14, 2016, http://www.torontosun.com/2016/11/14/public-support-for-public-private-partnerships-plummets-poll.

32. Blair Redlin, "Secretive, Risky, Unaccountable: How Public-Private Partnerships are Bad for Democracy," *Parkland Institute Conference*, November 21, 2004, https://cupe.ca/sites/cupe/files/rptbr_Secretive_Risky_Unaccountable_P3_Bad_for_Democracy_1.26.05.pdf.

Chapter 9

1. Sarah Aziza, "Body Politic," *Harper's Magazine*, January 2018, 57-62, https://harpers.org/archive/2018/01/body-politic-4.

2. Mark Mazzetti and Ben Hubbard, "It Wasn't Just Khashoggi: A Saudi Prince's Brutal Drive to Crush Dissent," *New York Times*, March 17, 2019, https://www.nytimes.com/2019/03/17/world/middleeast/khashoggi-crown-prince-saudi.html.

3. "Saudi Arabia Declares Online Satire Punishable Offence," *Yahoo News*, September 4, 2018, https://sg.news.yahoo.com/saudi-arabia-declares-online-satire-punishable-offence-133356688.html.

4. "Reposting in light of today's arms deal with Saudi Arabia. Principled foreign policy indeed. via @iyad_elbaghdadi" (@gmbutts, January 21, 2015), https://twitter.com/gmbutts/status/558031167837179906; Michael Petrou, "Why is Canada Making

Arms Deals with the Saudis?" *Maclean's*, January 14, 2016, https://www.macleans.ca/politics/worldpolitics/why-is-canada-making-arms-deals-with-the-saudis; J. Pederson, "We Will Honour Our Good Name: The Trudeau Government, Arms Exports and Human Rights" in *Justin Trudeau and Canadian Foreign Policy*, eds. Norman Hillmer and Philippe Lagassé (Cham, Switzerland: Palgrave Macmillan, 2018), 207-233.

5.   Memo from Global Affairs Canada, "Visit to Ottawa of H.E. Abdel Al Jubeir, Foreign Minister of the Kingdom of Saudi Arabia," obtained through an access-to-information request, https://www.dropbox.com/s/md3vev12ndp6trx/A201601091_2017-01-13_09-49-16.PDF?dl=0.

6.   David Pugliese, "John Manley Thinks An Armoured Vehicle With a 105mm Gun Is Just a 'Fancy Truck'," *Ottawa Citizen*, April 24, 2016, https://ottawacitizen.com/news/national/defence-watch/john-manley-thinks-an-armoured-vehicle-with-a-105mm-gun-is-just-a-fancy-truck.

7.   Steven Chase and Daniel Leblanc, "Armoured Vehicles In Saudi Deal Will Pack Lethal Punch," *The Globe and Mail*, January 6, 2018, https://www.theglobeandmail.com/news/politics/armoured-vehicles-in-saudi-deal-will-pack-lethal-punch/article28046099/; Army Recognition, *CMI Defence Cockerill CT-CV 105HP Weapon System (105 mm)*, 2019, Photograph, online digital database Army-Military-Defense, https://www.armyrecognition.com/belgium_belgian_light_heavy_weapons_uk/ct-cv_weapon_system_105_120_mm_turret_armoured_armored_cockerill_gun_vehicle_design_development_prod.html.

8.   The exercise in renaming was inspired by a report from *PressProgress*: "John Manley Claims These Things Canada Is Selling to Saudi Arabia Are 'Basically Fancy Trucks," April 25, 2016, https://pressprogress.ca/john_manley_claims_these_things_canada_is_selling_to_saudi_arabia_are_basically_fancy_trucks.

9.   Justin Ling, "Exclusive: Canada Isn't Being Totally Honest About Its Plan to Sell Weapons to Saudi Arabia," *Vice News*, July 12, 2016, https://news.vice.com/article/exclusive-canada-isnt-being-totally-honest-about-its-plan-to-sell-weapons-to-saudi-arabia.

10. Global Affairs Canada Memorandum for Action, "Export of Light-Armoured Vehicles and Weapons Systems to Saudi Arabia," March 21, 2016, http://www.international.gc.ca/controls-controles/assets/pdfs/documents/Memorandum_for_Action-eng.pdf.

11. Ethan Bronner and Michael Slackman, "Saudi Troops Enter Bahrain to Help Put Down Unrest," *New York Times*, March 14, 2011, https://www.nytimes.com/2011/03/15/world/middleeast/15bahrain.html.

12. Patrick Cockburn, "The Yemen War Death Toll is Five Times Higher Than We Think – We Can't Shrug Off Our Responsibilities Any Longer," *Independent*, October 26, 2018, https://www.independent.co.uk/voices/yemen-war-death-toll-saudi-arabia-allies-how-many-killed-responsibility-a8603326.html.

13. Palko Karasz, "85,00 Children in Yemen May Have Died of Starvation," *New York Times*, November 21, 2018, https://www.nytimes.com/2018/11/21/world/middleeast/yemen-famine-children.html.

14. Hannah Summers, "Yemen On Brink of 'World's Worst Famine in 100 Years' If War Continues," *The Guardian*, October 15, 2018, https://www.theguardian.com/global-development/2018/oct/15/yemen-on-brink-worst-famine-100-years-un.

15. Hugo Joncas, "Des armes fabriquées au Québec pour la guerre au Yémen," *Journal De Montreal*, January 12, 2019, https://www.journaldemontreal.com/2019/01/12/fabriques-ici-pour-tuer.

16. The following draws from my investigative report in the *National Observer*. Martin Lukacs, "Experts Say There's Proof Canadian-Made Weapons Are Being Used in Saudi War in Yemen," *National Observer*, November 30, 2018, https://www.nationalobserver.com/2018/11/30/news/experts-say-theres-proof-canadian-made-weapons-are-being-used-saudi-war-yemen.

17. Steven Chase, "Canada Now the Second Biggest Arms Exporter to Middle East," *The Globe and Mail*, June 14, 2016, https://www.theglobeandmail.com/news/politics/canada-now-the-second-biggest-arms-exporter-to-middle-east-data-show/article30459788.

18. Shanifa Nasser, "Saudi Arabia Put These 2 Men to Death. Now Their Families Are Calling on Canada to Stop Arming the Regime," *CBC News*, May 2, 2019, https://www.cbc.ca/news/canada/toronto/saudi-canada-executions-arms-1.5117422.

19. Human Rights Watch, "Saudi Arabia: Mass Execution Largest Since 1980," January 4, 2016, https://www.hrw.org/news/2016/01/04/saudi-arabia-mass-execution-largest-1980; Human Rights Watch, "Saudi Arabia: 14 Protesters Facing Execution After Unfair Trials," June 6, 2017, https://www.hrw.org/news/2017/06/06/saudi-arabia-14-protesters-facing-execution-after-unfair-trials.

20. United Nations Special Rapporteurs' letter to Saudi Arabia concerning the alleged demolition of the historic neighbourhood of Al-Masora in the town of Awamia, Eastern Province of the Kingdom of Saudi Arabia, March 27, 2017, https://spcommreports.ohchr.org/TMResultsBase/DownLoadPublicCommunicationFile?gId=23022.

21. Human Rights Watch, "Saudi Arabia: Security Forces Seal Off Eastern Town," August 13, 2017, https://www.hrw.org/news/2017/08/13/saudi-arabia-security-forces-seal-eastern-town.

22. "Despite our attempt to raise concerns and seek explanation from the Government about the planned destruction, bulldozers and demolition vehicles, assisted by armed military forces, have reportedly started on 10 May to destroy buildings and homes in the walled historic neighborhood and in other areas of Awamia, causing injury, deaths and material losses to the civilians residents," the group of UN experts said. "Historic buildings have been irremediably burned down and damaged by the use of various weapons by the military, forcing residents out of their homes and of the neighborhood, fleeing for their lives," noted the Special Rapporteur in the field of cultural rights, Karima Bennoune. Excerpt from: The United Nations Commission on Human Rights, "Saudi Arabia's Use of Force and Demolitions in the Al-Masora Neighborhood Violates Human Rights," May 24, 2017, https://www.ohchr.org/FR/NewsEvents/Pages/DisplayNews.aspx?NewsID=21657&LangID=E.

23. Sally Nabil, "Awamiya: Inside Saudi Shia Town Devastated by Demolitions and Fighting," *BBC News*, 16 August 2017, https://www.bbc.com/news/world-middle-east-40937581 https://www.reuters.com/article/us-saudi-security-awamiya/saudi-security-forces-flatten-old-quarter-of-shiite-town-idUSKBN1AP21S.

24. Fenton wrote an email describing his findings to *Globe and Mail* journalist Steve Chase, who, according to government documents released through access-to-information, forwarded the email to the Ministry of Global Affairs, asking for comment. A flurry of emails then passed between government officials and Minister Freeland.

25. "This is a very important issue, we're deeply concerned about it and we're looking into it to determine the facts carefully, very actively and energetically." Taken from Levon Sevunts, "Freeland Says Officials Urgently Reviewing Reports Canadian Arms Used in Saudi Crackdown," *CBC News*, August 8, 2017, https://www.cbc.ca/news/politics/saudi-arabia-armoured-vehicles-investigation-canada-1.4238564; "Ottawa

Investigates 'With Sense of Urgency' New Reports of Canadian Arms Used in Saudi Crackdown," *Radio Canada International*, August 7, 2017, http://www.rcinet.ca/en/2017/08/07/ottawa-investigates-with-sense-of-urgency-new-reports-of-canadian-arms-used-in-saudi-crackdown.

26. Melanie Marquis, "No Evidence Saudis Used Canadian-Made Armoured Vehicles in Human Rights Abuses: Freeland," *Canadian Press*, Feb 8, 2018, https://globalnews.ca/news/4014830/no-evidence-canadian-lavs-used-by-saudis.

27. Global Affairs Canada Memorandum for Action, "Export Permit Suspension: Munitions List Item to Saudi Arabia," October 10, 2017, https://www.international.gc.ca/controls-controles/assets/pdfs/documents/memorandum-memo.pdf.

28. When it released its first report in 2007, its president declared how well it reflected on the government. When Jamal Khashoggi was murdered by the Saudi government, the group praised the Saudi government's investigations and said the following: "We deeply regret the efforts of some regional, international and human rights bodies to politicize this case, with the aim of serving some agendas and attitudes against the Kingdom's policies, without any consideration for justice or consideration of the feelings of his family and relatives." There is a simple way to identify real human rights advocates in Saudi Arabia: they are behind bars.
   Americans for Democracy and Human Rights in Bahrain, "Mapping the Saudi State, Chapter 9: National Human Rights Institutions," December 2015, https://www.adhrb.org/wp-content/uploads/2015/12/MSS-Ch.-9_Final.pdf; Staff writer, "Human rights group: Khashoggi case should be left to investigators, not media," *Al Arabiya*, August 5, 2019, http://english.alarabiya.net/en/News/gulf/2018/10/14/Human-rights-group-Khashoggi-case-should-be-left-to-investigators-not-media.html.

29. Cesar Jaramillo, "Call for Independent, External Review into Reports of Misuse of Canadian Military Exports," letter to Minister of Foreign Affairs, 2018, https://group78.org/letter-to-minister-of-foreign-affairs-calling-for-saudi-arms-export-investigation.

30. Norman Webster, "Saudi Oasis Jumps As Trudeau Dances," *The Globe and Mail*, November 20, 1980.

31. "Saudi Arabians Behead 63 for Attack on Mosque," *Washington Post*, January 10, 1980, https://www.washingtonpost.com/archive/politics/1980/01/10/saudi-arabians-behead-63-for-attack-on-mosque/18063a57-ba6f-47e3-bdc0-05c1059b6961/?utm_term=.d1ef2915a49e.

32. There is another historical twist. Alongside the relaxing of the export policies, the Trudeau government helped a General Motors division—decades later to be bought by General Dynamics Land Systems—to convert their factory in London, Ontario. Until then, they had spent decades making parts for trains. Now they would make military vehicles.
   John Lamb and Ernie Regehr, "Time to Review Canada's Arms Export Policy," *Disarming Conflict*, January 31, 2016, http://disarmingconflict.ca/2016/01/31/time-to-review-canadas-military-exports-policy.

33. ITCOTT to ITCJEDDA on 21 January 1981, Subject line: Saudi Arabia - Armored Vehicles (AVGP*) RG25-A-3-C. Volume/box number: 16821. File number: 37-22-1-SAUDI. File Part 4, p. 96.

34. Anna Stavrianakis, "History Won't Look Kindly on Britain Over Arms Sales Feeding War in Yemen," *The Guardian*, November 30, 2018, https://www.theguardian.com/ global-development/2018/nov/30/history-will-not-look-kindly-on-britain-over-arms-sales-feeding-war-in-yemen; "France's Macron Evades Questions on Halting Saudi Arms Sales," *France 24*, October 24, 2018, https://www.france24.com/ en/20181024-french-macron-questions-saudi-arms-deals-merkel-german-khashoggi-murder.

35. Elise von Scheel, "Trudeau Tells Mohammed bin Salman Canada Will 'Always Stand Up Strongly' For Human Rights", *CBC News*, December 1, 2018, https://www.cbc. ca/news/politics/trudeau-putin-salman-g20-1.4928996.

36. Martin Chulov and Ashifa Kassam, "A Tweet, Then a Trade Freeze: Latest Row Shows Saudi Arabia is Asserting New Rules," *The Guardian*, August 7, 2018, https:// www.theguardian.com/world/2018/aug/07/saudi-arabia-canada-spat-analysis.

37. Ashifa Kassam, "Saudi Arabia Expels Canadian Envoy for Urging Activists' Release," *The Guardian*, August 6, 2018, https://www.theguardian.com/world/2018/aug/06/ saudi-arabia-expels-canadian-ambassador-for-urging-release-of-activists.

38. Ashifa Kassam, "Saudi Arabia Expels Canadian Envoy for Urging Activists' Release," *The Guardian*, August 6, 2018, https://www.theguardian.com/world/2018/aug/06/ saudi-arabia-expels-canadian-ambassador-for-urging-release-of-activists.

39. Samantha Wright Allen, "Arms Exports to Saudi Arabia Reach $1.2 Billion in 2018, Despite Calls for Canada to Suspend Permits," *The Hill Times*, July 3, 2019, https:// www.hilltimes.com/2019/07/03/arms-exports-to-saudi-arabia-reach-1-2-million-in-2018-despite-calls-for-canada-to-suspend-permits/206114; "Arms exports to Saudi Arabia reach $1.2-million in 2018, despite calls for Canada to suspend permits #cdnpoli" (@TheHillTimes, July 3, 2019). https://twitter.com/TheHillTimes/status/1146383082410242049.

40. Lisa Cox, "Australia Too Slow in Considering Saudi Teen's Asylum Bid, Rights Group Says," *The Guardian*, January 12, 2019, https://www.theguardian.com/ australia-news/2019/jan/12/australia-too-slow-in-considering-saudi-teens-asylum-bid-rights-group-says; Hannah Ellis Peterson, "Saudi Woman Fleeing Family Flies to Canada After Gaining Asylum," *The Guardian*, January 11, 2019, https://www. theguardian.com/world/2019/jan/11/canada-and-australia-in-talks-with-un-to-accept-saudi-asylum-seeker-rahaf-mohammed-al-qunun.

Chapter 10

1. Manny Fernandez, "You Have to Pay with Your Body': The Hidden Nightmare of Sexual Violence on the Border," *New York Times*, March 3, 2019, https://www. nytimes.com/2019/03/03/us/border-rapes-migrant-women.html.

2. Access-to-information documents shared by Solidarity Across Borders.

3. Patrick Cain, "These 14 Countries Have Taken More Refugees Than Canada," *Global News*, September 20, 2016, globalnews.ca/news/2951263/these-14-countries-have-taken-more-refugees-than-canada.

4. Sammy Hudes, "Ottawa's New Cap on Refugee Applications Upsets Sponsors," *Toronto Star*, December 24, 2016, https://www.thestar.com/news/canada/2016/12/24/ottawas-new-cap-on-refugee-applications-upsets-sponsors.html.

5.   Martin Lukacs, "Justin Trudeau's Tweets Won't Make Canada a Refugee Haven – But Popular Pressure Can," *The Guardian*, January 31, 2017, https://www.theguardian.com/environment/true-north/2017/jan/30/justin-trudeaus-tweets-wont-make-canada-a-refugee-havenbut-popular-pressure-can.

6.   Ashifa Kassam, "Activists Challenge 'Unsafe' US-Canada Pact That Prompts Refugees to Flee by Foot," *The Guardian*, July 6, 2017, https://www.theguardian.com/world/2017/jul/06/canada-us-refugees-safe-third-country-agreement-border-crossing.

7.   Amnesty International, "Legal Challenge of Safe Third Country Agreement Launched," July 5, 2017, https://www.amnesty.ca/news/legal-challenge-safe-third-country-agreement-launched; Nicholas Keung, "Canadian Law Profs Join Fight to Suspend Refugee Pact with U.S.," *Toronto Star*, February 1, 2017, https://www.thestar.com/news/immigration/2017/02/01/canadian-law-profs-join-fight-to-suspend-refugee-pact-with-us.html.

8.   Anna Mehler Paperny, "Canada Ramps Up Deportations Amid Growing Migrant Influx," *Reuters*, August 24, 2017, https://www.reuters.com/article/us-usa-immigration-canada-deportation/canada-ramps-up-deportations-amid-growing-migrant-influx-idUSKCN1B42QE.

9.   Immigration and Refugee Board of Canada. "Irregular Border Crosser Statistics," May 17, 2019, https://irb-cisr.gc.ca/en/statistics/Pages/Irregular-border-crosser-statistics.aspx.

10.   "The Tests Facing Canada's PM Justin Trudeau in 2018," *BBC News*, December 25, 2017, https://www.bbc.com/news/world-us-canada-42434702.

11.   Nik Barry-Shaw and Yves Engler, " November 2006: How Canadians 'Protect' in Haiti," *Canadian Centre for Policy Alternatives*, November 1, 2006, https://www.policyalternatives.ca/publications/monitor/november-2006-how-canadians-protect-haiti.

12.   Yves Engler and Anthony Fenton, *Canada in Haiti: Waging War on the Poor Majority* (Black Point, NS: Fernwood, 2004).

13.   Janice Gross Stein and Eugene Lang, *Unexpected War in Afghanistan: Canada in Kandahar* (Toronto, Viking Canada Press, 2007).

14.   Mike M. Ahlers and Mike Mount, "Radio Station in the Sky Warns Haitians Not to Attempt Boat Voyage," *CNN*, January 19, 2010, https://www.cnn.com/2010/WORLD/americas/01/19/haiti.broadcast.warning/index.html; Mark Thompson, "How the U.S. Military Will Help Haiti," *Time*, January 13, 2010, http://content.time.com/time/specials/packages/article/0,28804,1953379_1953494_1953445,00.html; Sgt. Angela Brees, "190th Trains in Cuba; Deploys to Haiti," *Air Force Print News Today*, August 14, 2014, https://web.archive.org/web/20140814030225/http://www.190arw.ang.af.mil/news/story_print.asp?id=123187603.

15.   Ed Pilkington and Ben Quinn, "UN Admits for the First Time That Peacekeepers Brought Cholera to Haiti," *The Guardian*, December 1, 2016, https://www.theguardian.com/global-development/2016/dec/01/haiti-cholera-outbreak-stain-on-reputation-un-says.

16.   Anna Mehler Paperny, "Canada to Take in Migrants at 'Gradual' Pace Amid Integration Concerns," *Reuters*, November 2, 2017, https://ca.reuters.com/article/topNews/idCAKBN1D22N3-OCATP.

17.   Teresa Wright, "Canada Deemed U.S. a Safe Country for Asylum Seekers After Internal Review," *National Post*, October 22, 2018, https://nationalpost.com/pmn/news-pmn/canada-news-pmn/canada-deemed-u-s-a-safe-country-for-asylum-seekers-after-internal-review.

18. Anna Mehler Paperny, "Canada's Trudeau Grilled on Efforts to Turn Back Asylum Seekers," *Reuters*, May 1, 2018, https://www.reuters.com/article/us-canada-immigration-border/canadas-trudeau-grilled-on-efforts-to-turn-back-asylum-seekers-idUSK-BN1I24L8.

19. Anna Mehler Paperny, "Canada Wants U.S. Cooperation in Turning Back Asylum Seekers," *Reuters*, April 30, 2018, https://www.reuters.com/article/us-canada-immigration-border/canada-wants-u-s-cooperation-in-turning-back-asylum-seekers-idUSKBN1I12AR.

20. Anna Mehler Paperny, "Canada to Take in Migrants at 'Gradual' Pace Amid Integration Concerns," *Reuters*, November 2, 2017, https://ca.reuters.com/article/topNews/idCAKBN1D22N3-OCATP.

21. Anna Mehler Paperny, "Flow of Asylum Seekers to Canada Begins to Slow Amid Traveler Crackdown," *Reuters*, July 12, 2018, https://ca.reuters.com/article/topNews/idCAKBN1K23D3-OCATP.

22. No One Is Illegal-Vancouver, "No Refuge, Conditional Home for refugees," *Never Home*, 2015, www.neverhome.ca/refugees

23. End Immigration Detention Network, "Detentions Watchdog Calls for Immediate Federal Action After Ontario Sanctions the Continued Imprisonment of Long-Term Detainee," October 5, 2017, https://endimmigrationdetention.com.

24. Nicholas Keung, "UN Alarmed by Canada's Immigration Detention," *Toronto Star*, July 23, 2015, https://www.thestar.com/news/immigration/2015/07/23/un-alarmed-by-canadas-immigration-detention.html.

25. Anna Mehler Paperny, "Exclusive: Canada Rushes to Deport Asylum Seekers Who Walked from U.S.," *Reuters*, October 31, 2018, https://www.reuters.com/article/us-canada-immigration-deportation-exclus/exclusive-canada-rushes-to-deport-asylum-seekers-who-walked-from-u-s-data-idUSKCN1N52V6.

26. "Against Borders, Against Prisons. Stop the Laval Migrant Prison," *Stop the Prison,* accessed April 20, 2019, https://www.stopponslaprison.info/en/home.

Chapter 11

1. Justin Haskins, "Alexandria Ocasio-Cortez's 'Green New Deal' Is Actually an Old Socialist Plan From Canada," *Fox News*, January 19, 2019, https://www.foxnews.com/opinion/alexandria-ocasio-cortezs-green-new-deal-is-actually-an-old-socialist-plan-from-canada.

2. "Ocasio-Cortez Sparks 'Socialism' Lookups," *Merriam Webster*, 2018, https://www.merriam-webster.com/news-trend-watch/ocasio-cortez-sparks-socialism-lookups-20180627.

3. United States Congress, "Introduction of House Resolution 109: Recognizing the Duty of the Federal Government to Create a Green New Deal," Introduced February 7, 2019, https://www.congress.gov/bill/116th-congress/house-resolution/109/text.

4. Tony Clarke, *Silent Coup: Confronting the Big Business Takeover of Canada* (Toronto: James Lorimer & Company Ltd., 1997), 20.

5. David Z. Berlin and Howard Aster, *What's Left? The New Democratic Party in Renewal* (Oakville,Ontario: Mosaic Press, 2001).

6. Brad Lavigne, *Building the Orange Wave* (Madeira Park, B.C: Douglas & McIntyre, 2013).

7. Murray Cooke and Dennis Pilon, "Left Turn in Canada? The NDP Breakthrough and the Future of Canadian Politics," *Rosa Luxemburg Foundation*, October 2012, http://www.rosalux-nyc.org/left-turn-in-canada-the-ndp-breakthrough-and-the-future-of-canadian-politics/.

8. Brad Lavigne, *Building the Orange Wave.*

9. LeftTurn, "Thomas Mulcair Shares His Views On Thatcherism," video, 1:18, August 15, 2015, https://www.youtube.com/watch?v=VZzSSp7ag-A; Susana Mas, "Tom Mulcair Defends Praise for Margaret Thatcher's Winds of Liberty and Liberalism," *CBC News*, August 19, 2015, http://www.cbc.ca/news/politics/tom-mulcair-defends-praise-for-margaret-thatcher-s-winds-of-liberty-and-liberalism-1.3196265.

10. The full resolution, passed by nearly 20 riding associations: "WHEREAS the Leap Manifesto, (https://leapmanifesto.org) already endorsed by tens of thousands of Canadians, proposes a model of climate justice; WHEREAS social, environmental and economic issues are intertwined; WHEREAS private action and unenforceable international declarations fail to reduce dependence on fossil fuels; WHEREAS democratically shared resources, respect for aboriginal rights, rebuilding of the public sphere, expansion of public transit, affordable green-engineered housing, and universal social services are needed to counter dependence on non-renewable resources; WHEREAS democratic control of non-renewable power sources is essential to foster an economy that places human need above profit; WHEREAS the Leap Manifesto provides an overarching narrative and goals that can inspire a vision for the NDP to unite with the climate justice and other social movements; WHEREAS the perception of the NDP as the vehicle for lessening income inequality, providing well-paying green jobs, committed to opposing the headlong drive to climate disaster is presently blurred in the electoral mind; THEREFORE, BE IT RESOLVED THAT the New Democratic Party endorse the Leap Manifesto; AND FURTHER BE IT RESOLVED THAT the New Democratic Party promote the vision of the Leap Manifesto in all its future electoral endeavors."

11. New Democratic conventions are byzantine affairs. The ranking of resolution is set in the months before convention by the party's central office. Under Jack Layton, the party had introduced a new element in the vetting of resolutions, modelled after the Saskatchewan provincial party's convention process. Resolutions would also now be discussed in "prioritization" meetings the early morning of the first day of the convention. Any delegate who showed up to these meetings could vote resolutions up or down on the initial priority list, thus improving or decreasing the chances of it being voted on at the main plenary. This model was lauded by party officials as a democracy-enhancing measure, giving more power to the delegates. But these "prioritization" meetings were closed to the media and lacking the scrutiny of an open and accountable debate, they in fact increased the central office's power over the prioritization of resolutions. Party officials could use their superior awareness of a complicated and opaque process to coordinate to stack the vote against resolutions they viewed as contro-

versial, which they often did. So, no matter the grassroots support that might be won for the socialist caucus's Leap Manifesto resolution, it was evident that the party's central office would not allow it through in its current form.

12. This resolution fused two resolutions passed by Vancouver East and Danforth ridings. The Vancouver East resolution read: "The NDP recognizes and supports the Leap Manifesto as a high-level statement of principles that is in line with the aspirations, history, and values of the party. We recognize and embrace the opportunity to confront the twin crises of inequality and climate change with an inspiring and positive agenda—to transform society as we transition to an economy beyond fossil fuels. The specific policies in the manifesto can and should be debated and modified on their own merits and according to the needs of various communities, but the goal of transforming our country according to the vision in the manifesto is entirely in line with the core beliefs and tradition of NDP." The Toronto Danforth resolution read, in part: THEREFORE, BE IT RESOLVED THAT the New Democratic Party looks forward to meaningful opportunity to debate [the Leap Manifesto] in riding associations across the country; AND BE IT FURTHER RESOLVED THAT these discussions be part of a pre-convention policy process leading up to 2018; The process mandated in the last paragraph must include a robust online mechanism. This would ensure broad inclusion in the proposal, debate, and prioritizing of policy leading up to the next election."

13. Kristy Kirkup, "Age Not A Consideration As Mulcair Eyes 2019 Election," *iPolitics*, January 20, 2016, https://ipolitics.ca/2016/01/20/age-not-a-consideration-as-mulcair-eyes-2019-election; Heather Libby, "Will Becoming Bernie Sanders Help Mulcair Keep His Job?" *The Tyee*, February 22, 2016, https://thetyee.ca/Opinion/2016/02/22/Bernie-Sanders-Mulcair; Kristy Kirkup, "Tom Mulcair Winds Up NDP Caucus Retreat Vowing Age Will Not Hold Him Back," *CBC News*, January 20, 2016, https://www.cbc.ca/news/politics/tom-mulcair-age-support-caucus-1.3412349.

14. "Tom Mulcair Will 'Do Everything' To Keep Oil in the Ground If Party Tells Him To," *CBC News*, April 6, 2016, https://www.cbc.ca/news/politics/tom-mulcair-oil-ground-manifesto-1.3523849.

15. Michelle Bellefontaine, "Alberta NDP Distances Itself From Tom Mulcair's 'Oil in the Ground' Remark," *CBC News*, April 8, 2016, https://www.cbc.ca/news/canada/edmonton/alberta-ndp-distances-itself-from-tom-mulcair-s-oil-in-the-ground-remark-1.3527947.

16. "'Leap Manifesto' is Not About Shutting Down Oilsands, Mulcair Insists," *Montreal Gazette*, April 8, 2016, https://montrealgazette.com/news/local-news/leap-manifesto-is-not-about-shutting-down-oilsands-mulcair-insists.

17. Laura Stone, "Notley Calls on NDP to Support New Pipelines, Takes Aim at Leap Manifesto," *The Globe and Mail*, April 9, 2016, https://www.theglobeandmail.com/news/politics/notley-calls-on-ndp-to-support-new-pipelines-takes-aim-at-leap-manifesto/article29579082; Stephen Lewis, "For the Record: 'I am, Truly, Insufferably Buoyant,'" *Maclean's*, April 14, 2016, https://www.macleans.ca/politics/stephen-lewis-for-the-record-i-am-truly-insufferably-buoyant.

18. Dias would flip-flop on the Leap Manifesto, making a bizarre statement at the convention's end. "You can't just come out with a statement that says we are going to eliminate all the use of fossil fuels, there is going to be a major reduction by this date and we're going to be fossil fuel-free in 2050," he said. "All I know is that when I left the [NDP] convention, I hoped in a taxi, then I hopped on a plane, and then I hopped in a taxi to get home. And I would suggest so did pretty well everybody else. I don't believe that there is going to be solar panels propelling 747s anytime in the future," he said.
Althia Raj, "Unifor President Jerry Dias: Leap Manifesto Debate At NDP Convention Was Thoughtless," *Huffington Post*, April 13, 2016, https://www.huffingtonpost.ca/2016/04/13/jerry-dias-leap-manifesto-ndp-rachel-notley_n_9682484.html.

19. Dave Ebner et al., "The Hermit Kings," *The Globe and Mail*, March 30, 2006, https://www.theglobeandmail.com/report-on-business/the-hermit-kings/article1096738.

20. Thomas d'Aquino, "The 40th Anniversary of the Business Council of Canada: Remarks and Toast by Thomas d'Aquino," April 18, 2016, https://thebusinesscouncil.ca/wp-content/uploads/2016/04/Toast-by-Thomas-dAquino-on-the-40th-anniversary-of-the-Business-Council-of-Canada.pdf.

21. Since leaving office, Mulroney had become a consummate conduit for the voice of Canada's corporate elite—sitting, at the height of his activity in the 2000s, on no less than 16 corporate or international advisory boards.
Jamie Brownlee, *Ruling Canada: Corporate Cohesion and Democracy* (Black Point, NS: Fernwood, 2005), 131;
Brian Mulroney, "Leadership in Uncertain Times," *Business Council of Canada*, April 19, 2016, https://thebusinesscouncil.ca/publications/leadershipinuncertaintimes.

22. CBC News: The National, "Rex Murphy – The Leap Manifesto and the NDP," video, 2:47, April 11, 2016, https://www.youtube.com/watch?v=-VIE2VumpQQ; Canadaland, "Rex Murphy is Paid by the Oil Sands and CBC Won't Disclose or Discuss It," interview with Guest Investigative Reporter Andrew Mitrovica, aired on February 17, 2014, 33:27. https://www.canadalandshow.com/podcast/rex-murphy-paid-oil-sands-cbc-wont-disclose-discuss.

23. "Wise Crowds and the Future," *Ekos Politics*, April 26, 2016, http://www.ekospolitics.com/index.php/2016/04/wise-crowds-and-the-future.

24. Jessica Elgot and Kevin Rawlinson, "People Saw Through It: Corbyn Hits Back at Daily Mail Attacks," *The Guardian*, September 27, 2017, https://www.theguardian.com/politics/2017/sep/27/people-saw-right-through-it-jeremy-corbyn-hits-back-at-daily-mail-attacks.

25. "Editorial: B.C. NDP's Adrian Dix Sends Dangerous Message to Resource Project Investors," *Vancouver Sun*, April 24, 2013, http://www.vancouversun.com/business/203/editorial+adrian+sends+dangerous+message+resource+project+investors/8290496/story.html; Gary Mason, "Adrian Dix's Opposition to Kinder Morgan and the Liberals' Hopes," *The Globe and Mail*, April 26, 2013, https://www.theglobeandmail.com/news/british-columbia/adrian-dixs-opposition-to-kinder-morgan-and-the-liberals-hopes/article11584071; "B.C. NDP Leader

Slammed For Opposition to Pipeline," *CBC News*, April 23, 2013, https://www.cbc.ca/news/canada/british-columbia/b-c-ndp-leader-slammed-for-opposition-to-pipeline-1.1311565; Personal communication with NDP organizer, Adam Friesen, May 2016.

26. "NDP Candidate Linda McQuaig's Comment On Oilsands Stirs Up Hornet's Nest," *CBC News*, August 9, 2015, https://www.cbc.ca/news/politics/canada-election-2015-mcquaig-oilsands-reaction-cp-1.3184704; Personal communication with Linda McQuaig, July 2016.

27. Donald Gutstein, *Harperism: How Stephen Harper and His Think Tank Colleagues Have Transformed Canada* (Toronto: James Lorimer & Company Ltd., 2014), 69-71.

28. "I have my differences w/ the Leap Manifesto, but it's a model of how to marshall intellectual/ activist opinion to maximum effect." (@acoyne, April 10, 2016), https://twitter.com/acoyne/status/719362000653053953.

29. The manual compared the Leap's policies to pre-existing NDP policies in their policy book. In itself it was excellent. But while there may have been good policies on the books, there was little on the stove.

30. Crawford Kilian, "The Leap Manifesto: When Did Stating the Obvious Become 'Political Suicide'?" *iPolitics*, April 15, 2016, https://ipolitics.ca/2016/04/15/the-leap-manifesto-when-stating-the-obvious-became-political-suicide.

31. Bob Weber, "Nunavut Sees Warmer Days Than B.C. During 'Unprecedented' Heat Wave," *Global News*, July 16, 2019, https://globalnews.ca/news/5499198/nunavut-heat-wave-environment-canada.

32. Jonathan Watts, "July On Course to be Hottest Month Ever, Say Climate Scientists," *The Guardian*, July 16, 2019, https://www.theguardian.com/environment/2019/jul/16/july-on-course-to-be-hottest-month-ever-say-climate-scientists.

33. Alex ballingall, "Majority of Canadians Support a 'Green New Deal', Poll Finds," *Toronto Star*, April 17, 2019, https://www.thestar.com/politics/federal/2019/04/17/majority-of-canadians-support-a-green-new-deal-poll-finds.html.

Index

AbitibiBowater, 115
Advisory Council on Economic
   Growth, 183, 185, 187, 239
Afghanistan, 81, 232
Al-Adeimi, Shireen, 200-201, 203
Amnesty International, 193, 217
Anti-Terrorism Act (Bill C-51), 33-34
Apotex Pharmaceuticals, 84, 86
Aristide, Jean-Bertrand, 219
asylum seekers, 211-212, 216-218,
   221-222, 224-225
Aurea Foundation, 245

Badawi, Raif, 193, 195
Bahrain, 199
Bains, Navdeep, 92, 187
Baird, John, 239
Barlow, Maude, 181
Barton, Dominic, 18-20, 183-185, 239
Beatty, Perrin, 92
Bellegarde, Perry, 133, 157, 158,
   163, 164
Bennett, Carolyn, 6, 136, 142, 147,
   156, 163-165, 168
bin Salman, Mohammad, 193,
   203, 210
Black, Conrad, 27, 191
BlackRock, 183-186
Blair, Bill, 224
Bombardier, 92, 191
Brazeau, Patrick, 43, 44
Brexit, 183
Brison, Scott, 40, 58, 84, 89
Brody, Leonard, 186
Bush, George W., 216, 219
Business Council of Canada:
   accomplishments, 239-240; and
   climate change policies, 113-116;
   and carbon tax, 123-124; foundation
   of, 229; history of, 76-82;

relationship with Harper, 25, 80-81;
   on infrastructure bank, 183; and
   National Energy Program, 111; and
   Saudi arms deal, 196; ties to WWF-
   Canada, 106
Butts, Gerald, 29-37, 41, 47, 104-109,
   111, 115-117, 122, 144, 188, 194

C.D. Howe Institute, 22, 24
Canada 2020, 31, 95, 248
Canada-European Union
   Comprehensive Economic and Trade
   Agreement, 175-181
   Wallon parliament opposition to,
   175-180
Canadian Association of Petroleum
   Producers, 61, 95, 115, 120, 123,
   126, 153
Canadian Border Services Agency, 225
Canadian Broadcasting Corporation,
   242
Canadian Commercial Corporation,
   197, 198
Canadian Council for Public-Private
   Partnerships, 18, 186
Canadian Council of Chief Executives,
   (see: Business Council of Canada)
Canadian Federation of Independent
   Business, 24
Canadian National Railway, 187
Carr, Jim, 96, 97, 116, 124, 126, 153
Carson, Bruce, 115, 116
Champagne, François-Philippe, 61
Chrétien, Jean, 22, 23, 33, 34, 37, 38,
   46, 60, 76, 78, 79, 82, 83, 118, 120-
   122, 141, 159, 160, 209
Clark, Christy, 241
Clark, Ed, 25, 80

Conservative Party of Canada: and
2015 election, 35, 38-39, 228,
232; and climate change politics, 3,
113-116, 117, 122, 124, 127-128,
243, 250; and neoliberalism, 8, 10,
20, 78-79, 188, 239-240; party
conventions, 60, 234; racism of, 8-9,
224; relationship with corporate
elite, 22-27, 79-82, 83, 88, 92, 239,
245; and rivalry with Liberals, 6,
8-10, 13-14, 37, 58, 85, 128, 182,
185; and zombie bureaucrats, 68-70;
and Indigenous peoples, 135-136,
140, 150, 153, 156, 168; and Saudi
arms deal, 192-194; and refugee
policy, 223-224
Cooperative Commonwealth
Federation, 36, 37, 237
Corbyn, Jeremy, 237, 243, 248
Council of Canadians, 181
Courtis, Kenneth, 184
Coyne, Andrew, 245
Cuba, 219

Davies, Libby, 235, 238
Demers, Charles, 233
Democratic Party, 226
Desmarais family, 240
Diabo, Russ, 158-166, 169
Dias, Jerry, 238
Dion, Stéphane, 84, 197-199, 201, 239
Dix, Adrian, 244
Dodge, David, 97
Doer, Gary, 230
D'Aquino, Tom, 77-81, 111, 113, 114,
116, 121

Earnscliffe, 92, 93
electoral reform, 70-73
Emerson, David, 88
Enbridge, 104, 131
environmental review process legislation
(Bill C-69), 127, 155
European Union, 175-180, 182,
183, 224
Extinction Rebellion, 249

extractive industries, 13, 24, 102, 109-
112, 114, 118, 120, 121, 127, 131,
132, 136-138, 140, 149-154,
161, 163

Fenton, Anthony, 201-203, 206, 209
Fink, Larry, 183, 185
First Nations, (see: Indigenous peoples)
Flaherty, Jim, 24
Florvilus, Patrice, 220, 221
Fontaine, Phil, 145, 153, 157
Ford, Doug, 127, 129
Ford, Rob, 51
fossil fuels, 8, 12, 13, 49, 100, 101,
111, 126, 236, 241, 249-251
France, 176, 210, 219
Fraser, Sheila, 82
Fraser Institute, 24
Freeland, Chrystia, 18-20, 38, 89, 175,
177, 178, 180-182, 204, 206,
211, 212

Gabriel, Ellen, 138-143, 155
Gagnier, Dan, 115-117
Gainey, Anna, 64
General Dynamics, 191, 192, 196,
197, 200
Germany, 216
Gibbins, Roger, 114
Goldenberg, Eddie, 160
Goodale, Ralph, 61, 64
Google, 61
Graham, Bill, 219
Granados, Lucy, 213-215, 223
Graves, Frank, 242
Green Party of Canada, 243
Guatemala, 213, 214

Haiti, 217-221, 225
Hampton, Howard, 36
Hansen, James, 104
Harper, Stephen, 1, 2, 10, 11, 17,
22-27, 31, 33, 38, 39, 51, 55, 67-70,
80, 85, 92, 93, 102, 111, 112, 115,
116, 122, 135-138, 148, 150, 151,
157, 159, 168, 176, 182, 218, 223,
228, 229, 232

Hoffman, Sarah, 237
Hubbard, Tasha, 135
Human Rights Watch, 205
Hussen, Ahmed, 61, 222
Hyndman, Al, 119

Idle No More movement, 17, 134-136,
    150, 159, 163, 165, 167
Ignatieff, Michael, 84, 232
immigration, 215-217, 221,
    223-225, 248
Imperial Oil, 229
Indigenous peoples, 2-4, 8, 10, 13, 17,
    21, 26, 27, 37, 43, 44, 50, 69, 96,
    98, 104, 110, 112, 124, 131-138,
    140-172, 174, 245
inequality, 3, 6-13, 16, 17, 20, 25, 27,
    35, 36, 39, 53, 54, 75, 183, 185,
    188, 192, 219, 224, 227, 235,
    248, 251
infrastructure bank 185, 187-189
Investor-State Dispute Settlement
    mechanisms, 177, 178, 181, 182
Iraq, 201, 216, 219, 232
Irving family, 88
Irving Shipbuilding, 92
Islamic State of Iraq and Syria, 194, 201

Kenney, Jason, 127
Keystone XL pipeline, 102, 112
Khashoggi, Jamal, 193, 210, 211
Kinder Morgan, 49, 52, 61, 95-98,
    103, 123, 124, 130, 154, 172,
    173, 244
King, William Lyon Mackenzie, 36
Klein, Naomi, 227, 228, 242
Klein, Ralph, 118-120
Koch brothers, 59
Kolber, Leo, 59
Kyoto Protocol, 10, 62, 114, 121, 122

Lalonde, Marc, 59, 78, 79
Lametti, David, 177
Laurier, Wilfrid, 1
Lavigne, Brad, 231

Layton, Jack, 22, 230-233
Leach, Andrew, 122
Leslie, Megan, 235, 238
Lewis, Avi 235, 242, 247
Lewis, David, 229
Lewis, Stephen 238
Liberal Party of Canada: and Bay Street
    interests, 25, 30, 32, 40, 59, 82, 83,
    87, 89, 107, 109; climate change
    policies, 95, 107-109, 116, 118, 119,
    121, 122, 125-128, 130, 228-230,
    232-234, 240, 247, 251; fundraising,
    33, 34, 59, 82-86, 88; Halifax
    national convention (2018), 57, 59,
    60, 63, 66, 156; and Indigenous
    peoples, 135-137, 150, 151, 153,
    156, 157, 160-169; influence of
    Obama administration on, 29,
    33-35, 48, 53, 84; infrastructure
    stimulus plan, 38, 40, 81, 87, 102;
    Laurier Club, 59, 60, 85, 86, 88;
    and neoliberalism, 174, 181, 185,
    187-189; pensions policy, 3, 4, 13,
    37, 63; polling, 10, 13, 19, 29, 33,
    34, 40, 41, 54, 55, 71, 110; refugee
    policies, 215, 218, 225; and Saudi
    arms deal, 193-195, 197, 198, 211,
    212; sponsorship scandal, 22, 82, 93;
    universal pharmacare, 8, 61, 63;
Liberal Party of Ontario, 29, 36, 85
Littlechild, Willie, 157, 164
Loblaws, 108
Lockheed Martin, 62

MacEachern, Allan, 78
MacFarlane, David, 92
MacNeil, Jim, 67, 68
Macron, Emmanuel, 52, 210
Magnette, Paul, 175-181
Manley, John, 75-78, 80, 81, 116, 123,
    124, 183, 184, 186, 196
Manly, Paul, 250
Manning Centre, 245
Mannix, Ron, 240
Mansbridge, Peter, 236

Manuel, Arthur, 145, 146, 149, 150, 167, 168, 172-174
Martin, Paul, 22, 23, 31, 34, 38, 39, 60, 80, 83, 84, 86, 93, 119, 120, 122, 135, 145, 167
McAuley, Lawrence, 61
McCarthy, Stuart, 95-97
McGowan, Gil, 238
McGuinty, Dalton, 29, 30, 36, 115, 188
McKenna, Catherine, 6, 49, 79, 116, 127, 155
McKinsey & Co., 18, 183, 185, 239
McLellan, Anne, 61, 88, 118-120, 122
McQuaig, Linda, 244
Mehr, Jay, 86
Mercredi, Ovide, 159-161
Merkel, Angela, 101
Mexico, 213, 215, 222
middle class, 4, 20, 34-36, 47, 53, 72, 87, 178, 182
Mintz, Jack, 22
Moe, Scott, 127
Morneau, Bill, 72, 75, 76, 86, 87, 89, 91, 239
Mulcair, Thomas, 31, 35, 37-39, 228, 229, 233-237, 239, 242, 247, 250
Mulroney, Brian, 8, 27, 46, 59, 75, 79, 92, 111, 114, 140, 187, 209, 241, 244, 245
Munk, Peter, 245
Murphy, Rex, 242

National Energy Program, 110, 111, 113, 240, 241
National Energy Strategy, 112-114
National Indian Brotherhood, 146
neoliberalism, 9, 10, 56, 109, 118, 120, 179, 229, 230, 233, 240, 244, 247, 251
New Democratic Party, 22, 27, 31, 34-41, 58, 60, 70, 99, 129, 156, 228-235, 237, 239, 241-246, 248-250
Newell, Eric, 119
Newman, Peter C., 33, 77, 79

newspapers, (see: media)
Nikiforuk, Andrew, 104
Nixon, Gord, 240
North American Free Trade Agreement, 168, 177, 181
Notley, Rachel, 122, 123, 235, 236, 238

Obama, Barack, 26, 51, 53, 84, 101, 112, 220
Ocasio-Cortez, Alexandria, 226
oil industry, 5, 24, 49, 59, 62, 88, 89, 98, 101-103, 106-123, 125-127, 129-131, 148, 150, 192, 193, 204, 208, 211, 229, 236-238, 240-242, 249
oil sands, (see: tar sands)
O'Regan, Seamus, 106

Palestine, 146, 233, 250
Pallister, Brad, 127
Paris, Roland, 193
Paris Agreement, 5, 49, 50, 52, 130
Pasternak, Shiri, 150
Pearson, Lester B., 37
Pelosi, Nancy, 226
Pembina Institute, 116, 121
pension funds, 185-187
Peters, Gord, 172
Peterson, Jim, 88
Petro-Canada, 110
Pettigrew, Pierre, 61, 88, 179, 180
pharmaceutical industry, 11, 61
Philipps, Shannon, 237
Philpott, Jane, 61
pipelines, 8, 12, 26, 49, 52, 95, 97-104, 112, 116, 117, 123, 124, 128, 130, 143, 151, 154, 170-173, 235, 238, 244, 251
Plutocrats: The Rise of the New Global Super-Rich and the Fall of Everyone Else, 18-20, 89
Podesta, John, 34
Powell, Rob, 105-107

Prentice, Jim, 117
Prime Minister's Office, 92, 114,
    136, 168
privatization, 8, 20, 24, 161, 176,
    185-189, 230
Privy Council, 69, 168
public-private partnerships, 18,
    185-187, 189
Putin, Vladimir, 210, 211

racism, 215, 218, 224, 227
Raitt, Lisa, 128
Raza, Omar, 57, 58, 61, 64
Reagan, Ronald, 110
Redford, Alison, 116, 124
Reid, Scott, 31
Republican Party, 34, 35, 183
Réseau express métropolitain, 188
Reynolds, Marlo, 116, 155
Rio Tinto, 92
Robinson, Eden, 134
Rogers Communications, 80, 92
Royal Commission on Aboriginal
    Peoples, 135, 140, 141, 149
ruling class, 3, 11, 12, 16, 21, 24, 26,
    28, 35, 59, 60, 83, 84, 87, 88, 183,
    184, 188, 248, 250
Runnalls, David, 67, 68

Sabia, Michael, 187
Saint-Pierre, Guy, 240
Sanders, Bernie, 21, 201, 235, 237,
    239, 243, 248
Saudi Arabia, 8, 26, 183, 191-212
Scheer, Andrew, 127, 128
Schwab, Klaus, 240
Scott, Duncan Campbell, 140
Sears, 24
Shaw Communications, 86, 92
Shell, 92, 115, 129, 131, 132
Sherman, Barry, 84, 86
Simpson, Leanne, 134
Sinclair, Murray, 135, 145
Singh, Jagmeet, 248
SNC-Lavalin, 12, 69, 84, 92, 131, 132,
    168-170, 186, 188, 240

socialism, 226, 233, 234, 236
social movements, 11, 17, 80, 107,
    135, 138, 161, 176, 199, 200, 220,
    226-231, 234, 243, 245-247, 250,
    251
social programs, 8, 9, 17, 19, 20, 22,
    24, 37, 53, 61, 63, 120
Sohi, Amarjeet, 184
Solberg, Janet, 235
Solidarity Across Board, 215
Spence, Theresa, 26, 135, 165
Statoil, 129
Stephens, Hugh, 182
Stewart, Keith, 103, 104, 106, 107
Stewart, Kennedy, 98
Suncor, 104, 115, 129, 131, 132, 136
Sutherland, Robert, 61
Suzuki, David, 117
Swanson, Jean, 100, 101
Syncrude, 119
Syria, 201, 216
Syrian refugees, 7, 69

Taft, Kevin, 116, 119
Taggaq, Tanya, 134
tar sands, 10, 26, 49, 52, 95, 98,
    103-106, 108, 109, 112, 114, 115,
    117-123, 126, 127, 130, 143, 173,
    236, 244
tax policies, 5, 8, 16, 17, 23-26, 35,
    39, 51, 75, 78, 93, 115, 229, 233,
    244, 250
tax havens, 5, 58, 60
TD Bank, 80, 91, 116, 117
Teck Resources, 131, 136
Telford, Katie, 115, 122
Telus Communications, 80, 92
Terradyne, 202, 206, 207
Thatcher, Margaret, 233, 235
Thomson family, 6, 88
Thunberg, Greta, 249
Topp, Brian, 122
TransCanada, 117
Trans Mountain pipeline, 8, 124, 154,
    181, 251

Trudeau, Justin: and 2015 election, 1-3, 29-41; accusations of class warfare, 15, 34, 35, 53; and Bay Street interests, 11, 15, 30, 32, 36, 40, 87, 89, 103, 107; Calgary Petroleum Club speech, 18, 111, 113; Canadian Club speech, 15, 21, 29, 34, 48; and climate change policies, 95-98, 101-104, 107-113, 115, 117, 122-124, 126-128, 228-229, 239, 241, 246, 248, 251; governance as Prime Minister, 59, 60, 62-73; and Indigenous peoples, 131-137, 144-146, 148, 149, 151-155, 157-174; and neoliberalism 176, 178-188; progressive image of, 2, 7-8, 10, 12, 13, 27, 34, 36-38, 40, 41, 43-57, 58, 67, 69, 70, 73, 102; on 1995 Quebec referendum, 55; and refugee policies, 215-218, 221-225; relationship with corporate elite, 15-18, 20-22, 25-28, 78, 81, 86-93; and Saudi arms deal, 193-195, 197, 202, 203, 208-212; selfies, 2, 31, 45, 50, 67; and social media, 11, 32, 41, 45, 47, 53, 67, 159; socks, 45
Trudeau, Pierre Elliott, 3, 30, 37, 59, 65, 67, 87, 88, 109, 111, 146, 149, 161
Trudeau, Sophie Gregoire, 51
Trump, Donald J., 7, 53, 102, 126, 181, 194, 210, 211, 215, 217, 223, 224, 227, 248
Truth and Reconciliation Commission, 135
Turner, John, 34, 59
Turp, Daniel, 198

Unifor, 236, 238
United Arab Emirates, 200, 201, 203
United Nations, 26, 49, 100, 136, 152, 200, 205, 206, 215, 217, 219, 223
United Nations Declaration on the Rights of Indigenous Peoples, 8, 136, 152, 153, 166

United States–Mexico–Canada Agreement, 181

Volpe, Joe, 84

Walmart, 24
welfare state, 10, 24, 67, 148, 230
Wernick, Michael, 69, 168
Weston family, 108
Wilson-Raybould, Jody, 86, 136, 147, 157, 163, 166-169
Wiseman, Mark, 185
working class, 3-5, 9, 17, 19, 20, 24, 35, 37
World Economic Forum, 12, 19, 185, 240
World Wildlife Foundation-Canada, 30, 103-108, 116
Wright, Nigel, 24
Wynne, Kathleen, 85

Yemen, 194, 199-204, 209-211

Also available from Black Rose Books:

Paperback: 9781551641782; Cloth: 9781551641799

Also, coming for Fall 2019:
Eduardo Galeano:
Wind is the Breath of Time, the Storyteller's Voice Travels On
(Paperback: 9781551647036; Cloth: 9781551647050; Ebook: 9781551647074)